Gen X TV

The Television Series

Robert J. Thompson, Series Editor

GenX
TV

The Brady Bunch to Melrose Place

Rob Owen

Syracuse University Press

First Paperback Edition 1999

99 00 01 02 03 04   6 5 4 3 2 1

Permission to reprint the article "'Placemats' Join to Watch 'Melrose' En Mass"
from the *Richmond Times-Dispatch*, Mar, 26, 1995, J1, is gratefully acknowledged.

The paper used in this publication meets the minimum requirements of American
national Standard for Information Sciences—Permanence of Paper for Printed Library
Materials, ANSI z39.48-1984. ∞

Library of Congress Cataloging-in-Publication Data
Owen, Rob, 1971–
    Gen X TV : the Brady Bunch to Melrose Place / Rob Owen.—
1st ed.
        p.   cm. — (The television series)
    Includes bibliographical references and index.
    ISBN 0-8156-0443-2 (cloth : alk. paper) 0-8156-0585-4 (pbk:)
    1. Television bradcasting—Social aspects—United States.
2. Generation X—United States. I. Title. II. Series.
PN1992.6.093 1997
302.23'45'0973—dc21   96-39043

Manufactured in the United States of America

For Mom, Dad,
and my big little
brother, Doug

Rob Owen, born in 1971, is television editor and critic at the *Pittsburgh Post-Gazette*. Previously he worked as TV/Radio columnist at the *Times Union* in Albany, New York. Owen began his journalism career as a features writer at the *Richmond Times-Dispatch* in Richmond, Virginia, where he helped create "inSync," a section for teen readers. His articles have also appeared in *NetGuide* magazine, and he is a member of the Television Critics Association. He can be reached via e-mail (GENXTVBOOK@aol.com) or on the Web (http://members.aol.com/genxtvbook).

Melrose Place is a *really* good show.
—Winona Ryder in the 1994 film *Reality Bites*

Contents

Preface Why write about television

and Generation X? That's pretty easy. The two were made for one another. Would the stereotype of Generation X exist if TV had not been invented? Probably not. Would television exist without Generation X? Yes, but its programming would certainly look different.

Some would argue that you could say the same thing about Gen X and movies or music. A snobbish member of Gen X would snort derisively at the idea that television is a medium worthy of study. Film (not movies) is what should be examined, they'd say as they drank their cappuccino and smoked their herbal cigarettes while wearing Exxon coveralls that they paid $50 for at an upscale thrift store. This person is probably a slacker, which is a subset of Generation X. The media began using *Generation X* and *slacker* interchangeably after the release of *Slacker,* Richard Linklater's 1991 film about do-nothing twentysomethings in Austin, Texas. Slackers are the members of Generation X who do not aspire to have careers, who sleep on a couch all day, and who wash their hair only a few times a year. Ethan Hawke's character in the movie *Reality Bites* was clearly a slacker. The 1996 edition of the *Random House Webster's Collegiate Dictionary* defined *slacker* in its new words section as an "educated young person who is antimaterialistic, purposeless, apathetic, and usually works in a dead-end job." In *The Official Slacker Handbook,* author Sarah Dunn writes, "The slack sensibility is part old-fashioned bohemianism and part fin de siècle exhaustion, placed against the backdrop of a crappy recession and intolerable suburban irony." It's worth noting that Dunn, 25, went on to write for the TV sitcom *Murphy Brown.*

This book is not about slackers; instead it will look at the broad-based Generation X made up of some slackers, some professionals, some bank tellers, some waiters, some students. As for the TV part, let me state right up front: I love television and feel no shame about that. I'm not a couch potato who beaches on the sofa, grabs the remote, and grazes mindlessly through the channels. I only watch shows I know I will enjoy, be it the moral quandaries of *Chicago Hope* or the guilty pleasures of *Savannah.*

Luckily, television today is better than it has ever been, and part of the credit for that must go to the discerning tastes of Generation X, a large segment of the viewing public that will not settle for the same old TV shows. Because Xers have such an acute awareness of TV and the media, Gen X demands more original and compelling programs. Yes, many twentysomethings watch such trashy fare as *Melrose Place* and *Beverly Hills, 90210*. These programs are escapist entertainment for some, but for many others, these two shows are more like sitcoms—they watch to laugh and, frequently, not alone but with a group of like-minded friends. It is possible to be a fan of both of these shows while also enjoying such highbrow fare as *Murder One, NYPD Blue,* or *Homicide: Life on the Street.*

Even those Gen Xers who proudly post "Kill Your Television" bumper stickers on their cars grew up watching the box, and whether they like it or not, it has influenced their lives. Popular culture is Gen X's specialty, and TV is a large part of pop culture. In the end, these two forces are inseparable. Other generations had wars and social movements to unite them, but for Xers, television is the common experience. Television may not be as spontaneous as Woodstock or as divisive as a war protest, but for Generation X, TV is the defining medium.

Rob Owen
Richmond, Va.
June 1996

Acknow-ledgments This book would have

been impossible to write without the technology that will forever be a part of Generation X life—the Internet. Some of the interviews in these pages were conducted via e-mail over the Internet and many of the quotes from Gen Xers came out of a survey I posted to Usenet newsgroups. I'd like to thank these cybernauts for taking the time to look at my posting and for following through with a reply. Many of their voices made it into this book, which could not have been written without their input. I especially thank Net experts Ian J. Ball, Heath Doerr, Ian Ferrell, Steve Joyner, Jol Padgett, Jon Singer, and Andy Williams, who all consented to interviews for this book. Thanks also to all the Xers not on the Net who took the time to respond to my survey or agreed to be interviewed, especially Erin Smith.

Thanks to all the people in the television industry and media who were willing interview subjects for this book, including Jeff Astrof, David Bianculli, Greer Bosworth, Yvette Lee Bowser, Adam Chase, Russell Collins, Kimberly Costello, Jennifer Elise Cox, Betsy Frank, Bob Garfield, Larry Gianinno, Robert Greenblatt, Jeff Greenstein, Eric Hirshberg, Winnie Holzman, Marta Kauffman, Charles Kennedy, Marty Krofft, Amy Lippman, Jonathan Murray, Rose Catherine Pinkney, David Poltrack, Charles Rosin, Karen Ritchie, Matt Roush, Sherwood Schwartz, Horst Stipp, Jeff Strauss, Dorothy Swanson, Ken Topolosky, Ira Ungerleider, John Wells, and Tom Yohe. In an industry in which life moves at the speed of light and sound, I appreciate that they took the time to help me with this project.

Special thanks go to the Museum of Television & Radio in New York, especially publicist Julie Charles, for help in research. Thanks also go to those who helped arrange interviews, including Carolyn Prousky of Fox publicity and Jamie O'Connor, who set up my visit to the set of *Friends* and interviews with the first-season writing staff.

Without my editor, Syracuse University professor Robert Thompson, this book would never exist. When I graduated from SU's S.I. Newhouse School of Public Communications in 1993, I didn't expect that a little more than one year later Thompson would ask me to contribute a book to the SU Press series of books about television. I never imagined that talking about the latest plot twist on *Picket Fences* during my years as an undergraduate could lead to a book deal.

I also extend thanks to my former employer, the *Richmond Times-Dispatch*, for allowing me the opportunity to pursue this extracurricular activity. I'm especially indebted to *Times-Dispatch* television critic Douglas Durden, who never discouraged my interest in TV or my desire to become a television critic. She helped me to continue TV coverage, allowing me space and freedom to write TV reviews and TV-themed articles for the *Times-Dispatch.* In addition, she's a fun person to talk with about this fascinating medium.

I also must mention my friends and family who have endured (and, in some cases, even encouraged) my TV talk. This includes my co-workers at Syracuse University's *Daily Orange* student newspaper during my undergraduate years (1989–93) and my friends at the *Times-Dispatch.*

Special thanks go to Yolanda Wright, my newswriting professor at SU, who has been a valued mentor and friend, and SU professor Bill Glavin, whose magazine writing classes taught me how to do the research necessary to write a book of this scope. Thanks also go to Carol Fay, my high school journalism teacher, who has always encouraged me in my writing pursuits. I also thank her daughter, Kristin, whose co-worker is the roommate of the cousin of *Melrose Place* producer Kimberly Costello. Sometimes it's not who you know, but who you know who your friends know.

Defining Gen X TV

One of the most frustrating things about writ-ing this book was defending the use of the term *Generation X*. A lot of people get upset that anyone would dare use such a label. When the cast of *Friends* appeared on *The Oprah Winfrey Show* in March 1995, Winfrey asked the show's six stars what they thought of the term. "I just hate the label in general," replied David Schwimmer, who plays Ross on the hit sitcom about six twentysomethings, "because to me it connotes a kind of slacker, and all my peers are aggressively pursuing either jobs or relationships or just trying to come to grips with their identities. And no one is kind of just lying back going, 'Let it happen, we're Generation X.'"

Generation X is not synonymous with *slacker*, but to many people these words have come to mean the same thing. That's what happens when the media names a generation after a piece of fiction (Douglas Coupland's 1991 book, *Generation X*) or a punk band (Billy Idol's late-1970s group), depending on who is asked. The same media that spilled gallons of ink over *Generation X* has already declared it dead. The *New York Times* ran the obituary in June 1995 on the "Styles" page under the headline "The Short Shelf Life of Generation X." Coupland himself announced the death of Gen X in the June 1995 issue of the Gen X magazine *Details*. This pronouncement just happened to coincide with the publication of his book, *Microserfs*. A planned cable network (called XTV and, later, Axon) that was to be devoted to short films made by Xers folded in May 1996.

Whether dead or alive in the minds of the media elite, a couple of million people still remain in the generation formerly known as X. When I posted a survey on Gen X TV viewing to several Usenet newsgroups, I expected to receive a few hostile replies. I was not disappointed. "Who the hell asked you to write a book about Generation X?" wrote one miffed respondent. "I never thought I would see an actual member of 'Generation X' call himself that. I'm

1

quite embarrassed, really." That wasn't the only negative response. "There is no Generation X," another person replied by e-mail. "Put that in your book and burn it."

So to get a working definition of Generation X out of the way, *Generation X* should not be viewed as a pejorative term, and it's not an inflexible definition. Not every Baby Boomer went to the original Woodstock, and not every Xer attends Lollapalooza. The same goes for television. Not every Xer watches *Melrose Place* or grew up playing with *Six Million Dollar Man* action figures, but many can relate to one or both of these things.

Who are the members of Generation X? The media stereotype is white, middle-class kids who grew up in suburbia, went to college, and are searching for a career but end up working at The Gap. In reality, a generation is more than a demographic unit, but because television and the media love to group people in target markets, Generation X often appears to be only white middle-class twentysomethings. In reality, Xers are one of the most diverse generations in American history. The 1990 census found that almost 35 percent of those in the 10 to 29 age group were nonwhite or Hispanic. The majority of Gen Xers grew up after the civil rights movements, and although Xers still encounter racial issues, they are just as likely to encounter gay rights issues. Whereas TV became separated into black shows and white shows in the early 1990s, many Gen X TV shows reflect the growing gay rights movement by including homosexual characters, including Matt on *Melrose Place*, Rickie on *My So-Called Life*, Ross on *Party of Five*, and Carol and Susan on *Friends*. Although Gen Xers are not all supporters of gay rights, Xers are certainly more understanding than previous generations. "We're as diverse as any ethnic group," said Yvette Lee Bowser, the 31-year-old creator of *Living Single*. "I think most of us who have

Xers Define *Generation X*

What is Generation X? That's a question for which there is no concrete answer. The November 1995 edition of *Webster's New World Dictionary* defines Generation X as "the generation of persons born in the 1960s and 1970s, the children of the Baby Boomers, often variously regarded as apathetic, materialistic, irresponsible, lacking purpose, etc." Clearly that was written by a Boomer. Not even dictionaries from the same publisher can agree on a definition: The 1996 edition of the *Random House Compact Unabridged Dictionary* says Generation X is "the generation born in the United States after 1960," whereas the *Random House Webster's College Dictionary* defines Gen X as "the generation born in the United States after 1965." Even Xers opinions vary on how to define the age group they were born into. Some Xers define Generation X as follows:

"A term invented by old fuddy-duddies who think that kids ages 18 to 26 are apathetic and without identities, but they're wrong."—Michelle Crouch, 22

"Someone born in the mid-to-late 1960s, perhaps as late as 1972." —Sal DeFilippo, 28

"A demographic seized by marketers to be exploited for the purpose of selling consumer goods." —Paul Waldman, 28

"It is a term given to people in my age group simply because they are lazy and apathetic." —Karla Vitale, 23

"Twentysomethings who often appear jaded and cynical to those of other generations; who are more into self-prophesying and saving the world than in being high on the corporate ladder in an office all day." —Jennifer Lyn Cather, 24

"The generation of the 1980s and 1990s and maybe of the next century. We are still trying to figure out what distinguishing features define this generation." —Helene Coplan, 22

"A marketing term inadvertently created by a really lousy Canadian writer." —Adam Lounsbery, 21

"A sarcastic, satirical, in-your-face generation that craves bigger, faster, more powerful technology and entertainment but somehow (paradoxically) finds extreme pleasure in the past (part of its childhood). References to the 1960s and 1970s proliferate in current media, and our generation eats them up with a spoon." —Chris Casdin, 25

"A class of young adults who society has forced to feel like failures and underachievers, thereby causing them to cling to hopes, dreams, and the successes of others like the drowning cling to a life jacket." —Jacob Palm, 22

"A group of misunderstood twentysomethings charged with cleaning up and dealing with the messes our parents have left us." —Laurel A. Sydlansky, 22

"It's what I most despise and am confused about in myself—a lack of being content with what you have—"You mean I have to take a job I hate?!?" The positive side is the wider awareness that most Xers have of world issues and their sensitivity to other people's (and peoples') needs. I think Xers generally want to make the world a better place to live but are too lazy to do it!" —Jonathan Spangler, 25

"I wish I knew how to define it because I'm supposed to be part of it. It seems to have something to do with Seattle grunge and disaffected youth. Long live Kurt Cobain." —Sue Bojdak, 24

"People who are nauseated by shows like *Donna Reed*." —Kathleen Scott, 24

"I suppose it merely categorizes people between certain [birth] dates. The problem is, people don't fit in neat packages like that; aren't labels what we're all trying to get away from?" —Tena Walters, 22

"A younger, disaffected but aware group that rejects the 'system' that's in place now, who are currently trying to find better alternatives. So far, however, they haven't. Despite that, they have their own values, common language, and media culture, which unifies them (e.g., *The Brady Bunch, Melrose*)" —Steve Sebelius, 28

"A whining, slacker stereotype popularized and perpetuated by youth-jealous Boomers who are finally realizing their mortality. Several studies show it's the Boomers who whine and see a dim future." —Kristina Sauerwein, 25

"Caffeine, emotional, angst, safe sex, politically correct, prochoice, pro-*Melrose*, pro-Brad Pitt, pro-Morrissey, and the inability to achieve selfish goals without guilt." —Michael Warner, 31

"Those who schedule their daily lives around certain TV shows." —Beth Kopp, 26

"Marketing scam." —David Ardell, 24

"Basically, the whole concept of Generation X is that of a generation of people who have grown up in the formidable shadow of the great and terrible Baby Boomers. I mean, to borrow from every Douglas Coupland rant and Goo Goo Dolls song, we have grown up with memories that aren't our own, hearing about Woodstock and Watergate and stupid Howdy-Doody reruns that were the end-all be-all of the Baby Boomer experience." —Jennifer Hale, 25

"A generation shaped by television, who base their actions on what TV portrays."—Sheri Fortier, 21

"A poorly thought, media-driven, poorly qualified excuse for a buzzword plastered upon the foreheads of an otherwise diverse group that defies catchy characterization." —Joshua M. Dillon, 24

"People my age, between 17 and 30." —Holly Bergstrom, 24

"A really over-hyped term for the twentysomethings raised on TV, Atari games, and fast food, now kind of lost in the shadow of their cause-oriented older siblings and parents. The term is over-hyped, however, just like everything that is made for this generation (be it sound-bite news, commercials, or videos). The name characterizes us all by what's probably a portion of our numbers. We don't all feel 'Gen X'." —Jeff Marcella, 28

"I despise that label; it excludes everyone but white, upper middle-class kids. It doesn't speak to everyone because it implies no ambition, a sense of being lost, which I am not at all." —Robin Hands, 26

"A label that big business and Baby Boomers thought of. Don't label us and try to reach us with cheesy commercials." —Craig Rechenmacher, 24

"Can't. No generation can define itself." —Rachael Conlin, 25

"Those under 30, above 20, who are working. *Not* slackers." —Scott Davis, 27

been given that label resent it, but we've found a way to turn it in our favor by exploiting it into television." Although there have been TV shows featuring black members of Generation X (*Living Single*, *New York Undercover*, *Martin*, *The Wayans Bros.*, *Fresh Prince of Bel Air*, *The Show*, *Homeboys in Outer Space*), these programs are rarely given the Gen X label. Instead, they're considered "black shows."

Douglas Coupland has said that Generation X is not a chronological age but a way of looking at the world. True, but most of the people who look at the world in this Gen X way (cynically, ironically, sarcastically) fall into the twentysomething age group. In their book, *13th Gen,* authors Bill Strauss and Neil Howe define Generation X as those born between 1961 and 1981, which means that in 1997 the ages of Gen Xers run from 16 to 36. Although people in this age group may have some things in common, when it comes to television, those born in 1961 can remember a time when MTV did not exist. The 1961 crowd grew up watching *The Brady Bunch* in prime time and the original *Land of the Lost* on Saturday mornings. The 1981 crowd entered kindergarten watching *The Care Bears.* As a result of the rerun, these two disparate age groups can share in a phenomenon such as *The Brady Bunch*, but in this book, I concentrate on the core group, those in birth years 1965–75 (ages 22 to 32 in 1997). That's not to say people born a few years earlier or later aren't Gen X, but for the purpose of studying TV, this more narrow definition works best.

It's tempting to define Generation X as simply an age group, but that classification ignores the fact that Xers are all members of one TV nation. Although not the first group of Americans to grow up on TV, Xers are the first group for whom TV served as a regularly scheduled baby-sitter. Gen X was the first to experience MTV and the Fox network, and they are an audience many advertisers are eager to reach. Xers are the most media-savvy generation ever.

"I thought MTV was just about the coolest thing I'd ever seen in my life, and I knew that my head was going to explode if we didn't get it at my house," said Jennifer Hale, a 25-year-old communications assistant for a nonprofit firm in Washington, D.C. "MTV turned everything up a notch. Action became faster, shots became shorter, women became nuder. Shows like *Miami Vice* and, now, *Baywatch* wouldn't exist without MTV. Producers realized that they could have more creativity by tying music and visuals together; they didn't just have to stick with theme songs and mood music as audio sources." MTV, in turn, changed television commercials, making quick cuts, funky camera angles, editing effects, and odd forms of lighting more commonplace in advertising. "The whole deal is tremendously more dynamic by orders of magnitude than advertising that existed even 15 years ago, thanks to MTV," said Bob Garfield, ad critic for *Advertising Age.* "Generation X, if it does have one thing in common through no fault of its own, is the most sophisticated viewer of film ever. As a consequence, advertisers are under pressure to up the ante in terms of visuals in advertising, and, as a further consequence, anyone over 50 is hard-pressed to follow the action of most modern advertising."

**TV =
Gen X
Literature**

Generation X has a much more extensive knowledge of television than any previous generation. Gen X speaks of a history of television viewing, said Larry Gianinno, vice-president of program research for ABC. "Boomers do too, but it's not something as prevalent as I see or hear with 18 to 29s and certainly teens today." This explains the rise of TV shows whose premises are the media or other TV shows. Many programs are littered with talk about other TV shows and inside jokes about the media. On the second episode of *Caroline in the City* in September 1995, Caroline's neighbor was shocked to find Caroline and her ex-boyfriend, Del, dating again. "I'm out of town two days, and it's like missing an episode of *Melrose Place*," she said. Only a few minutes later, Caroline asked Del, "Are you afraid you might go crazy and rent *Howard the Duck?*"

"Hey, *Howard the Duck* was underrated," Del replied. The studio audience and laugh track roared in appreciation of this inside joke: *Caroline in the City* star Lea Thompson played the human lead in this 1986 movie bomb.

Amy Lippman, the 31-year-old cocreator of Fox's *Party of Five*, said she has noticed a difference in letters her show receives from Gen X viewers. "People raised on TV have a real vocabulary for TV tradition," she said. "A lot of the mail I get from people in their twenties is incredibly savvy about the process of television. They say things such as 'Don't take the show off the air' and 'I will not watch Fox programming if this show is canceled,' but the fact that the word *demographic* appears in mail. . . . These people are really hip to network politics and the advertisers who want to advertise around the show. There's a real awareness of the process that I did not encounter on any other show." Accordingly, during the second season of *Party of Five*, the name of the band fronted by Bailey's girlfriend, Sarah (Jennifer Love Hewitt), was the Nielsen Family.

It's been a long time since Hollywood looked down on TV as the wicked stepchild of the film industry. Now films are frequently based on TV shows. Already viewers have seen big screen versions of *The Untouchables*, *Dragnet*, *The Fugitive*, *The Addams Family*, *The Beverly Hillbillies*, *Sgt. Bilko*, and *The Brady*

Bunch. TV-based features in development include *The Honeymooners, I Dream of Jeannie, Green Acres, The Partridge Family, Gilligan's Island, Leave It to Beaver,* and *Mr. Ed.* Even in movie reviews, the influence of TV is cited. The 1995 release *Clueless* (which depicted the younger members of Gen X using the Strauss and Howe timeline) brought this review from Joe Brown in the *Washington Post*: "A *Gidget* for the millennium, a perfect time capsule for this Attention-Deficit-Disordered decade, *Clueless* is a live-action *Sassy* magazine (the *real Sassy,* not the pop-*People* impostor on the newsstands now)," Brown wrote. "It's *My So-Called Life* x *Beverly Hills, 90210* + *The State*."

Erin Smith, a 23-year-old TV connoisseur and editor of the 'zine *Teenage Gang Debs*, said TV is now at the center of popular culture. "You lose a tremendous amount by not knowing about TV," she said. "It permeates the culture. A lot of my friends are total geniuses, but they're so handicapped by not watching TV. Anything that is ever-present in anyone's life should be taken seriously. You can't go to the movies everyday and a lot of people I know don't subscribe to a newspaper, so TV is the common thread."

David Poltrack, executive vice-president of research and planning for CBS, said the lives of the *Friends* cohort have been more culturally shaped by television than were those of previous generations. "If you watch *Friends* and the sitcoms done by Generation X writers for the Generation X audience, they're totally filled with allusions to TV," Poltrack said. "The utilization of TV series as time stamps is much stronger than it was in the earlier Baby Boomer programs. This may be the true television generation. For the Baby Boomers, it was a transitional medium. We watched a lot of TV, but we didn't have TV in our classrooms; we didn't have computers with TV screens. In the educational experience of Generation X and the people coming up behind them, everything has a visual element, so they are even more TV-centered culturally than we were."

Just look at all the TV-related products geared toward Generation X. Fan books about *Friends, The X-Files, Mad About You, Seinfeld, The Brady Bunch, ER,* and *The Real World* litter bookstore shelves. Suncoast Video stores stock T-shirts and hats with logos from *Schoolhouse Rock, Charlie's Angels,* and *The Partridge Family*. Similar items are advertised in *Entertainment Weekly*, and that magazine's parent company, Time Warner, even has its own mail order catalog devoted to TV and movie merchandise, *Viewer's Edge*. Even a theme restaurant was scheduled to open in fall 1996 in Manhattan called Television City. More than a year before this TV version of Planet Hollywood arrived, the restaurant's gift shop was open and selling TV show trinkets.

Eric Robeson, 27, founded Mamba Merchandising (1-800-41-MAMBA) in 1992 to sell TV, movie, and cartoon T-shirts. Along with T-shirts similar to the ones sold through *Entertainment Weekly,* Mamba also featured *Starsky and Hutch, That Girl, Fat Albert, Gong Show, Welcome Back, Kotter, CHiPs, Happy Days, Bewitched, Banana Splits, Scooby Doo, Speed Racer,* and *Brady Bunch* items in its summer 1995 catalog. Robeson said the majority of his customers are in the 16 to 35 age group.

Karen Ritchie, author of the book *Marketing to Generation X,* pointed out another difference between Boomers and Xers. Baby Boomers differentiate news from entertainment and entertainment from advertising in a strict way, she said. Whereas a Boomer with a zapper is more likely to zap a commercial, an Xer doesn't differentiate among news and entertainment and advertising. "It's kind of all entertainment," Ritchie said. "It's partly because there's more mass media and partly because they've grown up with a lot more advertising. They watch TV differently, and they're a lot more comfortable with the technology that allows them to tape and time delay and switch channels. They can watch several programs simultaneously or surf 90 to 100 channels without viewing it as a waste of time. They can watch TV, do homework, and chew gum at the same time. They just simply have more control over the medium."

Generation X is the first generation to grow up with VCRs and multiple remote controls. So it should come as no surprise that the most often-taped TV shows are *The X-Files, Melrose Place, Beverly Hills, 90210, Party of Five,* and *Frasier,* all programs with a high number of Gen X viewers. This makes sense because the older generations are well known for their inability to set the VCR clock, let alone program it to record a program. "We were the guinea pigs of the electronic media," said *Friends* story editor Ira Ungerleider during a March 1995 interview on the *Friends* set where he was joined by writing partner Adam Chase. "Computers, video games, television—all that came into its own during our generation."

While Generation X gained Pac Man, Donkey Kong, and *The A-Team,* this generation also lost something far more important—faith in the nuclear family, church, the government, and U.S. leaders. *Friends* story editor Adam Chase attributes the change in attitudes to a loss of political idealism just as many Xers were born. "Kennedy was shot and then Nixon happened, an era of the president as God, someone who is a little more than human, was very much over," Chase said. "I think it's an overstatement to say that our cynicism defines us, yet I think that is an element. I don't think people our age have a lot of faith in institutions."

"We're all really cynical, and I don't think we've found our identities yet," Ungerleider added.

"Oh, I forgot to tell you," Chase replied.

"We found our identities?" Ungerleider said. "Well, scratch that last one."

"Did the people in the 1960s know they were hippie radicals?" Ungerleider said. "Did the people in the 1970s know they were, like, cheesy, cocaine-snorting, me-generation people? I don't think we know what we are yet. I think a lot of what we do is to emulate other decades, other generations. The 1970s have come back, and pretty soon the 1980s will be back. We all look at people in the 1960s, which was a simpler time, but it seemed like people cared about so much more and knew how they felt about things, and now it's kind of like society runs itself and its hard to figure out where your place is." Gen X was shaped by a changing society that experienced divorce rates that rose from less than 10 percent in 1950 to almost 20 percent by 1980, according to U.S. Public Health Service data presented in *13th Gen* by Strauss and Howe. Strauss and Howe also found that in 1988 only 50 percent of American youth aged 15 to 17 lived with both their biological parents. Is it any wonder that TV, an easy parental substitute, had such an impact on the lives of Gen Xers?

The job market, once booming for Boomers, is difficult, at best, for college graduate Xers. In addition, many of the jobs Gen Xers want are held by 45-year-olds who don't plan to retire for a long time. In this respect, the portrayal of Xers on TV has hurt them in real life. Mike Suerdieck, a 25-year-old construction company estimator, said programs like *Friends* and *The Real World* give older generations the impression that Xers are well-off living in great apartments and that all Xer problems are minor social issues. "That's far from the reality," Suerdieck said. "The vast majority of my generation is paid far less than the older generations made coming out of school, and that's the lucky ones who did find jobs related to their college degrees. Whenever a TV show depicts someone from our generation not living in well-furnished pads, it makes the characters out as losers who just don't try. What is ultimately frustrating is to hear the older generation talking in public, and you can tell they assume that the TV shows depict real life correctly."

Charles Rosin, executive producer of *Beverly Hills, 90210* during its first five seasons, makes the point that the term *Generation X* hadn't even emerged when his program, the first Gen X ensemble drama, premiered in September 1990. "I remember the day when one of my colleagues came in and used the term *Generation X* and said this is what this is," Rosin said in a May 1995 interview. "We'd been writing about Generation X for the three years that preceded it. We tailored our show in some ways to be consistent with the attitudes of an age group not being serviced in a fair and forthright way by broadcast television up to that point. We were not part of the merchandising campaign to appeal to Generation X. Now TV is utterly and completely demographically drawn. We went counter to conventional wisdom. *Ferris Bueller, Hull High,* and *Parker Lewis Can't Lose* [which came on at the same time as *90210*] were geared to the notion of carefree, happy youth. *90210* not only deals with the inner lives, the emotional lives of our characters, but in context with this, [our characters] need to be connected socially to issues."

That's not why everyone watches *90210.* Some watch it for a good laugh. Generation X loves irony, postmodernism, and, basically, goofing on things that are presented seriously—things like "a very special episode of *90210.*" Simply put, it's the cheese factor. Comedy Central's *Mystery Science Theater 3000* became a hit because it consists of characters making fun of really bad movies. That's what Xers do every week while watching *Melrose Place.* But with *Melrose,* there's a difference. After the first rocky season, the people creating the show went out of their way to make it "bad," which is really "good." There's a self-consciousness about *Melrose* (and, to a lesser degree, *90210*) that Xers are drawn to.

It's also the reason Generation X likes the *Late Show with David Letterman, The Simpsons,* and *Talk Soup* because they're poking fun at the establishment. In the Gen X lifetime, there's been corruption in just about every institution—families, churches, the government. That's why Xers laugh at them, why they appear to have so little respect for them. That's why the audience roars when

Letterman calls his CBS bosses "corporate weasels" and makes fun of the network's pitiful prime time ratings. Gen X viewers like to see *The Simpsons* make fun of a politician who sounds like Ted Kennedy (Mayor Quimby) or a mean-spirited kid's TV show host (Krusty the Clown, supposedly based on David Letterman).

Despite a distrustful nature, cynicism, and resistance to marketing, Generation X holds some things dear. Hollywood has figured those things out, and they're now appearing with greater regularity in TV shows in an effort to lure Xers in. What's more, it's working. Friends as family, serialized storylines, and the use of music are three ingredients found in every Generation X TV show.

Friends as Family

With the rising divorce rate, young Xers turned to their friends more often than their parents or relatives. Male-female relationships were just as likely to be based on friendship as romance. For Xer youth, a group of friends often became more important than their families, especially when their home lives were in turmoil. This reordering of priorities and restructuring of relationships came to be reflected in TV shows aimed at Generation X. Look no further than the sitcoms *Friends* or *Living Single* for quintessential examples. When a nuclear family is featured, there's nothing *Leave It to Beaver* about them. "Shows such as *Roseanne, My So-Called Life,* and *Party of Five* tend to portray more realistic families," said Jennifer Elise Cox, the 22-year-old actress who played Jan Brady in *The Brady Bunch Movie* and its sequel. "I think people crave to have a family. You aspire to have one. You create one in any way you can, and I think [Gen X] can relate to dysfunctional families because I think everyone's in a dysfunctional family. I don't really know a functional one."

Kimberly Costello, a Boomer-age producer on Fox's *Melrose Place,* has a theory about how day care shaped the *Friends* generation. "This generation has the ability to socialize in packs, which is incredibly interesting to someone like me who didn't," Costello said. "At age two, they were taught how to get along with others [in day care] and what it means to respect others and somebody's space. So they value those friendships more than family because they spend so much time with them. The people I know from that age group just love being in groups." Costello created a pilot in 1995 for Aaron Spelling called *Pier 66* that didn't get picked up by ABC, but she did learn a lot about Gen X socialization by hanging out with the actors. "We had eight actors ages 20 to 27 and none of them would go to the store without calling all the others," she said. "They were careful not to hurt anyone's feelings or leave anyone out, which I found incredibly kind and wonderful. Then they'd stay up until two or three in the morning and talk about music and film."

The importance of friendship also helps explain why many of the Gen X shows have become hits. ABC's Gianinno said that *Friends* is well written, well acted, and has the edgy humor young adults and teens find appealing. "Another thing you're getting that's different on shows that appeal to 18 to 29-year-olds is the nature and importance of friendship," Gianinno said. "There's always been male-male and female-female bonding, nothing about that is new, but what's different is male-female relationships characterized by friendship as opposed to just a sexual relationship. That's something they've grown up with, which is unlike the nature of male-female relationships that previous generations have grown up with."

Doing things in groups also applies to TV viewing of specific shows, especially *Friends, Melrose Place,* and *Beverly Hills, 90210.* These shows have become a reason to watch with other people and to socialize as the show is taking place, Gianinno said. "When *90210* or *Melrose Place* is on, we've heard in various forms of qualitative research that people are talking about those as appointment shows not only in terms of watching them but also in terms of having the gang over. This gets back to the issue of friendship and just how important friendship is and how important maintaining those friendships is to 18 to 29 year olds."

Serialized Storylines

Because Gen Xers were exposed to so much more than Boomers were (broken homes, sex, violence) and at earlier ages, they grew up much faster than their parents did. Sex ed started in the fifth grade (if not sooner), and in some schools, visiting the nurse was just an excuse to grab a handful of condoms. Like it or not, that's the reality, and realism is something Xers demand from

TV. Before the 1980s, TV shows almost always wrapped up a storyline within an episode. If any questions were left hanging, then it was a two-part story that was concluded the next week. That's not the case in 1990s TV. Thanks to the quality drama genre (which borrowed serialized storylines from daytime soaps), Gen X TV shows and others are almost all serialized. Viewers would expect a prime time soap such as *Melrose Place* to have continuing stories, but what about a sitcom such as *Friends* or *Partners*? In the past, sitcoms rarely carried over stories from week to week other than their basic premises. In the 1980s *Cheers* had continuing stories, but not for every character every week. On *Friends*, the will-they-or-won't-they relationship between Ross and Rachel carried on for a whole year, and each of the other characters had a continuing storyline, too. Medical shows of the 1970s featured doctors with a new set of patients each week, whereas on *ER* and *Chicago Hope*, a patient may be part of a story arc for several weeks. Likewise, the relationships among the workplace staff on a 1990s drama are far more intertwined and complicated.

Music and Multimedia

Music also plays a much more important role in Gen X TV than it ever has before. How could it not after MTV? First, music video stylings crept into prime time in *Miami Vice;* now it's the quick-cut look of *ER* and *NYPD Blue*. Even if the look of TV isn't always MTV, the sound frequently is. *Beverly Hills, 90210* always uses a new and different song during its opening guest star credits. The show frequently features rising acts performing within the episodes, including the Flaming Lips and the Goo Goo Dolls. With the onset of the Seattle grunge scene and Nirvana in the early 1990s, TV quickly got behind this music trend. First, Fox tried it by depicting a garage band in *The Heights.* When that proved too blatant, *Melrose Place* started slipping "alternative rock" music into its opening guest credits and running videos for the songs from the show's soundtrack during the end credits. *My So-Called Life* used truly alternative songs throughout its 19-episode run and included guest spots by singer Juliana Hatfield and the band Buffalo Tom.

If nothing else, members of Generation X are voracious consumers of entertainment of all types. With all the media mergers of recent years, this is good news for the entertainment industry as a whole, but it makes it difficult to lure Xers to any one medium, especially an older medium such as broadcast TV. "Unless you're just trying to get counterprogramming for *Matlock,* you're not going to be getting any buzz unless you look like no other show on TV," said *USA Today* TV critic Matt Roush. "You've got to look or sound different. With *ER,* it's because it packs so much information, so much story content, into every hour, and it's got the young cast. This sense of the 1990s is that they're trying to get people [to watch] who have so many other things to play with now. That is the generation thing. They don't need to amuse themselves by watching network television, and that's the dilemma all the programmers are facing as they try to come up with new program concepts—how to hook them."

For Xers, seeing something new and different is definitely necessary. "I grew up on video games and TV," said Craig Taube-Schock, 27, a researcher/consultant in Alberta, Canada. "Technically strong visual images and sound have always been something I've been interested in. Very often, I will go to a movie simply to see the special effects."

Jonathan Murray, executive producer of *The Real World,* said pace is an important component in shows targeted at Gen X viewers. He pointed to *Murder, She Wrote* as an example of a TV show that's paced too slowly for Xers. "You see Angela Lansbury go to the door, knock on the door, the door opens," Murray said. "We wouldn't go through that process. We'd jump cut her inside. You don't have to connect the dots. These people are used to getting information in a fast way, in a way they can comprehend it. We're busy people who don't have time for Angela Lansbury to walk up the sidewalk."

One of the most important mediums competing for the interest of Xers is the Internet. TV accustomed Xers to spending hours looking at a box, so sitting at a PC for hours on end is easy to accept. Whereas Xers stared at TV, they interact with computers, especially on the Internet where talk about television is prevalent.

"I think the Internet can be used to reinforce loyalty to good TV," said Ian J. Ball, a 25-year-old graduate student who has cataloged all the TV-related Internet sites. "It can also be used as a means to promote new shows and to facilitate deeper understanding of shows, plots, and characters. As far as the networks are concerned, it can be used to canvas viewer opinion to improve shows; however, if I were a network, any opinions on the Net must be taken with a grain of salt."

The on-line universe is also part of Xers' search for community and friendship, impersonal though it may be. Even when they're home alone, there are others out there who are like them and have similar thoughts and interests. Betsy Frank, executive vice-president/director of strategic media resources at Zenith Media Services in New York, said that Internet chatter about TV mirrors a growing societal acceptance of TV discussion. "Not too many years ago it was not a particularly cool thing to admit you did," she said. "Nobody admitted they watched anything but PBS and the news. Suddenly everybody is an expert and a critic and has an idea and feels passionate about certain programs. Everyone feels entitled to pass on judgments and criticisms of TV shows, and I like to graze [the Internet] just to see what people are talking about. There are stupid [posts] too, but there's a lot of very astute observations."

Although Generation X may not be the target market of all advertisers, it's clear that many are trying to reach people in that age group. John Wells, executive producer of *ER*, said that economics play a large role in TV today, especially among advertisers looking for new customers. Advertisers are especially fond of people between ages 24 and 35 because they don't own anything. "Those are the years you have to buy everything you own as an adult," Wells said. "When you reach 40 you tend to have amassed a lot of stuff. Generation X is going to shape TV in the same way the 1960s generation hippies and posthippies shaped all of the viewing. This will now change to reflect this generation entering their prime buying age, which is what TV, whether it wants to admit it, is all about. We're all proud of what we do, but it is a medium for selling stuff."

Although some people interviewed for this book downplayed the importance of Generation X in current TV programming, there's no denying its effect, especially when one considers that three broadcast networks have been launched in the past 10 years that target Gen X specifically. "Fox proved there's room for a fourth network, which is why UPN and WB want to prove there can be a fifth and sixth network," said *Richmond Times-Dispatch* TV critic Douglas Durden. "Fox also pushed demographics to the forefront, unapologetically pursuing 18 to 34 year-old viewers without worrying if it was turning off older viewers. By the start of the 1995–96 season, the other networks had decided to follow Fox's lead, emphasizing twentysomething characters almost to the exclusion of older characters in the majority of their new series."

In this book, I examine how these ingredients came together and were used in both successful and unsuccessful Gen X programs. I explore the TV shows Generation X grew up watching, the TV shows Xers watch now, and the programs that depict their lives. It's also important to look at technology and the impact it has on Xers and the impact Xers have on TV via the Internet. Throughout this book Gen Xers both inside and outside the entertainment industry express thoughtful, intelligent views on Generation X and TV that should dispel the slacker myth. Whether people use the labels Generation X, 13ers, twentysomethings, slackers, the Free generation, or a dead media creation, the fact remains that millions of Xers are very much alive and will influence TV culture for decades to come.

Growing Up with the Ultimate Baby-sitter

When Jennifer Elise Cox was born in November 1973, *The Brady Bunch* was eight months away from its final regularly scheduled prime time broadcast. This sitcom to end all sitcoms began in 1969, but during its run of 117 episodes, it never made much of a splash. At the time Cox was born, no one could have guessed that the Bradys would live on the way they have. As Cox watched reruns of middle child Jan Brady going through the angst of wearing glasses that made her look "totally goofy," little could she have guessed that one day she would recreate Jan on the big screen. A lot changed between 1973 and the release of *The Brady Bunch Movie* in February 1995. When it all began, the show's creator, Sherwood Schwartz, couldn't have realized he would plant something in the minds of America's children that they wouldn't forget. People remember the names of the Brady kids long after they've memorized and forgotten the names of all the state capitals. Even *The Brady Bunch* theme song is more American for some people than, say, the national anthem.

"Two summers before I auditioned for the part, my whole family went on a trip to Ireland," Cox recalled. "We were staying in a kind of castle hotel and we went downstairs to the dungeon room where you have dinner and there were all these people from all these different countries. Everyone from each one of the countries had to get up and sing his or her national anthem. For some reason that evening, my family got up and sang *The Brady Bunch* theme. I don't know, it was the first thing that came into our minds."

2

Although it has become a cliché that *The Brady Bunch* is the childhood favorite of Xers (seen mostly in syndicated reruns), a survey of more than 200 random people in this age group bears out the cliché. I conducted this unscientific survey via the Internet and among groups of fellow twentysomethings in America and Canada. These were the results.

Actress Jennifer Elise Cox portrayed Jan Brady in *The Brady Bunch Movie*. Paramount Pictures.

The Top 10 most memorable TV shows while respondents were growing up:

1. *The Brady Bunch*
2. *Happy Days*
3. *The Love Boat*
4. *Family Ties*
5. *Little House on the Prairie*
6. *M*A*S*H*
7. *Laverne & Shirley*
8. *Star Trek*
9. *Three's Company*
10. *The Facts of Life*

Other shows that ranked just below the Top 10 included *The Cosby Show, Dukes of Hazzard, Cheers,* and *Gilligan's Island.* Still other programs that received numerous nominations included *The Six Million Dollar Man, The Bionic Woman, Silver Spoons, Welcome Back, Kotter, Diff'rent Strokes, The A-Team, Scooby-Doo, Super Friends,* and *The Muppet Show.* The average birth year of survey respondents was 1970. *The Brady Bunch* was 5 percent ahead of the second-most-nominated TV show in this survey. "It amazes me when you meet someone around our age group who never watched the show," Cox said. "That blows my mind."

The number of articles that look to those involved in *The Brady Bunch* for an explanation of the show's phenomenal success is rivaled only by the number of articles that try to explain the *Star Trek* legacy ("It was the hope and depiction of a future where everyone got along," the *Trek* cast members always say). For *The Brady Bunch,* the response falls into one of two categories: (1) they were dorks we now know we should make fun of, or (2) they remind us of a happier, more simple time when families weren't as dysfunctional. Cox said the appeal of the show to her as a child was the opportunity to have "brothers and sisters for a half-hour and then turn it off and they were gone." But the Bradys are really never gone.

Just like *Star Trek,* their one-time sibling on the Paramount lot, the Bradys won't die. They have become ingrained in American culture, so it comes as no surprise that the Bradys came up during a writer's meeting for the NBC Gen X sitcom *Friends* in March 1995. The show's first-season writing staff, aged 24 to 31, were debating how to rework a scene in the episode "The One with the Ick Factor" in which Monica (Courteney Cox) dated a guy who turned out to be only 17. The writers were working on the scene in which she dumped him because she couldn't handle the nine-year age difference. At one point, a writer suggested that the guy's voice should crack. Another writer suggested the punchline should be "It happened to Peter Brady too." Although the joke never made it into the program, it shows the cultural implications of *The Brady Bunch.* "For me, [watching] *The Brady Bunch* and *Gilligan's Island* was almost like a legal drug," said *Friends* story editor Adam Chase. "When I watched it, I wouldn't laugh like I did when I watched *The Odd Couple;* I'd watch the three episodes they'd show in a row and just zone. It was like heroin."

Remnants of the Bradys remain, from the 1995 movie incarnation, *The Brady Bunch Movie* (and its 1996 follow-up, *A Very Brady Sequel*), to the appearance of original cast members on talk shows (which seems to occur during every sweeps month). There have been *Brady Bunch* tell-all books, fan books, and cookbooks, but perhaps the best source of everything Brady is a 'zine called *Teenage Gang Debs* created by a Maryland brother and sister. Erin Smith and Don Smith created the first (now out-of-print) issue of *Gang Debs* in 1989. In 1996 they were at work on issue 7. Both graduates of the University of Maryland, Erin (born in 1972) and Don (born in 1968) have created a publication that has about 2,000 readers per issue. *Gang Debs* isn't exclusively devoted to *The Brady Bunch,* but this sitcom is the primary focus. Erin said she started writing for *Gang Debs* in 1987 (before *Entertainment Weekly*) because she was disgusted by the sorry state of television coverage by the mass media.

"I remember looking at the 'Summer of Love' issue of *People* in 1987 and saying, 'This does not speak to me'," Erin said. "I was very upset because I did not like the way TV was discussed. Either the stuff was very dry, just bad writing, or boring and totally Boomer-centric. So I just wanted to do it the way I wanted it to be. I just thought about getting my ideas out. So doing this was just necessity because I just could not find discussion of pop culture. No one wanted to discuss film study 30 years ago, and I think TV just takes longer to get respect."

With *Gang Debs,* Erin created the ideal outlet. Each issue (except the rare first issue) features a grainy picture of one of the Bradys taken off a video freeze frame from a *Brady Bunch* episode. Especially frightening is issue 2, which features what looks like a demonic Cindy Brady in midscream. Throughout its existence, *Gang Debs* has featured original interviews with Eve Plumb (Jan Brady), Robbie Rist (Cousin Oliver), Stanley Livingston (Chip Douglas on *My Three Sons*), Joseph Barbera (cocreator of Hanna-Barbera cartoons), David Garrison (next-door neighbor Marcy's first husband on *Married . . . with Children*), and Barry Williams (Greg Brady).

Operators Are Standing By Copies of *Teenage Gang Debs*
(issues 2–6) are available for $3 plus two stamps each from *Teenage Gang Debs,* P.O. Box 1754, Bethesda, Md. 20827-1754.

In these interviews, Erin and Don don't ask the regular questions. "In the Hawaiian episodes, you carried this nutty Jan bag . . . whatever happened to that?" Don asked Eve Plumb in issue 4. When Plumb said Imogene Coca was her favorite *Brady Bunch* guest star, Erin asked, "Were you ever afraid you were going to grow up to look like Imogene Coca?"

Perhaps the best *Gang Deb* pieces are the "take you there" articles that describe meeting Joseph Barbera, attending a Frankie Avalon–Annette Funicello concert, and the experience of being on *The Sally Jessy Raphael Show.* In the last account, Erin wrote about being asked to appear on *Sally Jessy* as an obsessed *Brady Bunch* fan along with celebrities such as Barry Williams and Florence Henderson of *The Brady Bunch* and Lisa Welchel and Charlotte Rae from *The Facts of Life.* In the Green Room before the show, Williams looked at a copy of *Gang Debs* and asked why they took photos of the TV screen for the cover: Erin's written response in issue 5 was, "Because we don't have access to the Paramount vaults, dumbass."

In issue 3, Erin took aim at *The Brady Bunch Book* by Andrew J. Edelstein and Frank Lovece, which at that time was the first retrospective Brady book to be published. Erin took exception to the book because some of the material presented as fact was wrong. She also felt that the authors pretended to be experts on a subject they really didn't know or care about. "What really upsets me is that everybody seems to think that Marcia's first boyfriend was Harvey Klinger," Erin wrote. "He wasn't! Even in the book, they actually fell for that one. Her first boyfriend was Alan Anthony. ALAN ANTHONY, God damn it!"

Perhaps one of the best examples of *Gang Debs'* insider dirt is in issue 5, which features an account of Robert Reed's memorial service by Elizabeth Moran, author of the book *Bradymania*. Moran described being in the "Brady room" after the service and hearing cast members squabble. She wrote that Maureen McCormick let Barry Williams know her displeasure about his tell-all book, *Growing Up Brady*. Moran also reported that McCormick and Eve Plumb both refused to participate in a group photo for fear Williams would sell it for use in a future Brady book. In articles like this, *Gang Debs* has plenty to say about *The Brady Bunch* and Gen X pop culture that still can't be found in mainstream media coverage even in this age of entertainment overload.

Erin said she first remembers watching *Brady Bunch* reruns as a kid. "I loved the big family, just like I love *The Sound of Music* [for the large family]," Erin said. "My mom has brothers and sisters in the same makeup as the Bradys. She's the Cindy. I like having one brother, but I remember getting excited about memorizing [the Brady kids'] names and ages. It was my favorite back then of the live-action stuff because it was so warm and fluffy. I remember preferring it to *Family Affair*."

Brady Bunch creator Sherwood Schwartz, 78, said the friendship of the Brady kids was a key ingredient in the show's enduring success. "There's a great deal of affection in the *Brady* show, even separate from love," he said in a 1995 interview. "You don't see that in television anymore. That was knocked out in the 1980s. In the 1980s kids became wiseguys. They now insult their mothers and fathers. Kids insult each other. The tone was radically different from the *Brady* tone."

By the mid-1980s, *The Brady Bunch* barely registered on the pop culture radar. Sure, it was still in syndication, but it didn't seem to show up quite as

often, and it certainly wasn't a topic of conversation. Now it's considered weird if people don't reminisce about watching the show. With the advent of Melanie Hutsell's Jan Brady impression on *Saturday Night Live* and the stage production of *The Real Live Brady Bunch* in the early 1990s, clearly the show was making a comeback. In 1991, Sherwood Schwartz even saw his beloved program reproduced in the form of the ABC series *Step by Step*, which also featured a man and woman falling in love, marrying, and setting up a home for their blended family.

"I think they stole my show," Schwartz said. "As a matter of fact, they advertised themselves as a '*Brady Bunch* for the 1990s.' I think that's intrusion or certainly riding on coattails, and I resented it. I discussed the advisability of a lawsuit, but we came to the conclusion it would not be a lawsuit we could win."

The same thing happened in 1996 when ABC added *Aliens in the Family* (from Jim Henson Productions) to its TGIF lineup. The premise featured a guy abducted by aliens who fell in love with a female alien. The couple returned to Earth to raise their mixed family of human and alien offspring. Although there were five kids instead of six (three alien, two human), the name of the family was Brody, they had a housekeeper, and in publicity photos they posed on stairs as in the traditional *Brady Bunch* cast shot. In the pilot, the father even delivered a Mr. Brady-like moral lesson at the end.

When *The Brady Bunch Movie* came out in 1995, even the *New York Times* was hip to Bradymania. In the "Metropolitan Diary" by Ron Alexander, a very

Opposite: The Brady Bunch cast and the show's creator: (from left) Susan Olsen, Mike Lookinland, Eve Plumb, Christopher Knight, Maureen McCormick, creator Sherwood Schwartz, Barry Williams, Ann B. Davis, Florence Henderson, and Robert Reed. Courtesy Sherwood Schwartz and Paramount Pictures Corp.

A Very Brady Chronology

"**Here's the story,** of a lovely lady." With those lyrics began the most famous TV show theme song this side of *Star Trek's* opening narration of "Space, the final frontier." *The Brady Bunch* began as just another sitcom, but years after its final first-run episode aired, the show became a pop culture phenomenon. *Brady Bunch* creator Sherwood Schwartz said he came up with the idea for the show after reading a statistic in 1965 that said marriages in which one or both spouses already had children were approaching 30 percent. "No show had ever been done like that, so it set me to thinking because as a writer this opened a new world," Schwartz said. "Here was the possibility of not just sibling rivalry, but cross-sibling rivalry."

Schwartz said he attributes the show's emergence as a cultural phenomenon to the reruns airing in syndication. "We became an extended family for a lot of kids who had been subjected to divorce or single parents," he said. "They longed to be in a family that was getting along that well. Most people don't even think of the fact that it's a blended family."

A difference with *The Brady Bunch* that many kids did notice is that they actually went on location for filming. Among the famous *Brady Bunch* trips were visits to a ghost town, the Grand Canyon,

Hawaii, and Kings Island amusement park. Even though the show occasionally went outside, the Bradys were never perceptive enough to notice that the exterior and interior of their suburban home didn't match. How could they walk in the front door and be facing the stairs when the upstairs portion of the house on the exterior is to the left, not straight ahead? "I have no idea," Schwartz said. "Maybe [Mr. Brady] was an incompetent architect." Schwartz pointed out that every bedroom had a window that managed to look out into the backyard. Schwartz said other gaffes occurred when the young actors called each other by their real names. "If you listen closely, in two different episodes Barry Williams calls Jan 'Eve'," Schwartz said. "In one, he says, 'Out of my way, Eve,' and nobody caught it."

But such mistakes are easily forgiven by true *Brady* fans such as Erin Smith, coeditor of a Brady-focused 'zine, *Teenage Gang Debs.* "It's the most perfect show ever," she said. "I do not think it's corny and heavy-handed. I'm not ashamed to watch it. I think adults can enjoy it, and so can kids."

The original series was canceled after a healthy five seasons. Schwartz said if it had continued, Mike Brady would have been written out of the show because of clashes with actor Robert Reed. "There was talk of extending the show for another two years, and we would have killed off the dad, because he was a source of big problems to me, to the show, to the network right from the very beginning because he was doing a show he didn't want to do," Schwartz said. "We would have replaced him or just changed the direction of the show—kill him off and have the adventures of the widow with six kids who are trying to fix her up with another guy."

In the book *Bradymania,* Schwartz told author Elizabeth Moran thought was also given to bringing back Carol's first husband. It would have been ex-

Show Stats

The Brady Bunch
Premiered: September 26, 1969, on ABC
Created by: Sherwood Schwartz

Primary cast:
Robert Reed as Mike Brady
Florence Henderson as Carol Brady
Maureen McCormick as Marcia Brady
Eve Plumb as Jan Brady
Susan Olsen as Cindy Brady
Barry Williams as Greg Brady
Christopher Knight as Peter Brady
Mike Lookinland as Bobby Brady
Ann B. Davis as Alice Nelson
Allan Melvin as Sam "the Butcher" Franklin
    (occasional)
Robbie Rist as Cousin Oliver (last six episodes)

Plot:
Carol Martin was either a widow or divorcée who married Mike, a widower with three sons. This newly created family unit, including Carol's three daughters and Alice the housekeeper, moved in together and went through its share of trials and tribulations. From Jan's middle-child angst to Greg's attempts to establish a music career, the Bradys stuck together through good times and bad. At the end of 30 minutes, however, everything was always good. The exterior of the Brady home was not a studio facade but an actual suburban home located at 11222 Dilling St. in Studio City, California.

plained that he had been missing and had had amnesia for five years! Mercifully, the show was canceled and none of these proposals came to fruition. At the same time as the original series, an animated version, *The Brady Kids,* ran from 1972 to 1974 as part of ABC's Saturday morning cartoon lineup. After the original series and the cartoon show went off the air, it would be two more years before anyone heard a peep from the Bradys.

Once, Twice, Three Times a Brady

Then the reincarnations began. The first, and most dreadful, was *The Brady Bunch Hour,* which even Schwartz has trashed. "I had nothing to do with that," Schwartz said. "I didn't create it; I didn't write a word; I didn't have anything to do with it except that I hated it."

Schwartz said *The Brady Bunch Variety Hour* came about after an ABC executive saw Henderson and some of the other Brady kids on Sid and Marty Krofft's *Donny and Marie* variety show. The network wanted a Brady variety show, so the entire cast (minus Eve Plumb, who was replaced by Geri Reischl as Jan) returned for *The Brady Bunch Variety Hour,* which was broadcast November 28, 1976, on ABC. That one outing served as the pilot for *The Brady Bunch Hour,* which ran for eight episodes. Schwartz said Paramount never gave permission for the Bradys' foray into a variety show, but the studio was reluctant to sue ABC "because they were in bed with the network and had other things to sell them."

"We had discussions about [a lawsuit], but we decided [the show] would probably be a failure because it looked so awful," Schwartz said. "It was just so distorted from the *Brady Bunch* series that I just resented it and would have gladly burnt that celluloid."

It would be another four years before the Bradys returned to series television. What started out as a two-hour TV movie called *The Brady Girls Get Married* morphed into a short-run series called *The Brady Brides.* "We sold it as a two-hour special,"

Show Stats

The Brady Bunch Hour
Premiered: January 23, 1977, on ABC
Produced by: Sid and Marty Krofft

Primary cast:
Robert Reed as Mike Brady
Florence Henderson as Carol Brady
Maureen McCormick as Marcia Brady
Geri Reischl as Jan Brady
Susan Olsen as Cindy Brady
Barry Williams as Greg Brady
Christopher Knight as Peter Brady
Mike Lookinland as Bobby Brady
Ann B. Davis as Alice Nelson

Plot:
What plot? Mike ditched his job as an architect and moved the family into a beachfront home so they could all star in a variety show. The Water Follies Swimmers made frequent guest appearances.

Schwartz recalled, "but after [the network] saw the show and loved it, they said this was too good to kick away in one evening."

Schwartz was ordered to chop it into four pieces, which caused Sherwood and his son Lloyd (his producing partner) to spend four days in an editing room trying to cut it into sensible, coherent episodes. The four episodes have since been put back together for subsequent airings on network TV and on Nick at Nite. Six more episodes were ordered, and *The Brady Brides* project was born, but the honeymoon was short-lived (February–April 1981). "I was not pleased with it," Schwartz said. "I thought it was OK, but they insisted that we stick in extraneous characters. We did not want Florence in and out of the show. We wanted two couples sharing the same house and the couple's problems. They felt we had to include Florence, Alice, and a child who had no place in the show at all."

The show's funniest moment came when Jan and Phillip arrived at the Brady homestead to announce their engagement. Carol said, "We weren't doing anything important," to which Mike replied, "You don't consider reruns of *Gilligan's Island* important?"—a ha-ha in-joke for those who knew *Brady Bunch* creator Sherwood Schwartz also cre-

---

Show Stats

The Brady Brides

Premiered: February 6, 1981, on NBC
Created by: Sherwood Schwartz

Primary cast:
Maureen McCormick as Marcia Brady Logan
Eve Plumb as Jan Brady Covington
Jerry Houser as Wally Logan
Ron Kuhlman as Phillip Covington III
Florence Henderson as Carol Brady
Ann B. Davis as Alice Nelson Franklin

Plot:
Jan and Marcia had both gotten married, and to save on expenses the two couples moved in together. Marcia married a goof-ball toy salesman, Wally Logan (Jerry Houser), and Jan married an uptight college professor, Phillip Covington III (Ron Kuhlman). The actual wedding segment of this series marked the last time the entire original cast appeared together in a Brady project.

---

ated *Gilligan's Island*. It was probably even funnier for viewers who knew about the disdain actor Robert Reed had for such fluff. Schwartz said they originally didn't even plan to have Reed in *The Brady Girls Get Married*.

"To our surprise he insisted on being in the show after five years of agony with him," Schwartz said. "He was actually in a Broadway play at the time, and he had to leave the play for five to six days as I recall, fly back here, do this, and give up whatever monies he'd have been getting for the play to be their father. I said, 'You don't have to come back,' and he said, 'Are you kidding? No one's going to get those girls married except their father.' That was the last attitude I thought I'd get from him. Each time he came back it surprised me."

Another seven years would pass before the gang returned for a two-hour movie, *A Very Brady Christmas*, which debuted December 18, 1988, on CBS. Everyone was back except Susan Olsen (replaced by Jennifer Runyon as Cindy), and now the clan multiplied even further. Greg married his nurse, Nora (Caryn Richman of *The New Gidget*); Peter was in love with his boss; Marcia and Wally were raising two kids; Jan and Phillip were on the verge of divorce; Sam dumped Alice; Bobby quit school to become a race car driver; and Cindy, who was a college freshman in the 1981 reunion, was a college senior in 1988. She must have been on the special seven-year plan. "That one, I think, was terrific," Schwartz said. "We were able to give each of the kids a grown-up personality stemming from the original, and we tried to be honest about it. It all seemed to evolve naturally."

Bradysomething

The ratings for the Yuletide special were better

than anyone expected, so CBS ordered a new series that hit the air just a little more than one year later, *The Bradys.* "We wanted to treat the family more seriously," Schwartz said. "They had adult problems now." Schwartz said he was happy with the show but blames its failure after six episodes on the CBS decision to air the show in the Friday 8:00 P.M. time slot against ABC's successful comedy lineup. "We took the kids, who used to be kids, and treated them like grown-ups with grown-up problems. Maybe it was just unacceptable that way, but I'm positive that the time period had a great deal to do with it. Kids are not interested in these kinds of problems."

Again, because of bickering between Schwartz and Reed, Papa Brady almost bought the farm. "We were going to have Mike accidentally killed in a helicopter accident," Schwartz told Elizabeth Moran in *Bradymania.* "As a city councilman, he was going to check out a fire to see if the fire department needed more backroads, and the helicopter [was going to go down]. Bob [Reed] didn't know about this. I was fed up with him. The story would go on with the kids trying to fix up their mother."

Once again, cancellation saved Mike Brady from death. Erin Smith said it was difficult to accept *The Bradys* without the real Marcia Brady. "You had this feeling already that we were being betrayed," she said. "I remember thinking, how did Martha Quinn get this job? Couldn't I have been the next-door neighbor? The Christmas show succeeded because people hadn't seen them since the *Brides.* Why they thought people would watch an hour-long drama . . . no one wants to see them in a drama."

Except for gatherings on talk shows, the Brady cast has yet to reunite as their characters for another television project. With the death of Robert Reed, that may never happen, but because they've replaced each of the Brady daughters at one time or

Show Stats

The Bradys
Premiered: February 9, 1990, on CBS
Created by: Sherwood Schwartz

Primary cast:
Robert Reed as Mike Brady
Florence Henderson as Carol Brady
Leah Ayres as Marcia Brady Logan
Eve Plumb as Jan Brady Covington
Susan Olsen as Cindy Brady
Barry Williams as Greg Brady
Christopher Knight as Peter Brady
Mike Lookinland as Bobby Brady
Ann B. Davis as Alice Nelson Franklin
Jerry Houser as Wally Logan
Ron Kuhlman as Phillip Covington III
Caryn Richman as Nora Brady
Martha Quinn as Tracy Wagner Brady
Gary Greenberg as Ken Michelman
Michael Melby as Mickey Logan
Jaclyn Bernstein as Jessica Logan
Jonathan Weiss as Kevin Brady
Valerie Ick as Patti Covington

Plot:
The most populated Brady incarnation (dubbed by critics *bradysomething*), this time there weren't just nine squares for the opening credits—there were 18! After trying to conceive a child on their own, Jan (at one point seen vacuuming in her silk underwear) and Phillip decided to adopt a Korean girl; Alice and Sam were back together; womanizing Peter had been through four failed engagements; Bobby was crippled in a racing accident and then married the much-too-perky Tracy (former MTV VJ Martha Quinn); Cindy was a DJ (even though she still had a lisp); Mike ran for city council; and (fake) Marcia (played by replacement actress Leah Ayres) became an alcoholic, but only for one episode.

another, anything is possible. When last quoted in newspaper articles and on talk shows, however, Eve Plumb refused to talk about *The Brady Bunch.* "They take turns not doing something," Schwartz said of Plumb and her TV sister, Maureen McCormick, who has also been a somewhat reluctant Brady in recent years.

Although a *Brady Bunch*-based series hasn't been introduced since 1990, there have been plenty of Brady sightings on other TV shows before and since. Plumb appeared in the 1988 blaxploitation spoof *I'm Gonna Git You Sucka.* And in 1989, Florence Henderson, Robert Reed, Christopher Knight, Mike Lookinland, and an obviously pregnant Maureen McCormick appeared as their Brady selves in an episode of the NBC sitcom *Day by Day.* The early 1990s also produced *The Real Live Brady Bunch,* a stage version of real episodes from the sitcom. It started in Chicago and moved to New York in 1992 before traveling to other cities. Melanie Hutsell played Jan in the stage show and went on to join the cast of *Saturday Night Live,* where she played Jan in a 1992 spoof that pitted the Bradys against *The Partridge Family* in a battle of the bands.

The Bradys hit the big screen in February 1995 with *The Brady Bunch Movie,* starring a new cast as the Brady characters with cameos from some of the original cast members. "That was affectionate satire," Schwartz said of the film. "We weren't making serious fun, not black satire. We loved them, we still love them, but we know what we're doing here. That was the tone we wanted—Mr. Brady's overlong lectures, everybody a little over-the-top—but the aim was to keep it affectionate, or we would have lost the audience who loved it. You can't destroy the people and expect the audience to like it."

But earlier drafts of the script called for just that. "They were really travesties," Schwartz said. "They were beyond parody. As I once put into a memo, it was like somebody wrote the script with an axe, chopping all the characters to pieces. I think we achieved that balance."

The Brady Bunch Movie led to other TV specials, including Nick at Nite's hilarious *Brady: An American Chronicle,* a spoof of the PBS Ken Burns documentary *The Civil War.* In May 1995, Susan Olsen produced *Brady Bunch Home Movies* for CBS. That same month, members of the *The Brady Bunch Movie* cast appeared on the sitcom *Wings* as their Brady characters in a pointless dream sequence.

The entire cast from the first *Brady Bunch Movie* returned for the 1996 *A Very Brady Sequel,* which featured a trip to Hawaii (as in the TV series) and an imposter claiming to be Carol's first husband (played by Tim Matheson). "Alice, this is Carol's first husband, Roy," Mr. Brady said as an introduction. "He's not dead like we originally thought." Roy was out to steal the family treasure, the horse statue located beneath the stairs that has been part of the Brady house set in almost every incarnation.

Brady moment was overheard while waiting in line at an uptown deli: "I saw *The Brady Bunch Movie* last weekend," a female patron said.

"I did, too," replied her male companion.

"On TV, I always identified with the youngest girl," the woman explained enthusiastically. "We both had curls, were cute and funny. Who did you identify with?"

"The same," the guy replied.

The Brady Bunch wasn't the only show Xers watched in the 1970s. Another, more musically inclined family also fought for viewer attention, but *The Partridge Family* never became the icons the Bradys are. Schwartz said *The Brady Bunch* continued to appeal to kids in reruns because the characters experienced problems young viewers of any generation could relate to. "The show was written from a child's standpoint," Schwartz said. "To a young girl, if there's a junior high prom and she has a zit on her face, that's a more important problem than world peace, and we treated it that way. If a kid is afraid of getting beaten up by another kid at school, that's a bigger problem than the national debt. I think only twice did we do a story that featured the parents. It was always a kid-driven story; that's the reason that it worked. With all due respect to *The Partridge Family,* which was a higher-rated show, their problems were too individual. What do we sing? Should we go on the road? It was all directed to that. They did not deal with the problems we dealt with that affect every child watching."

Erin Smith felt that *The Partridge Family* didn't hold up because it was such a product of the 1960s. "It didn't translate well because it was very specific, and *The Brady Bunch* was very general and could go into moral issues [that apply] at any time," she said. "The Partridges would discuss Indian rights and go into a long ecology sermon and celebrate the 1971 Earth Day. And it seems goofy and tacky now because of the music. They were trying harder to be cooler, and it became dated faster. I think *The Brady Bunch* has a timeless quality to it. I know people talk the other way, but it wouldn't be on all the time if that were true."

Schwartz also gave the world *Gilligan's Island,* which only ran for three seasons, but he said most people think it was on much longer because (as a result of syndication) it's never been off the air. Schwartz said that show was a hit with older Gen Xers because it aired originally during 1964–67, before *The Brady Bunch.* "The ideal age for a complete *Brady* fanatic is 24, whereas a *Gilligan* fan is about 31," Schwartz said.

"I thought *Gilligan's Island* was funny in a strange sort of way," said Jack Pelligrinelli, 28, a newspaper editor in Hartford, Connecticut, "almost like it was a test to see how far in advance you could figure out the plot. They could do whatever they wanted for a story every week. Although it always took place on an island, they could bring in characters from the outside (Russian cosmonauts or the Mosquitoes band). The storyline had no limits."

Gilligan's Island appealed to Xers in the late 1960s (and in reruns in the 1970s) because even though it starred adults at least one of the characters always acted like a child. Schwartz said his biggest argument over *Gilligan's Island* was with the head of CBS programming, who wanted the professor to have a nephew to get a kid's point of view in the show. "I won that argument," Schwartz said, "because if you have a nine-year-old kid, that destroys Gilligan: he's a nine-year-old kid no matter what his age is. Sure enough every kid identified with Gilligan because no matter how hard he tried to be helpful, he always screwed things up. That's how most kids view life."

Gen X TV
Nostalgia

Other TV shows that made impressions on young Generation Xers (both in prime time and reruns) included *Happy Days, CHiPs, Charlie's Angels, Battlestar Galactica, Buck Rogers in the 25th Century, Good Times, What's Happening!!, The Muppet Show, New Zoo Revue,* and PBS shows such as *Sesame Street, The Electric Company, Zoom, Villa Alegre,* and *3-2-1 Contact.*

"*Happy Days,* it's like, why did I love it so much?" said *Friends* story editor Ira Ungerleider. "It's so simple; the stories were pretty linear and uncomplicated. But it all really depends on the age you're coming at it from, which is why I try not to judge too harshly the shows that are on now that are aimed at younger viewers. Because to children, maybe they're great like *Happy Days* was to us. I just remember *Happy Days* and *Laverne & Shirley* back-to-back was, like, the greatest hour of television. The writing was so incredibly funny, it was such a pleasure to watch, and the characters were really great."

For Andy Perry, a 26-year-old graduate student at Brown University, *The Six Million Dollar Man* was a favorite. "I was really into the slow-motion running thang," he wrote in an e-mail. "As soon as the show was over, it was bed-time, and I would make my dad watch as I ran into my bedroom in slow motion and jumped onto the bed, trying to simulate the 'bionic' sound effects that accompanied such feats in the show." The creation of a female equivalent helped spark young girls' interest too. "[*The Bionic Woman*] had a female role model," said Kelli Biggs, 28, an English teacher in Silver Spring, Maryland. "The Jaime Sommers character was hip, progressive, beautiful, and in charge."

Reruns of *The Mary Tyler Moore Show* also helped inspire young Gen X women. "I loved Mary and Lou," said Elizabeth Muslin, a 31-year-old graduate student living in Chicago. "Lou reminded me of my dad; he was stern on the outside but a teddy bear inside. I liked the relationship between Mary and Lou and Mary and Rhoda. Mary was beautiful, but she had problems too."

Science-fiction came into its own briefly in the 1970s after the success of *Star Wars*. "[*Battlestar Galactica*] was the best science fiction show that was out there," said Craig Taube-Schock, 27. "*Star Trek* was good too, but after seeing *Star Wars*, I think I was hooked on better special effects."

Xers didn't only watch the silly shows. Many who responded to my survey recalled watching *M*A*S*H*. "It was funny—can't explain why—but over the course of my youth I became very intrigued with adult shows to the point of taping them (audio) and wanting to reenact them," said Erika Grams, a 26-year-old graduate student at the University of North Carolina at Chapel Hill, in an e-mail. "*M*A*S*H* was second in the trend (*Alice* first and *Benson* third). It had one character I always liked in particular—Major Winchester (David Ogden Stiers). Maybe I also liked it because it was about history, and because of it, I started reading books about the Korean War. I am now a World War II–early cold war historian-in-training."

In her book, *Platforms,* author Pagan Kennedy noted that during the 1970s, television had to become more relevant to match a society engulfed in the Vietnam War: exit *I Dream of Jeannie,* enter *All in the Family.* Kennedy also pointed to the 1970s as the time when TV first began to revel in the self-references that have become commonplace today. TV began to go from bionic to ironic. For examples, she pointed to the *Happy Days* episode that served to spin-off *Mork & Mindy.* In a scene with Ron Howard, Robin Williams points to a TV set that's playing the theme from *The Andy Griffith Show* and says, "I love that kid, Opie." In an episode of *The Love Boat,* Florence Henderson and Robert Reed appeared in two unrelated storylines, but they did manage to exchange one significant, knowing glance.

Saturday Morning's Greatest Hits

A uniquely Gen X TV staple in the 1970s was ABC's *Schoolhouse Rock*, a series of three-minute Saturday morning lessons on grammar, civics, science, and math that ran from 1973 to 1985 and returned in 1994 with new installments. From "Conjunction Junction" to "I'm Just a Bill" and "Lolly Lolly Lolly, Get Your Adverbs Here," these little ditties entered the Gen X consciousness and stayed there. They even got mentioned in the 1994 flop film *Reality Bites.*

Tom Yohe was 34 when he, along with David McCall and George Newall, created *Schoolhouse Rock.* All three worked at McCaffrey and McCall, a New York advertising agency, and used their experience with the short sell to bring learning to Saturday morning TV. It all started when McCall saw that one of his sons had no problem remembering the lyrics to rock songs but had trouble with his multiplication tables. So, he thought, kids might learn better if the information were put to music.

Yohe and Newall got to work, joining forces with jazz musician and songwriter Bob Dorough, who came up with the first installment, "Three Is a Magic Number." Michael Eisner, ABC's 27-year-old vice-president for children's programming (now chairman and CEO of the Walt Disney Company), gave the project the green light, and the first installment was soon on the air. It was followed by "Grammar Rock," "America Rock," "Science Rock," and the early 1980s segments, "Scooter Computer and Mr. Chips." Now 58, Yohe believes that the short length of each *Schoolhouse Rock* installment (three minutes) along with the number of times each one aired led to the show's popularity. The segments were never on long enough for kids to realize they were being educated. "I don't think kids would have accepted education in the half-hour format," Yohe said. "*Sesame Street* started a year before we did [with their short learning segments], CBS had *In the News*, a 90-second thing. I'm sure the reason they created this drop-in format was as a way to satiate the critics of children's television." The *Schoolhouse Rock* segments were originally dropped into ABC's Saturday morning schedule five or six times, Yohe said, allowing for enough variety to keep kids interested and enough repetitions to make an impression. By the mid-1980s, *Schoolhouse Rock* began to be preempted by three-minute spots featuring flash-in-the-pan musical group Menudo and, later, by exercise spots starring Mary Lou Retton. "We were gone, and it was sort of out of sight out of mind," Yohe said. "I'd get phone calls every now and then from somebody doing a thesis on children's television, and then in 1990, I got a phone call from kids at Dartmouth. They were having a senior symposium on education and asked me to participate."

Yohe's *Schoolhouse Rock* presentation was scheduled for a Saturday night in the biggest auditorium on campus, and 900 Xers showed up for the event that turned into a sing-along when Yohe played segments on video. "That was the first time I realized what kind of impact it had had on that generation," Yohe said. "That was my rebirth, my catechism. I realized we really affected this group because they all sang along."

At a Museum of Television & Radio seminar in May 1995, Yohe said it was the efforts of college students that helped get *Schoolhouse Rock* back on the air. An undergraduate at the University of Connecticut collected thousands of signatures and sent them to ABC, and another fan kept calling Yohe from phone booths all over the United States. "He was traveling around on his own to campuses, trying to drum up pressure to put *Schoolhouse Rock* back on the air," Yohe said at the seminar.

By 1994, *Schoolhouse Rock* was back on TV with its 44th installment, "Dollars and Sense," the first in the "Money Rock" series. ABC didn't even order any changes in the style. Newall said Jennie Trias, the president of ABC's children's television division, didn't want them to do *Schoolhouse Rap*, she wanted *Schoolhouse Rock*. "It's really a misnomer to call it *Schoolhouse Rock*," Newall recalled at the seminar. "Bobby [Dorough] is too good to stick to rock. He used whatever musical language was appropriate for the concept [of each segment] and that's why it has such variety and that's why I think it has lasted."

About the same time, in 1994, *Schoolhouse Rock* moved to the stage in Chicago with a production called *Schoolhouse Rock Live!* by Theater BAM. This musical production by a group of Xers included 20 songs from the 1970s *Schoolhouse Rock* framed by an original story about a young school teacher who, fearing that he won't remember what to teach his students, turns to the tube. "It's a combination of cynicism and hope," said Nina Lynn, producer of *Schoolhouse Rock Live!* in an interview with Sid Smith of the *Chicago Tribune*. "People come because they think it's a nostalgia thing." Like *The Brady Bunch Movie*, which parodied the Bradys but also treated them with some reverence, *Schoolhouse Rock Live!* didn't make fun of its subject. "[Audiences] see we're playing it partially straight," Lynn said. "These songs bind us as a generation, and it's nice to know there are some things we can actually feel good about."

At the same time, Chicago was also home to *Hooray*, a takeoff on the PBS show *Zoom*, and *Saturday Morning Live*, which featured actors portraying characters from *Scooby Doo*, *Land of the Lost*, and *Fat Albert*, along with songs from *Schoolhouse Rock*. By the summer of 1995, *Schoolhouse Rock Live!* made it to Manhattan and an appearance on ABC's *Good Morning America*. When that happened, even MTV took notice, devoting a segment of the August 4, 1995, *Week in Rock* to the theatrical production. "I remember seeing 'Sufferin' till Suffrage' and being like, 'Yeah! I love this song'!" cast member Dina Joy Byrd told MTV. "Like, I was this tiny kid who thought this stuff was so great. And I think that's how a lot of people feel. It touches a part of them." Cast member Thomas Mizer recalled the dark days when *Schoolhouse Rock* went off the air. "It was pretty frightening," he said. "Actually, I remember because it went from *Schoolhouse Rock* to Mary Lou Retton doing scary, evil gymnastics. You were expected at nine in the morning to get up and be rolling on the floor."

Yohe, now vice-president and creative supervisor at Grey Advertising, said he thinks the impact of *Schoolhouse Rock* is evenly split between educational and cultural. "I think a lot of people love it just because it brings back fun memories of childhood or of sitting in front of the TV on Saturday mornings," Yohe said. "And a lot of people claim to have really learned something. And there's the recognition. You say to someone, 'Conjunction junction,' they say, 'What's your function?' That's purely a rote cultural thing, but I think it made learning very palatable."

There's another Gen X connection with *Schoolhouse Rock:* these three-minute snippets of education were actually a forerunner to music videos. "In a way, we were because we visualized music in animation," Yohe said. "This group [of people] who have grown up on *Schoolhouse Rock* have also grown up on MTV; we just beat them out there by 10 years. There is a tremendous

"Conjunction junction, what's your function?" asked one of the most memorable installments of *Schoolhouse Rock*. Courtesy Tom Yohe and © American Broadcasting Companies, Inc. *Schoolhouse Rock* is a registered trademark and service mark of American Broadcasting Companies, Inc.

correlation. It's almost like *Schoolhouse Rock* was the primer for MTV. Music used to be very much of an aural experience, and now, with the onset of MTV, it's very visual as well. We weren't the first people, but I think we're very similar to MTV in many respects."

Other tidbits that came out of the Museum of Television & Radio's "Reading, Writing, and *Schoolhouse Rock*" seminar included George Newall's revelation that the original title was *Scholastic Rock* until lawyers from *Scholastic* magazine heard about it. Music director Bob Dorough also attended the seminar and told about being hired to sing *Schoolhouse Rock* songs at wedding receptions. The creators spoke about future endeavors, including a series called "Ecology Rock," educational CD-ROMs based on *Schoolhouse Rock*, T-shirts, a fan book written by Yohe and Newall, a new release of the segments on video in August 1995 (some stores couldn't keep them in stock), a boxed set of original *Schoolhouse Rock* tunes, and the Atlantic Records April 1996 release of *Schoolhouse Rock Rocks* featuring *Schoolhouse Rock* tunes sung by alternative rockers.

Finally, Yohe commented on the longevity of what is probably the most memorable *Schoolhouse Rock* segment, "Conjunction Junction." He said it has endured in particular because of the alliterative quality of the song. "We have a test in which we walk into any restaurant and if a waiter or waitress is between the ages of 25 and 33, we just say, 'Conjunction Junction,'" Yohe said. "If they don't respond, 'What's your function?' they've been on Mars for the past 20 years."

Those Wacky (and Sometimes Disturbing) Krofft Shows

Another series of programs that caught the attention of Gen X youngsters were those from prolific producers Sid Krofft and Marty Krofft. These shows, which generally aired during the Saturday morning lineup, were a nice break from the same old cartoons for many Xers. The Kroffts kicked things off with *H. R. Pufnstuf* (NBC, 1969–71 and a 1970 theatrical film; reruns later aired on ABC), a series about a boy named Jimmy (Jack Wild) who, with his magical talking flute, Freddy, hopped aboard a boat, was kidnapped by the evil Witchiepoo (Billie Hayes), and was taken to Living Island where he was befriended by a dragon, Mayor H. R. Pufnstuf. Jimmy and Freddy also encountered sneezing houses, talking animals, and other oddities. With its paths through the forest, menacing talking trees, and a witch as the antagonist, *Pufnstuf* looked a lot like a low-budget *Wizard of Oz*.

Like many of the Krofft programs that would follow, *H. R. Pufnstuf* had a psychedelic quality that some have speculated was inspired by drug use by the show's producers. For instance, doesn't the name Pufnstuf suggest a slang term for marijuana? And why include a magic flute that Witchiepoo constantly craves? Did the talking flute symbolize a massive joint? A September 1995 America Online chat session suggested that there may have been some underlying drug themes in the Krofft shows. Someone on AOL asked, "Your creations (characters, sets, songs) are beautiful, psychedelic, and horrifying, often all at the same time. What were/are some of your influences? Be honest. . . . Did you guys take a lot of drugs in the late 1960's?"

Sid and Marty responded, "The question should be: Do we take drugs in the 1990s?"

In a later interview, Marty Krofft said that drugs really didn't play a role in the creation of their programs. "That was our look, those were the colors; everything we did had vivid colors, but there was no acid involved," Krofft said. "I'm no goody two-shoes, but you can't create this stuff stoned."

Their second series was *The Bugaloos* (NBC, 1970–72), a Saturday morning version of *The Monkees*. Four British musicians (Caroline Ellis, John Philpott, John McIndoe, and Wayne Laryea) starred as a bunch of bugs who formed a band while avoiding Benita Bizarre (Martha Raye), who lived inside a giant jukebox. Billy Barty played Sparky the firefly.

For *Lidsville* (ABC, 1971–73), The Kroffts sent a young boy named Mark (Butch Patrick, who played Eddie Munster on *The Munsters*) into a strange world populated by giant talking hats, an evil magician named Hoodoo (Charles Nelson Reilly), and the kind Weenie the Genie (Billie Hayes).

A friendlier creation was *Sigmund and the Sea Monsters* (NBC, 1973–75), the tale of a sea monster family who disowned their youngest, Sigmund (Billy Barty), because he refused to scare humans. Sigmund ran away and lived with human kids Johnny (Johnny Whitaker, who played Jody on *Family Affair*) and Scott (Scott Kolden). Mary Wickes played Johnny's family housekeeper; Rip Taylor was added to the cast as Sheldon the Sea Genie. One episode also featured a guest appearance by H. R. Pufnstuf, Jimmy, and Freddy.

Aside from *Pufnstuf*, the most enduring Krofft show was undoubtedly *Land of the Lost* (NBC, 1974–77; reruns later appeared on CBS), which featured a dad (Spencer Milligan as Rick Marshall) and his two kids (Wesley Eure as Will and Kathy Coleman as Holly) who fell through a time tunnel and landed in the prehistoric age. Each week they tried to find a way back home while battling dinosaurs and lizardlike humanoids called Sleestaks. They also made some friends in this prehistoric world, including Chaka (Philip Paley), a curious apelike creature called a Pakuni.

Later, the Kroffts produced *Far Out Space Nuts* (CBS, 1975–76), which starred Bob Denver (who played Gilligan on *Gilligan's Island*) and Chuck McCann as two guys who accidentally launched themselves into space. Space was also explored in *The Lost Saucer* (ABC, 1975–76), which starred Ruth Buzzi (of *Laugh-In*) and Jim Nabors (of *Gomer Pyle, U.S.M.C.*) as extraterrestrials who accidentally kidnapped a boy and his babysitter during a visit to Earth.

Another popular Krofft program was *The Krofft Supershow* (ABC, 1976–78, renamed *The Krofft Superstar Hour* for NBC in 1978), which was hosted by a rock group called Kaptain Kool (played by Michael Lembeck) and the Kongs. The band introduced the show's various segments until 1978 when a Scottish recording group called the Bay City Rollers took over those duties. Edited episodes of *The Lost Saucer* were featured on *The Krofft Supershow* along with several new series. *ElectraWoman & DynaGirl* starred a pre-*Days of Our Lives* Deidre Hall and Judy Strangis as Lori and Judy, two magazine reporters who turned into superheroes and battled criminals (much like the 1960s *Batman* series). *Wonderbug* starred a talking dune buggy; *Dr. Shrinker* featured a bad guy who shrank a group of kids; *Magic Mongo* was about an untalented genie; and *Bigfoot and Wildboy* followed Sasquatch and a teenage human. In prime time, the Kroffts inflicted the airwaves with *Donny and Marie* (ABC, 1976–79) and *The Brady Bunch Hour* (ABC, 1977). Even an indoor theme park called The World of Sid & Marty Krofft existed in Atlanta for seven months in the mid-1970s at the site of what is now CNN headquarters.

Young Xers loved these shows because they offered something different from the multitude of cartoons on the TV schedule. They had the psychedelic look that was alien to kids at that time and was, therefore, "cool." The

Krofft shows starred other kids, which was a great way to grab young viewers' attention. Most of the shows had the same theme at their cores: kids cut off from their world who learn to survive on their own. "The Kroffts never talked down to kids, never wrapped up with a moral, and made the best of their budgets," said Grant Goggans, a 24-year-old writer. "Many of the series had the astonishingly stark image of someone or some people leaving our known universe to become trapped forever somewhere and never coming home."

Marty Krofft said this theme of kids cut off from their parents probably stemmed from his and his brother's childhood. "I think part of it had to do with our own upbringing because my brother and I didn't have much adult supervision growing up," Marty said. "My brother was out touring with his puppets, my dad died when I was 12, and mom was not that involved. She was there for me, but my mother and father trusted me."

Joseph Nebus, a 23-year-old graduate student at Rensselaer Polytechnic Institute said he liked the science fiction aspects of the Krofft shows. "I liked the many ways in which it was about exploration and discovery and attempting to understand the world. I liked the storylines in which the show would explore new aspects of the *Land of the Lost*, looking for the boundaries and discovering what was there. It was recently pointed out to me that the entire show has a subtext, which I think I appreciated without understanding back then, about the search for identity."

Although Gen Xers have remembered the Krofft shows over the years, few of the programs were brought out of the vaults until September 1995 when Nick at Nite aired eight hours of the programs in a bit of stunting called Puf-A-Palooza. Among the Krofft entries shown were *H. R. Pufnstuf*, the original *Land of the Lost*, *The Bugaloos*, *ElectraWoman and DynaGirl*, *Lidsville*, *Sigmund and the Sea Monsters*, and *The World of Sid & Marty Krofft Live at the Hollywood Bowl*, featuring songs by Johnny Whitaker (from *Sigmund*), Jack Wild (from *Pufnstuf*), and the Brady [Bunch] Kids.

At the time of Nick's Krofft-fest, Sid and Marty discovered that—horrors of horrors—Freddy the Flute from *H. R. Pufnstuf* had been stolen from their warehouse. A reward of $10,000 was offered (Freddy was returned anonymously to a Los Angeles television station two months later). Around the same time, the alternative rock group Tripping Daisy released an album (*I Am an Elastic Firecracker*) that included this line in the song "Rocketpop": "Well all is great / and everything's nice / with H R Puffinstuff [*sic*] by our side." In December 1995, MCA Records released *Saturday Morning Cartoon's Greatest Hits*, a compilation of kids' show theme songs (mostly from the 1970s) recorded by 1990s modern rock artists. Tripping Daisy covered the theme from *Sigmund and the Sea Monsters*, Collective Soul tried to sing like *The Bugaloos*, and The Murmurs offered their rendition of the *H. R. Pufnstuf* theme.

Just as *The Brady Bunch* and *Schoolhouse Rock* have been revived, so has the Kroffts' *Land of the Lost*. New episodes ran for several seasons on ABC Saturday mornings beginning in 1991. The new version featured another family, consisting of a father (actor Timothy Bottoms) and his teenage son and younger daughter. Instead of encountering Sleestaks, the bad guys were another lizardlike race. Although Chaka didn't return, a new character named Stink (who looked like a Pakuni) was introduced along with the jungle girl, Christa, and a baby dinosaur that lived with the family.

In 1995, the Kroffts entered into an agreement with Walt Disney Pictures to bring their TV shows to the big screen, starting with *The Land of the Lost*. *H. R. Pufnstuf* is expected to be the second Krofft property to be remade as a movie, and a new *Bugaloos* TV show is in development at Fox. "Sid and Marty Krofft are kind of a brand name today, and that's why we're doing it all again with the [age] 20 to 35 audience in mind," Marty Krofft said. "Those are the kids who grew up with it, and they are very loyal. We sold 10,000 T-shirts during Puf-A-Palooza. They never sold more than 1,500 during a marathon before that."

The Kroffts aren't the only ones making a comeback. ABC announced in July 1995 that the Muppets would return in *Muppets Tonight!* and gave the updated series a 13-episode order for the 1995–96 season. The original *Muppet Show* was rejected by all the networks but became a syndicated hit in the 1970s and still airs on Nickelodeon. When *Muppets Tonight!* joined the ABC TGIF lineup in March 1996, Kermit and company ran a TV station instead of an old theater. Like the original show, the new adventures of the Muppets included sketch comedy, music, and a major guest star each week. Despite critical acclaim, the ratings were low, but ABC still renewed the show with plans to bring it back during the 1996–97 TV season. Often accused of recycling culture from the past, now Gen X gets to see its own culture recycled.

The TV Set: Another Parent?

Although the later Baby Boomers were the first to grow up with television, for them, watching TV was generally a family affair. Everyone would gather around to watch the tube and see what delights Ed Sullivan had to offer on a Sunday night. Some Boomer youth watched alone too, but mom was probably cleaning or in the kitchen making dinner. Just look at the opening credits of HBO's *Dream On*; the show's main character, Baby Boomer Martin Tupper (Brian Benben), grew up in front of a TV set (while his mother vacuumed around him). Even the Boomers who did grow up with the tube as a parent experienced a television landscape without a VCR or cable TV. In addition, they more often than not had a flesh and blood parent nearby, which wasn't always the case for Gen X. As kids, television was more often a solitary experience for Generation X as a result of the rise in single-parent and dual-income families. The percentage of working mothers (with children under age 6) rose from 20 percent in 1960 to 60 percent in 1990, according to the U.S. Bureau of Labor Statistics. This change left many kids home alone with the tube.

"We're the first generation who were really raised on television," said *Friends* story editor Adam Chase. "Television was virtually another parent. I certainly used to come home from school and watch three hours of television."

The term *latchkey kids* (children whose parents worked who returned home from school to empty houses that they unlocked with their own keys) never existed before the birth of Generation X. These kids often returned home to TV as their after-school companion. For the youngest of Xers, teething rings were quickly replaced by remote controls: one for the TV, one for the VCR, one for the cable box. Boomers had no remotes and were able to watch only a few channels. For Xers, the number of channels boomed. Xers quickly learned how to program the VCR and how to surf through the various cable networks. While their working parents climbed the corporate ladder, Xers watched TV.

"My parents were divorced when I was five, and my mother and I moved from Puerto Rico to Georgia where it was just the two of us," recalled Jennifer Hale, 25. "I remember playing with other kids and catching fireflies, but I also remember lots and lots of TV. I'd watch it when I was at the baby-sitter's after school, and then my mom would pick me up and we'd go home and eat dinner while watching TV. I think I even watched it in the mornings before school. And Saturday morning was an animation-fest, not like this crap now with live-action science shows and the *Today* show that they air on Saturdays. TV was the cheapest baby-sitter my mother could buy. My sister has two kids, and I tell you, there's a reason she owns every Disney movie on video."

Gregory M. Weight, a 24-year-old graduate student in English at the University of Delaware, agreed, calling himself "one of those latchkey kids *and* an only child. I definitely used the TV as baby-sitter, teacher, friend, and entertainer."

Many Xers who responded to my Internet survey described the TV as an "electronic baby-sitter." Even baby-sitters often passed their responsibilities along to the TV. "My TV babysat my baby-sitter," said Prashant Sridharan, a 22-year-old student at the University of Maryland. "And because she babysat us, we were, by some weird, twisted logic, babysat by a TV."

"I watched it constantly," said Renee Drellishak, a 25-year old administrative assistant in Sunnyvale, California. "It raised me. . . . TV wasn't just a baby-sitter, it was a member of the goddamn family." Although this certainly wasn't the case for everyone in Generation X, TV as a babysitter was far more prevalent with this age group than it was with Boomers. With more dual-income families in the 1980s and 1990s, this phenomenon is even more common with children today.

When Prime Time Was Not So Prime

There's no way around it, by and large, television in the 1970s was a vast wasteland of superheroes and substandard sitcoms, with few quality programs available to discerning viewers. "It was horrible," said *New York Daily News* TV critic David Bianculli. "It was amazing to me how bad TV was pre-*Hill Street Blues*."

Bianculli said the shows acknowledged as "good TV" (*All in the Family, Mary Tyler Moore, Bob Newhart*) were carryovers from the 1960s. "You could have entire nights when there was not only not anything good on one network, there was nothing good on any of them," he said. "There was *Sheriff Lobo, B. J. and the Bear, Supertrain,* and *Pink Lady and Jeff. Hill Street Blues* really did change that. TV rematured after it hibernated in the 1970s."

As Xers aged, they saw a change in television with the emergence of shows based in reality. Whereas the 1970s had only a few pioneering programs, the 1980s had a new breed of program with the creation of the "quality drama." Prime time began to grow up as stories became more dense, production values improved, and programs became more arresting with the likes of *Hill Street Blues* and *St. Elsewhere.* Many Xers were too young to appreciate these particular shows, instead embracing their offspring: *NYPD Blue* and *ER.*

At the same time that the doctors of St. Eligius grappled with realism mixed with the occasional self-conscious inside joke, the same old silly sitcoms bombarded the airwaves with *Diff'rent Strokes* and its spin-off, *The Facts of Life,* topping the Nielsen charts. For a few years, uttering the catch phrase "Whatyoutalkin'bout, Willis?" became the zenith of TV pop culture literacy among young Xers.

"I started watching [*The Facts of Life*] when Molly Ringwald was still part of the cast," recalled Sara Emily Whitford, a 20-year-old undergraduate at North Carolina State University. "As a little girl, I wanted to watch shows that gave me ideas about what it would be like to be a teenager. To be honest, I don't know of anyone who didn't watch *The Facts of Life.* The character mix was so unusual. You had all of the major social classes represented (at least those that existed in the early 1980s). Blair was the rich, cosmopolitan girl. Tootie was the minority girl who always rode around on roller skates and had most of the artistic talent. Natalie was the not-so-pretty, but lively 'class clown'-type character."

"I just thought [*The Dukes of Hazzard*] was a great show," said Chris Lesher, a 22-year-old student in Jonesboro, Arkansas. "Any show with all those car chases and crashes just *had* to be great. All the kids in my elementary school watched it, and we'd talk about the show during the day. I even played *Dukes of Hazzard* and *CHiPs* quite a bit. I had many favorite shows and cartoons. It's hard to believe the amount of time I spent in front of the TV when I was younger. Somehow, I still managed to go outside and play in the afternoons, too."

The 1980s served as a transitional decade during which shows like *The Dukes of Hazzard* and *Moonlighting* could be on the schedule during the same TV season. Even as TV began to shed its traditional mantle of goofiness for more sophisticated fare, programming aimed at kids remained in the goofy mode. *Silver Spoons* and *Punky Brewster* typified the shows of that day; then things started to change. *Voyagers*, a relatively intelligent (by comparison) sci-fi show at least gave kids some history along with the high jinks, but it only lasted one season. The sci-fi miniseries *V* (not the series, which eventually turned into the first sci-fi soap) also captured the imagination of young Xers with its premise that Nazi Germany could happen again, only this time with alien lizards disguised as humans.

With the success of *Family Ties* and, especially, *The Cosby Show,* family shows returned in the mid-1980s, including the hit *Growing Pains.* It was almost like a *Brady Bunch* revival. "If you examine *The Cosby Show,* they duplicated two-thirds of our stories," said *Brady Bunch* creator Sherwood Schwartz. "The parents were always paying attention to their children, teaching moral lessons. It was the same sort of show really. I was doing a family values show before there was such a phrase."

These values didn't last. By the late 1980s, *Roseanne* had come to embody the dysfunctional family sitcom. Whereas *Roseanne* presented a more realistic approach, *Married . . . with Children* simply took the sleaziest route. "Morality is sorely lacking in a lot of the situation comedies," Schwartz said. "You can just say 'condom' and get a laugh. That's sad. It's dishonest humor, it's shock humor, and very often shock humor is schlock humor. They'll do anything to get a laugh."

Sophisticated Sitcoms

As prime time content became more mature, it also became more relevant. This was certainly the case with *Roseanne*, which premiered on ABC in 1988, offering what was then an atypical sitcom family. Unlike June Cleaver or even Clair Huxtable, Roseanne Conner is a sarcastic woman who lives in a home that doesn't look like it's been cleaned by a maid (or anyone else for that matter). Unlike those earlier TV shows in which dad was in charge, on *Roseanne*, mother knows best. Whereas Norman Lear's 1970s sitcoms dealt with race and abortion issues, *Roseanne* reentered the arena of sensitive social issues on sitcoms after a decade of near dormancy. Whereas earlier sitcoms had episodes about condoms without using the word *condom*, *Roseanne* shirks from no issue: racism, religion, teen sex, gay issues, masturbation, rape, drugs, and unwed mothers.

Kenny Hom, a 25-year-old student in Ontario, Canada, said he watches *Roseanne* because of what he considers the show's realism. "Besides being funny, Roseanne's show hits home about their place in society," Hom said. "The characters are average-looking. Some even have weight problems. They don't live in a nice house with nice furniture. They don't act nice to everybody. They have dead-end jobs. The characters are neurotic. The women are manipulative. It reminds me a lot of close friends, relatives, and my situation. It is funny to watch your life on TV; in reality, it's not that funny."

In its early seasons, *Roseanne* held special interest for Gen Xers because of Darlene (Sara Gilbert), the wisecracking middle child. Darlene was smart, independent, and able to exceed her mother's level of sarcasm. She was a typical Xer. *Roseanne* was also the first Gen X sitcom to implement continuing storylines; from Jackie's string of lovers to Roseanne's series of jobs, *Roseanne* didn't wrap up every storyline in a half hour as did most 1980s sitcoms. By not allowing each episode to be a neat package, *Roseanne* came across as more realistic. Real life doesn't happen in 30-minute blocks; why should sitcoms? "There's always been a tension about that because people can get frustrated," said *USA Today* TV critic Matt Roush. "People can't watch all TV all the time. There's a fear that if they fell out of the show's sync, they'd be unwilling to come back to it. Now, the other argument is [that] those kinds of [continuing] threads have proved beneficial because people will discuss them and talk about them around the water cooler."

Roseanne also preceded all the other 1990s sitcoms in making an art of self-referential jokes. Perhaps the best running joke was the changing of the Beckys when actress Lecy Goranson was replaced by Sarah Chalke in 1993. At the end of Chalke's first episode, the whole gang gathered around the TV to watch an episode of *Bewitched*.

"I cannot believe they replaced Darrin," Roseanne said.

"Well, it was a hit show," Jackie replied. "They knew they could get away with anything."

"Well, I like the second Darrin much better," said the second Becky.

The joke continued in a flashback episode during the 1994–95 season when an adult D. J. (played by John Goodman) was traumatized, saying repeatedly, "They say she's the same, but she's not," as images of the two different Beckys flashed in his head. In fall 1995, Goranson returned to the role.

"Where the hell have you been?" Roseanne said to Goranson in her first scene in September 1995. "It seems like you've been gone for three years." Although Goranson was named in the opening credits (both actresses were pictured as a result of a bizarre morphing process), throughout the 1995–96 season, Chalke frequently filled in as a substitute.

At the end of Goranson's return episode, a black and white ditty to the tune of *The Patty Duke Show* theme aired, featuring both Chalke and Goranson. Even William Schallert, who played the father of one of the Pattys on *Patty Duke*, smiled on as the dueling Beckys mimicked one another.

"Meet Lecy, the one you used to see, from '88 to '93, but Sarah came and took her place because she had a similar face, that's what's on TV," went the specially created, peppy theme song. "But they're Beckys, nearly identical Beckys, one pair of matching actors, but only one part to play." For the 1996–97 season, Chalke returned to the role full-time.

The fact that a sitcom continued through the closing credits was a new twist itself. *Roseanne* was the first to do it, and now nearly every sitcom on TV has followed that lead. By continuing the show through the end credits, viewers are conditioned to stay tuned for the end credits and, the network hopes, the next show too. For viewers who pay close attention, this final scene is a bonus; for those with short attention spans, it's a way to keep them tuned in. By the 1995–96 television season, *Roseanne* had become tired and predictable, reaching its lowest point in the ridiculous Roseanne-directed Halloween episode, which for years before had been a highlight. *Roseanne* did return to form at the end of the season when Dan suffered a heart attack, which led to Roseanne leaving him in the season finale. Goodman planned to make occasional appearances during the 1996–97 season, which was planned as the last hurrah.

Just as *Roseanne* helped 1990s sitcoms grow up, *Seinfeld* made sitcoms grow weird. Although critics dubbed it "a show about nothing" when it debuted as a summer series in 1990, it's really a show about strange idiosyncrasies everyone can relate to (looking through someone's medicine cabinet, thinking your dry cleaner is wearing the jacket you brought in for cleaning, being embarrassed by a date, trying to take back a message left on an answering machine, pretending you're something you're not). Granted, these are all exaggerations, but they're also extremely funny. More importantly, they're all situations viewers can relate to. Kristen Buchanan, a 23-year-old student at Syracuse University, said *Seinfeld* is her favorite TV show. "It's a comment on the relevant issues in society today," she said. "Topics like homosexuality, dating, and masturbation are discussed in a humorous fashion while showing how 'normal' members of society deal with them."

"It has the greatest writing, and the characters are real," said Syracuse University student Craig Sender, 21.

Seinfeld also makes expert use of the friends as a family device. None of the characters ever has a relationship that lasts longer than a few episodes (until George's failed engagement in 1995–96), which makes their shared desperation for a successful romance even more laughable.

"The pieces just fall together," said Joanne Cosker, a 25-year-old executive assistant in Centreville, Virginia. "It pulls from different episodes. It's inside jokes."

Her husband, Glynn Cosker, also pointed out *Seinfeld's* serialized elements. "Something in episode three will be referred to in episode 12, just a one-liner or a look from Jerry," said Glynn, a 25-year-old employee at the British embassy in Washington, D.C. "*Seinfeld* makes fun of everyone you hate or who gets on your nerves, like people who talk in the third person. It's people you want to tell to get a life, and Jerry does it for you."

Seinfeld also has a knack for winding all the elements of an episode together. The storylines converge in what is often a funny (other times, forced) mess of coincidences. *Seinfeld* has been able to tackle subjects that once were taboo in a funny, realistic manner from the "master of my domain" episode about masturbation to the episode in which Jerry is thought to be gay, "not that there's anything wrong with that." Although the characters are at the trailing edge of the Baby Boom, *Seinfeld* appeals to Gen X because it is unafraid of being frank and honest in its depiction of silly but realistic situa-

The *Seinfeld* gang poses for an uncharacteristically warm and fuzzy cast shot. Courtesy Castle Rock Entertainment and NBC.

tions. Far from being "a show about nothing," *Seinfeld* is a show about some tiny aspect of life week after week.

Although neither *Seinfeld* nor *Roseanne* can be called a strictly Generation X show, both sitcoms appeal in large part to that age group because they are different and take chances. *Roseanne* features a sarcastic Gen X daughter; *Seinfeld* features continuing jokes among the gang just like in real-life friendships. These weren't the same old shows. In the 1980s, teenagers were only seen on TV as part of a family sitcom unit. Single twentysomethings were almost unheard of. That's what changed in the 1990s. After a decade of programming aimed at Boomers, TV finally began to recognize, depict, and make an appeal to another age group.

A Changing TV Culture

Television in the 1980s began to show society more accurately as it existed, but it wasn't just a matter of sitcom writers waking up and realizing it was time to get real. Technology was pushing the entertainment industry. For all the TV shows that made it to the airwaves in the late 1970s and 1980s, none had as much influence on the future of Gen X culture as two new technologies—cable TV and the VCR. As cable became more prevalent, its permissive nature trickled down to the networks, leading to such shows as the realistic *Roseanne*, the coarse *Married . . . with Children*, and the blue *NYPD Blue*. Both cable and VCRs had a great impact on the development of younger Xers (and even more impact on the millennials, the post-Xers born during the 1980s and 1990s), but it still didn't take older Xers long to figure out how to work the remote controls for either the cable box or the VCR. Granted, those were the days when tapes were loaded into VCRs from the top, not the front, and their remote controls were not wireless. But the ability to record TV shows and play them back at a time of the viewer's own choosing is significant in the study of Gen X's current viewing habits and demands. Just as the VCR was an important new must-have gadget, one cable network in particular stands out as an influence on Gen X culture.

On August 1, 1981, MTV first went on the air to the tune of "Video Killed the Radio Star" by a British band called the Buggles. This new network, which targeted the 12 to 34 age group, got the attention of Generation X like nothing else has before or since. Although Xers today (particularly the older ones) look down on MTV, there's no denying that it greatly influenced both Gen X culture and American culture on the whole.

"I think the more obvious effects were seen in the 1980s with a show such as *Miami Vice*, which incorporated a music-video look into the traditional cop drama," said Douglas Durden, TV critic for the *Richmond Times-Dispatch*. "On a more long-term basis, MTV can probably be credited for TV series having shorter scenes and moving at a faster pace. But MTV itself has already decided to be less MTV and more mainstream TV by adding its own nonmusic series, such as *The Real World*, and news segments."

Before MTV, music was just music. After MTV, music had a visual component. When many people hear Bruce Springsteen's "Dancing in the Dark" they also picture the video (which introduced the world to Courteney Cox). This visual component has changed the way TV and movies look today. Quick cuts, fast-paced scenes, computer graphics, rock music as underscore, and the further emergence of cable (to some extent) can all be traced to MTV.

"I thought it was the most wonderful thing in the world, worthy of all my young time and attention," said Parley Stock, 24, a hotel reservations center employee in Phoenix, Arizona. "MTV changed TV by showing advertisers and network executives what the newly budding consumers responded to. I think we saw a whole new wave of commercials full of splashy graphics, attitude, and youth, as well as all of the high school/college soapy shows like *90210*."

"I was 15 years old," said John D. Frazier, a 26-year-old federal contract administrator in Springfield, Virginia. "I remember this because a friend had cable and a Betamax. I only had the Betamax. I asked him to tape four hours of MTV onto a Beta tape. Back then, MTV was all music videos and the occasional VJ[video jockey]. I got an entire summer's worth of videos off that tape. It was interesting because [before that] the only interpretations we got from the music were from the broken lyrics we tried to pick up off the tape or radio. With the videos, we could piece together the lyrics better by reading the lips of the artist, and we could understand the imagery and symbolism of the songs with pretty pictures behind the artists."

"All of my friends and I thought that it was the greatest thing ever," said

Andrea Bright, a 27-year-old graduate student living in Alexandria, Virginia. "I think MTV changed television a lot. It demonstrated that a network devoted to young adults and teenagers could not only survive but thrive. I think that the reactions of advertisers to MTV's audience is probably responsible for a lot of the young adult programs on other networks today."

"[Because of MTV], everything must be in video form for my generation," said Alex J. Millar, a 23-year-old student in West Lafayette, Indiana. "It has decreased our attention spans like nothing else. It has made bands that may not have made it on the radio, and it has killed bands that don't fit the MTV mold. Everything geared for my generation must be 'extreme' or 'in your face' or 'intense' or 'cutting-edge.' I don't blame Dan Cortese for this, it is all MTV's doing. It has changed rock and roll more than anything since long hair. I think it has made TV a bit hipper, but I wish I could watch a commercial without squealing guitar, odd camera angles, and an 'alternative' look."

It's interesting that MTV had this effect on commercials because music videos are basically nothing more than three-minute commercials for compact discs and tapes. So MTV insisted that record companies provide music videos with the record labels paying production costs—voilà, instant programming at no cost to MTV. But MTV's selling of itself, its personalities, music, and movies often comes under criticism.

"I worry that MTV gets a bit too much credit everywhere, including in the media," said *USA Today* TV critic Matt Roush. "Everything about MTV is about self-promotion and about being sold and marketed to a very media-savvy population that sort of pats themselves on the back and makes people feel hip just by having tuned into it whether there's anything good about it or not. I can't believe *Beavis and Butt-head* became the sensation it was. I think it became the sensation because the media validated it [and] because to criticize it makes it look like you're not cool."

Many Xers agreed.

"There's way too much calculated marketing and programming on there," said Jack Pelligrinelli, 28. "They've lost the true spirit of rebelliousness and innovation they once had."

Before MTV, if people wanted to hear music from a popular movie, they had to listen to the radio or buy the soundtrack album. Now they can watch MTV and see a video from the movie, see an interview with the star of the movie, and see the star host videos. This synergy is especially true if it's a Paramount movie because MTV is part of the Paramount-Viacom conglomerate. *Clueless* was a perfect example. MTV is not alone in this approach; Fox also has stars host nights of programming to coincide with 20th Century Fox motion picture releases. Once MTV makes a band a hit, the band will appear on *Saturday Night Live* with a guest host who is almost always there to promote his or her latest film project. *SNL* itself has become a breeding ground for movie stars and sketches that can be turned into feature-length movies that will be promoted on MTV. "MTV's about nothing if its not about the hard sell," Roush said.

For all its influence, many in the industry think MTV's clout is overstated. *Rolling Stone* reported in May 1996 that MTV's ratings have remained flat for five years at one-half of one rating point. During the final quarter of 1995, about 300,000 homes were tuned to MTV during any 15-minute period, the magazine reported. Even Nickelodeon has 1 million viewers in the same time span while TBS draws 800,000. "I admire MTV for all their marketing and imaging and the clever things they've done, but I think the cleverest thing they've done is to convince the world that Generation Xers and teens watch MTV all the time," said Horst Stipp, director of social and development research for NBC. "According to the Nielsens, most sitcoms on the old traditional networks and Fox [have] ratings among Gen X that are 10 times as high as the average rating for MTV."

Since its launch 15 years ago, MTV has evolved dramatically. In the beginning, it was condemned for many reasons, including a lack of air time for black performers, presenting women as sex objects, and promoting sex and violence in videos. One way the network sought to add more black artists to its lineup was by creating shows such as *Yo! MTV Raps* and *MTV Jams Countdown*. This segmentation has carried over to the rest of MTV's schedule as well, resulting in a lineup that is far more like a traditional network than like a video jukebox. Now there are fashion shows, sports shows, soap operas, and animated programs. These changes don't sit well with many Xers, who no longer consider themselves MTV viewers.

"MTV has more TV than music nowadays, and much of the TV is geared toward semiliterate, uninspired young twentysomethings who like to whine and party," said Mary Burnside, a 26-year-old special events coordinator at the Northwestern University School of Law.

"Quite frankly, I think it sucks now," said college student Sara Emily Whitford, 20. "Back then it was about musicians and bands and music videos. Now it's about how many shows they can create using former *Real World* guinea pigs to host. I liked it back when all they had was music videos, none of that extraneous stuff."

"I'm stuck between the generation that watches MTV, and those that watch VH-1," said John Frazier, 26. "I have no icons to cling to, no VJs to lust over. I grew up; MTV didn't grow with me."

That's the dilemma that will eventually be faced by all the networks that have sprung up since the 1980s. Do they want to age and change along with their target audiences, or will they stick to one specific age group that generation after generation will pass through? MTV has chosen to remain stationary so that its first generation of viewers is about to leave it behind. MTV will not lack for viewers as the next generation fills its viewing ranks. Still, the music network will have to deal with disgruntled Xers who want their MTV.

"These days MTV tries too hard to be a cultural icon—the voice of a generation," said Benjamin E. Bryant, a 19-year-old college student in Austin, Texas. "Back in its infancy, it just was an icon because it was new and different. It brought a new focus on the youth of America as a viewing (and buying) force. It also introduced the psychedelic taping technique, the quick edits, and the young (not youth-oriented, but young) VJs who proved that youth will watch youth. MTV only appeals to a select group of people at any given time these days because of its specialization. Thus, 80 percent of the time, I'm not interested."

MTV realizes how far it has strayed from its original concept, and in summer 1996 introduced M2, a cable channel that airs only music videos. Clearly, the original MTV gears itself toward the younger end of its age 12 to 34 target audience, which explains the dissatisfaction among these Xers now that they're older. But that doesn't diminish the link between MTV and Generation X, nor does it mean that no Xers are watching MTV. *The Real World* stars and is watched by many in the Gen X age group, but Xers are not as likely as today's teens to tune in regularly. Still, by melding music and television, MTV created a combination that eventually became de rigueur in almost all Gen X programs.

Dave, ALF, and the Rise of Irony

If the MTV innovation is one hallmark of Gen X, another important attribute is this generation's sense of humor, which is self-conscious, self-deprecating, and filled with irony, but also tends to be somewhat subversive and antiestablishment. The king of this kind of comedy is Baby Boomer David Letterman, whose *Late Night* premiered on NBC in 1982. With an hour-long show that didn't hit the air until after midnight, Letterman remained a cult hero to older Xers (college students and insomniacs) for many years, but by the mid-to-late 1980s the cult grew. "I started watching him probably in 1986," said Julie Ayotte, a 25-year-old educational travel coordinator in Boston. "I used to videotape the show when I was in high school and watch it the following afternoon, and in college I watched all the time."

Because Letterman was older, Xers appreciated an elder who had the guts not to fawn over his celebrity guests if he didn't like them. Here was an adult who was actually "cool." Letterman was basically a smartass who could get away with such behavior because the people who were most likely to find him objectionable were in bed hours before his show came on the air. Letterman made his mark with a sarcastic sense of humor that was foreign at the time. "Now it's hip to be sarcastic, and it was more of a rarity in the 1980s," Ayotte said. "It's really bizarre to me because he's almost as old as my dad, but I don't think of Letterman as being my elder; I think of him as being my peer. He's still with it; he's still fresh. He still can really relate to the younger generation, so it's strange to me that he's in his forties."

It's interesting that a Baby Boomer has been the ringleader of Gen X humor. Letterman's audience has always been younger mostly because of the time of night his TV shows have aired, but it's his style of humor—angry, sarcastic, cynical, ironic—that has come to be known as Gen X humor. Xers have always dwelled in the shadow of the Boomers, even to the point of earning the title Baby Busters, a nickname that makes it sound as if the whole X generation is a failure because it did not continue the glorious reign of the Boomers. It's kind of discouraging for Xers to strike out on their own when a nickname for their generation implies that failure is a part of their birthright. The fact that the parents of many Gen Xers left them at home with TVs in order to pursue their own career goals or simply to work to make ends meet led to much of the anger manifest in Gen X humor. It's not just divorce and career-minded parents who have had an impact on Generation X. This is the first generation expected not to do as well financially as the previous generation; Xers know that they will be left with a huge national debt even after the Boomers have sucked the Social Security system dry, not to mention that Xers can't get the jobs they want now because Boomers will have them for the next 20 years. By the time the Boomers do retire, Xers will be bypassed for the next generation. Xers have seen news footage from dozens of airplane crashes, the space shuttle explosion, the bombing of the World Trade Center and the Oklahoma City Federal Building, and still people wonder why Xers are unwilling to trust their elders, the government, and even each other. According to *The Shelter of Each Other* by Mary Pipher, by 1990, 72 percent of Americans did not know their neighbors, and the number of people who never spent time with their neighbors had doubled since 1970. The rising rates of poverty, violence, and incarcerations also contribute to Xers' overall negative outlook. This negativism may explain why the humor of Gen X is regarded as mean-spirited, rude, and often inappropriate. Out of this anger comes cynicism, sarcasm, and irony. Alanis Morissette even named one of her songs "Ironic," but Boomer elders were quick to point out that most of the situations she describes in the song are not examples of irony. The *Washington Post* tackled the whole irony issue and concluded that the definition of *irony* has eroded to the point where anything self-referential, satiric, or coincidental has come under the classic definition of *ironic*. Naturally, the *Post* blamed David Letterman and Gen X culture for the tendency to label anything ironic. That in itself is not ironic because it's what most Xers have come to expect from the Boomer-controlled media establishment.

One of the first fictional TV characters to capture the sarcastic nature of Gen Xers wasn't even human. He was from the planet Melmac, ate cats, and went by the name ALF, which was also the title of his show. Granted, *ALF* (one of the last fantasy-based, outsider-looking-in sitcoms until NBC's *3rd Rock from the Sun*) had a standard fantasy sitcom premise (alien crashes into garage, family adopts alien, alien threatens to eat cat, nosy neighbors never figure out what's going on), but it was ALF's wisecracks, snide remarks, and comments on human habits and customs that qualify the show for mention in a discussion of the shows Gen X grew up watching.

The Fourth Network

During the same season that *ALF* premiered, Generation X passed another major TV milestone—the premiere of Fox. This so-called fourth network began October 9, 1986, with the ill-fated debut of *The Late Show Starring Joan Rivers* on 96 stations (about 76 percent of the country). Fox first moved into prime time April 5, 1987, with 106 stations, and the programs *Married . . . with Children* and *The Tracey Ullman Show.* Other programs that first season included *21 Jump Street, Mr. President,* and *Duet.* Second season duds included *The New Adventures of Beans Baxter, Karen's Song,* and *Down and Out in Beverly Hills.*

"There's an acceptance of the hip and off-center and the unusual," said Betsy Frank of Zenith Media about the Fox plan. "A lot of people think Fox really changed the whole level of standards for the networks. They may have raised the level of what was tolerated in terms of language [in prime time] most especially."

Relying on the sensationalism of *Married . . . with Children,* which was considered overly raunchy at the time, and niche marketing (the teen girl appeal of Johnny Depp in *21 Jump Street*), Fox made a name for itself with in-your-face programs that mom and dad hated but the kids loved. Fox also differentiated itself with its name. Although sometimes referred to as FBC in media accounts during its early days, on the air the network was always called Fox. In an interview with Arthur Unger of the *Christian Science Monitor* in July 1987, Fox's then president, Jamie Kellner, said he was targeting a more narrow audience than were the big three networks.

"They try to appeal to everybody, and we believe that has resulted in derivative, homogenized programming, although I applaud their occasional efforts to do unique things like *ALF,*" said Kellner, who was 40 when Fox launched. "We are going after the young-adult audience. A large percentage of the network audience is over 50, and, in order to win the household ratings game and be no. 1, they must appeal to the older viewers. Fox is not in that household ratings game. We believe that the future of television is going to be directed toward pinpointed demographic audiences."

This niche targeting of untapped segments of the viewing public began with shows targeted at teens in Generation X and eventually moved on to go after young males with reality programs such as *America's Most Wanted* and *Cops* and young black audiences with *In Living Color, Roc,* and *Martin.* The young female audience was targeted later with a spate of Aaron Spelling shows and the revival of the prime time soap with *Melrose Place.*

"Maybe Fox was the one to be the pioneer [for Generation X programming] just like ABC had been [for Boomers] back in the 1960s with *The Mod Squad,*" said *USA Today*'s Matt Roush. "Fox, I guess, would be seen as the ABC of Generation X. To me, ABC seems like it's always been there, and to this generation, Fox has always been there. They're not really going to remember [the time] before Fox was one of the networks—that's like life before computers."

Indeed, even as late as the 1960s, ABC was viewed as the loser network. It had to fight throughout the 1950s with the fledgling DuMont network for stations in many markets, but even after ABC finally won its place as the third national TV network, it still lagged behind CBS and NBC. ABC didn't have a top-rated series until *Marcus Welby, M.D.* in the 1970s, and the network never ranked no. 1 in prime time for a complete season until 1976–77.

David Poltrack, executive vice-president for research and planning for CBS, also compared the Fox intense interest in young viewers to the ABC campaign for acceptance in the late 1960s and early 1970s with the Baby Boomers. "When ABC first started, it didn't have full national coverage, so it programmed and targeted for a younger audience," Poltrack said. "Then it started to market the audience it had and convinced the Nielsens to publish age breaks in surveys and started promoting that at the time when Baby Boomers started hitting the adult market place. So what happened was that the Boomers became the major target audience of marketers. So advertisers started to place buys based on [ages] 18 to 49."

That 18 to 49 demographic remains the favorite of many advertisers today, but as the Baby Boomers aged, that ideal demo aged with them, shifting to the 25 to 54 age group for a time. With the introduction of cable, the networks' share of the audience shrank from a one-time high of 90 percent to 60 percent (divided three ways). "The networks found that if the target audience is now 20 percent instead of 30 percent, you might as well go after the 20 percent that gives the biggest return," Poltrack said. "So the relative orientation of advertisers to young people has always been there, but the nature of network TV was to reach everyone and try to be as competitive as possible. As the potential audience available to them narrowed, the networks started to focus more on the younger audience, which was the most lucrative in terms of advertiser appeal. From the perspective of totality of advertising, the middle-age audience is as important as the younger audience, but for advertisers who want to target younger viewers—movie companies, soft drinks, automobiles to a certain extent, Blockbuster Video—these people came in and were willing to pay the highest premiums." By 1992, advertisers were suddenly clamoring for a younger demo again, which led to the orientation toward Gen X TV as advertisers went after the 18 to 34 demographic.

Age and the Networks

Although the networks don't agree on the average age of their viewers, they did agree on the order the networks ranked by the average age of viewers in 1995. Network executives more reluctantly agreed with the stereotypes associated with each of the networks: CBS is for the 50 plus crowd; ABC for the kids; Fox for teens, twentysomethings, and minorities; NBC for hip, white urbanites, 18 to 49. The approximate average age (based on different figures from different networks) of viewers for the four broadcast networks are listed below in parentheses.

Fox (29)
ABC (35)
NBC (39)
CBS (48)

X Marks the Spot

By targeting a specific segment of the market, the Fox network has been able to not only survive but to thrive. During the 1993–94 TV season, *60 Minutes* finished second in the Nielsen household ratings, whereas *The Simpsons* ranked forty-ninth. Yet 30-second ad rates for both shows during the 1994–95 TV season were both set around $160,000. Even though *The Simpsons* had fewer viewers, it had younger viewers, which to advertisers is more important than the millions of older viewers who watch *60 Minutes*. People in the

18 to 24 age range only watch between 20 to 25 hours of TV per week, whereas people in the 55 plus age group watch between 35 to 40 hours per week. Because younger viewers aren't watching as much TV, they're more difficult to reach, so advertisers are willing to pay a premium to reach them. Advertisers who want Gen X customers are also sometimes willing to pay more (or an equal amount) to reach fewer viewers if they think there's a greater chance those viewers will pay attention to their commercials.

"The problem for us as a network is that we don't get paid by the intensity [with which] a show is watched, we get paid by the number of people that watch," said Charles Kennedy, Fox vice-president of program research. "Now we've tried to incorporate that into our rate structure and into our selling of the ads. We go to advertisers and say, you know when people are watching a *Melrose Place*, they're watching with more intensity; they're not switching channels because there's a large group [watching together] and nobody wants to miss what comes on in the next minute. So your ads get seen at a higher rate. Your ads have a chance to be exposed to groups rather than individuals and to be reacted to that way. So there is value to an intensely and loyally watched show."

This helps make up for the fact that Xers brought up on TV have too much going on in their lives to watch as many programs as they once did. "My TV viewing now is an extreme fraction of what it once was," wrote Jennifer Hale, 25, in an e-mail message. "It used to be that I'd turn on the TV the minute I got home and just use the audio as background noise, but now I only turn it on when there's a specific thing I want to watch. That sound you just heard was millions of advertisers bursting into tears. I'd still say I probably watch between 10 and 15 hours a week, total, but in high school or before it was easily 35? 40? I'd come home from school at 4:00 P.M., and the TV would go on and stay on until 10:00. And the weekends were a video orgy as well . . . Yeesh. Makes my eyes blur just thinkin' about it!"

Charles Kennedy of Fox cites these as the main reasons advertisers target Generation X. He says younger viewers are valued because

1. Xers are more willing to try new brands or switch brands because they haven't developed intense brand loyalty.
2. Younger people need to buy more things, because they're just beginning

to establish households. They do a lot of first-time purchasing of a variety of products, and some are even raising kids.

3. They spend a lot. Older people grew up during recessions and wars; younger people grew up during an era of consumerism. Xers will buy not only what they need but also what they want. "They may not make a lot of money, but they'll still own Gap jeans and go to Starbucks," Kennedy said.

4. Xers place more value on image. "They may not want to admit it," Kennedy said. "And often times that's part of the image too. Younger people have a need to say things about themselves and to define who they are. And they define who they are in one small way, however superficially they think it is, by the products they use and surround themselves with."

Many Xers will undoubtedly read this and say it's untrue. "I'm an individual," they'll cry. "I can't be classified; I'm unique!" That may be, but how else does one explain the success of The Gap? Or what about Urban Outfitters, a Gap-like store for the grunge crowd that specializes in clothing that looks like it came from a thrift store but is sold at a department store price? Although I can't say I would buy a deodorant because "it's cool," I think to a greater or lesser extent Xers do buy items based on TV advertising. If they didn't, would companies still advertise there?

Karen Ritchie, author of the book *Marketing to Generation X*, points out the unusual dynamic working between the public and advertisers. Although the popular perception is that people don't want to be targeted by advertisers, at the same time, if a generation is ignored by the advertising establishment "that means you're being ignored by corporate America, that you're not functioning as part of the economic structure, and that historically has been a bad thing," Ritchie said. "Some people say, 'We

Brought to You in Part by . . .

Not surprisingly, the companies that advertise on Gen X TV shows are selling products bought by people in the 18 to 34 age range, this means lots of ads for movies, videos, beer, hair care products, and cars, all items young people buy. Below is a list of four shows that appeal to Gen X and the national commercials that aired during a single episode in March 1996.

Melrose Place

1-800-COLLECT
The Birdcage (movie)
Burger King
Elantra car from Hyundai
Jhirmack shampoo
Levi's 501 jeans
Mountain Dew
Oral B Toothbrush
Pantene Pro-V shampoo
Pepsi
Playtex tampons
Pulp Fiction (home video)

Revlon
7-Up
Women's Reebok

The Simpsons
Ace Ventura: When Nature Calls (video)
Coke
1-800-COLLECT
Gillette deodorant
McDonald's (twice)
M&Ms candy
Mountain Dew
Ocean Spray drinks

Friends
Ace Ventura: When Nature Calls (video)
Aquafresh
The Birdcage (movie)
Clairol Ultress shampoo
Coors Light
Fargo (movie)
Kraft Singles
Mazda cars
Olive Garden restaurant
Orudis KT
Polaroid
Reebok
Wow! (on-line service)

ER
Bissell
Doritos
Equal
Ethan Allen
A Family Thing (movie)
Fidelity Investments
Hallmark cards
Honda cars
Intel Pentium Processor

Kellogg's Nutrigrain Bars
Olive Garden restaurant
Playskool toys
Polaroid
Primal Fear (movie)
Purina Dog Chow
Revlon
Sears Craftsman tools
Tagamet HB
Tylenol PM

It's clear that the ads in some of these programs are aimed more at one gender than at the other. *Melrose Place* is a good example of this bias, with ads for women's shoes, shampoos, and tampons. At the other end of the spectrum, commercials that aired during *The Simpsons* are clearly more geared toward young males who guzzle soda, fast food, and candy. The commercials shown during *Friends* tend to be more unisex in nature and a little more hip, too. There was even an ad for CompuServe's spin-off, the Wow! on-line service. That's something not likely to be advertised during *Murder, She Wrote*. *ER*'s commercials are also fairly unisex in appeal, but the products advertised are not as clearly aimed at Gen X. Ads for Playskool toys and Craftsman power tools are probably targeted at a slightly older audience than are Doritos.

Each of these programs appeals to different types of people. Some shows have more male viewers, others more female viewers. Some appeal to older folks; others appeal to younger people. But in each program products from fast food to entertainment to cars are aimed at Gen X. Generation X may not be the sole target of any of these commercials, but people in this age group are certainly a part (and, in some cases, a large part) of each commercial's target demographic.

haven't been targeted by advertisers. Don't mess that up because we don't miss it,' and I think there's some truth in that. But if you're not valued as a customer when you walk into a store, don't you find that somewhat off? I would."

Charles Kennedy of Fox said the rationale for reaching Gen X outlines why the network continues to pursue the younger demographics. Although Fox is fighting to broaden its appeal to include the complete age 18 to 49 audience, Kennedy said the network will never target people over age 50. Instead, people will stop using Fox at a certain point, and they'll be replaced by younger viewers. Fox is viewed by many as the Gen X network today, but if Fox sticks with its plans to remain a network for the under-50 crowd (and, in most cases, Fox appeals primarily to the under-40 set), Gen X will be out of its target demographic by 2020.

Although all the TV networks want to attract Gen X viewers, Fox is certainly courting them more aggressively than are the traditional networks. "They were very effective at it, and once they got the hang of it, they were very effective at it to the point where they were able to cannibalize viewership from the other networks," said Betsy Frank of Zenith Media. "But this is not the be-all, end-all audience that advertisers want to reach. In general, this is not a terribly affluent audience. It's not a terribly loyal audience, but if you're selling soft drinks or jeans, it's absolutely where you want to be."

Advertising Age critic Bob Garfield said Xers are important consumers to manufacturers of these specific products. "At the ages they are now, they're buying the vast majority in certain categories like soft drinks, fast food, low-cost fashion wear and music," Garfield said. "In those specific categories,

Desperately Seeking Consumers
The melding of Generation X and TV hasn't been limited to TV programs. Commercials have also been targeted to reach the Baby Busters and to get them to buy, buy, buy. Just because they've been targeted doesn't mean the commercials have hit the spot. *Advertising Age* critic Bob Garfield, 41, said in a phone interview that advertisers have been making big mistakes in their attempts to reach this age group. "They think of this young, feckless group of people who listen to Pearl Jam all day, all the time, who wear flannel and are underemployed," Garfield said. "They're just caricatures that will not impress those who do look that way, and they will put off those who do not look that way, who are the vast majority. They're trying to tap into a mind-set that is the subject of a few op-ed pieces but in no way is applicable to an entire generation of people."

The first obviously Gen X slacker spot was Subaru's 1993 commercial featuring actor Jeremy Davies as a grunge-clad Xer who compared the Subaru Impreza to punk rock. Garfield trashed the spot in his *Advertising Age* review, calling Davies's stereotypical character "a Rebel Without a Chest who couldn't sell David Koresh a grenade launcher. . . . Compared to this grungy little cheesesack, Dan Cortese [the grungy pitchman in Burger King's BK TeeVee campaign] looks like David Niven." Garfield said the Subaru spot made a poor assumption. "I hated it because from a marketing point of view it made little sense, but also you don't assume the entire generation looks like a refugee from a Seattle coffee house," he said. "If you do assume, you'll be wrong. That was the most extreme example."

Another series of spots from Budweiser made more of an effort to connect with Gen Xers reared on 1960s sitcom reruns. In these ads, Xer guys played pool while discussing which *Gilligan's Island* character they'd rather sleep with, Ginger or Mary Ann. A young woman commented, "Ginger was a bimbo."

"They were a little smarter in the sense that if people in this generation do have anything in common, it's what they grew up watching on TV," Garfield said. "By trying to tap into some sort of shared experience or mutual nostalgia, you have a better shot than you do trying to get into peoples' points of view about the environment, the economy, or even music."

Garfield said the one Gen X campaign that he thinks successfully avoided clichés was for Janus Mutual Funds, which encouraged Xers with a small amount of money to think about investment plans.

"There was not a molecule of flannel in the whole campaign," Garfield said. "It ran heavily [in 1994], and there was no punk rock music, no victims of the transformation from a manufacturing economy to a service economy, just advertising without mentioning any demographic."

Most recently, the depiction of Xers has been a backlash on the initial slacker image. A 1995 commercial for Bold laundry detergent featured an electric guitar version of "Pomp and Circumstance" and the voice-over of a 1995 college commencement speaker, who assured Xers "We are not a generation of slackers, we are the future, and we have come for what's ours." Garfield said this depiction is likely to change further as Xers age. "As Generation X gets a little older and they have grown-up jobs, the stylistic, superficial characteristics that are the basis of the stereotype will dissipate," he said. "Once Generation X gets into the foray of clothing opportunities that the adult world offers them, it will be harder and harder to pretend there is some sort of common thread weaving them together as people on a single monolithic course. At 35, we won't see flannel in advertising aimed at them."

they are an economic force and as they age will work their way through other categories and continue to spend large amounts of money as a generation. And a time will come when they will be the heaviest users of incontinence diapers."

Betsy Frank pointed out that many of the Gen X shows, such as *Friends*, appeal to a wide audience. "I think a lot of the programs on the air now that seem to be targeting that group, even shows like *Friends*, focus on people in that age group but are really not necessarily trying to reach those people alone," Frank said. "I think a lot of people like to watch that show. You could probably go broke if the only people you're trying to reach are between 25 and 35. Shows these days have to have broader appeal."

Frank said Fox shows seemed to typify the life-style associated with Generation X, so they have now become synonymous with Generation X shows. *"The Simpsons* may do just as well with that target audience," Frank said, "but it's less likely to be called a Generation X icon because it's not glamorous and young."

"Don't Have a Cow, Man"

Show Stats

The Simpsons
Premiered: January 14, 1990, on Fox; originally created in 1987 as a series of 30-second spots on *The Tracey Ullman Show*
Created by: Matt Groening

Primary cast:
Dan Castellaneta as Homer Simpson
Julie Kavner as Marge Simpson
Nancy Cartwright as Bart Simpson
Yeardley Smith as Lisa Simpson
Harry Shearer as Mr. Burns, Principal Skinner, Ned Flanders, Smithers, Otto the bus driver, and other characters
Hank Azaria as Moe, Apu, Chief Wiggum, Dr. Nick Riviera
Marcia Wallace as Mrs. Karbappel

Plot:
Not since *The Flintstones* has a prime time cartoon captured so much attention and led to so much mass marketing. This dysfunctional cartoon family lives in Springfield, a typical cartoon town somewhere in middle America. Homer works at the nuclear power plant run by the evil Mr. Burns; Marge stays at home with the kids, including brainy Lisa, Bart the brat, and pacifier-sucking Maggie.

Ah, but how *The Simpsons* has become a Gen X icon. It's a show whose humor is totally in sync with the sarcasm, cynicism, and media obsession that appeals most to Generation X. *The Simpsons* was the show most directly responsible for bringing Gen X self-consciousness to the forefront. "Every episode has something satirical that makes me laugh," said Glynn Cosker, 25. "The show has no boundaries. Because it's an animated show, they can do things with the characters and to the characters that can't be done on real-life shows. The kids won't get older [as they would] in a live-action show. It's not set in the limits of everyday life like other shows, so they can do fantasy shows. It's sledgehammer wit, blunt, to-the-point, and funny. It's a series of one-liners that make you laugh out loud. They parody every movie and every current thing."

"I love *The Simpsons* because it is so referential and deep," said graduate student Gregory Weight, 24. "I mean, any show that can have a day-care center founded on the principles of Ayn Rand is amazing. In addition, it is incredibly subversive. With characters such as Smithers, Krusty, and Lisa, there is so much room for social comment, which the writers take advantage of."

The Simpsons first appeared in short segments on Fox's *Tracey Ullman Show* in 1987 and was spun-off into its own

30-minute series in January 1990 after a Christmas special in 1989. Each week, the show follows the trials and tribulations of Springfield's dysfunctional (yet loving) family, the Simpsons. From Homer's job at the local nuclear power plant (just where one wants an idiot to work) to the trials of Apu, the stereotypically foreign owner of the local Kwik-E-Mart, there's always plenty of satire in this creative series. In the beginning, *The Simpsons* also created controversy. Parents objected to Bart's pride in being an underachiever, crying that he was a poor role model. What they failed to notice was the show's humor that poked fun at politicians, religion, and any sort of establishment imaginable. This humor also allowed the show to survive beyond its phase as fad TV that generated Bart Simpson T-shirts, toothbrushes, and sleeping bags.

Originally, supporters of *The Simpsons* were attracted to the fact that it made fun of the *Leave It to Beaver* family life displayed on *The Cosby Show.* Even as *The Simpsons* reveled in the depiction of a less-than-perfect all-American family, the show did offer clear moral lessons and showed that even though Bart and Lisa fought, they always loved each other. To combat any perceptions that the Simpsons and the Huxtable clans were more similar than either one would like to admit, *The Simpsons* became more and more a parody of current popular culture and media figures as it aged.

In a sixth-season episode, Lisa visited a tarot card reader who showed the future. In 2010, Lisa would fall in love with a charming Brit named Hugh (clearly trading on the fame of actor Hugh Grant). The couple went to a film festival featuring "40 classic films starring Jim Carrey," Lisa lived in Dr. and Mrs. Dre Hall (from the name of rap star Dr. Dre), and she had a poster on her wall from the Rolling Stones' "Steel Wheelchairs Tour 2010." Back at home, Homer watched one of the 1,500 cable channels, "CNNBCBS (a division of ABC)," which covered the lives of celebrities.

"Heather Locklear Fortensky remains at large," the news reader explained, referring to the *Melrose Place* star who evidently followed in the footsteps of Elizabeth Taylor and married former construction worker Larry Fortensky. "Remember, if you see a celebrity, consider them dangerous."

This episode of *The Simpsons* also made fun of the futuristic gimmick often used on sitcoms where the audience learns that in the future one of the beloved family members has died. When Lisa called home to tell her family that she and Hugh were to be married, Marge said, "If only your father were here . . . (dramatic pause) but he's run to the store."

These are all examples of *The Simpsons* parodying other forms of media, and because the show's audience is so media savvy, viewers love it. Although the show began more as a showcase for Matt Groening's dysfunctional family creation, *The Simpsons* evolved into a pop culture barometer. If it's made fun of on *The Simpsons*, then it's an important piece of popular culture. *The Simpsons* ushered in a minianimation revolution as well, but the makers of these other shows failed to realize that *The Simpsons* didn't become a hit because of animation. It became a hit because of its style of humor. Whereas *Fish Police* (CBS 1992), *Capitol Critters* (ABC 1992) and *Family Dog* (CBS 1993) flopped, *The Critic* (ABC 1994, Fox 1995), from the producers of *The Simpsons*, was at least a critical success. *The Critic* took the media-obsession/parody portions of *The Simpsons* and created a separate show around them. Jay Sherman (voiced by John Lovitz) was a movie critic who worked for a cable station owned by Duke Phillips (a thinly veiled Ted Turner parody). Jay had a *Siskel & Ebert* type review show so there were plenty of opportunities to make fun of current films. Jay also continued the Simpsons' habit of mocking Fox.

"You're watching Fox, shame on you," Jay frequently scolded as the show went to a commercial break. Another bumper featured this gem: "You're watching Fox; give us 10 minutes, we'll give you an ass."

Although the humor was aimed at adults, *The Simpsons* also had an impact on kid's animation. When Steven Spielberg's *Tiny Toon Adventures* came along in 1990 (followed later by *Animaniacs*), it also included pop culture references. Even though these weren't prime time shows, the creators still put in enough intelligent humor that they appealed to teens and some Xers. In September 1995, Steven Spielberg's *Pinky & The Brain* (a spin-off of *Animaniacs*) premiered in prime time on WB. In the first episode, the Brain tried to raise funds to sabotage everyone's voice mail in a continuing effort to take over the world.

"There must be a way to get this money without working for Eisner," he said in a reference to Disney chief Michael Eisner that surely sailed over kids' heads but amused their media-savvy older siblings and parents.

Seeking Younger Demographics

After the MTV revolution of the early 1980s and the emergence of Fox as the Gen X network in the late 1980s, in the mid-1990s two more upstart networks compete for a slice of the broadcast pie. Like Fox, both the Warner Bros. Network (WB) and United Paramount Network (UPN) are aiming young. "Jamie Kellner is heading up their whole thing [at WB], and he learned a lot from working at Fox," said Fox research vice-president Charles Kennedy. "It is easier to go after the younger audience because they are less into the habit and are more likely to take chances to seek out something that's specifically for them. It's harder to change older people."

Because Warner Bros. already has a strong kids' business with the success of *Tiny Toons* and *Animaniacs*, Kennedy said WB can gradually promote their younger viewers from the morning cartoons into watching the prime time network. WB began its prime time run in winter 1995 with a Wednesday lineup of sitcoms with an appeal to a primarily young, urban male demographic. *The Wayans Bros.*, Robert Townsend's *The Parent 'Hood*, *Unhappily Ever After* (dubbed *Divorced . . . with Children* by critics), and *Muscle* were the debut shows. By the fall 1995 season, WB had dumped *Muscle*, a *Soap*-like sitcom that didn't fit in with the rest of the lineup, and had added a second night of programs, including Kirk Cameron in *Kirk*, ABC's canceled *Sister, Sister, Simon* (a Gen X *Forrest Gump* for TV), *First Time Out* (a Hispanic *Living Single*), *SNL* alumnae Ellen Cleghorne in *Cleghorne!* and *Pinky & the Brain*. By January 1996, *First Time Out* and *Cleghorne!* had been canceled and had been replaced with an Aaron Spelling soap set in the South, *Savannah*. "WB was going the Fox route and going it worse," said Matt Roush of *USA Today* in July 1995. "How low can you stoop and try to mimic something? But anybody new is trying to establish itself by going for this [young] generation."

In January 1995, UPN was launched with the goal of attracting a young, suburban male audience with its flagship show, *Star Trek: Voyager*. Although that show had built-in appeal to legions of Trekkers, UPN's other offerings that were also aimed at young males attracted little interest. The sitcoms *Pig Sty* and *Platypus Man* and dramas *Marker*, *The Watcher*, and *Legend* were all

Brothers Marlon Wayans and Shawn Wayans helped launch the WB network with their sitcom, *The Wayans Bros.* Courtesy WB Network.

canceled in May 1995. "Paramount certainly is putting on better shows than WB in terms of trying to attract a younger audience," Roush said. "*Legend* looked like [Fox's] *Adventures of Brisco County, Jr.* In a Freudian slip, I [set my VCR to tape an episode], but I set my machine for Fox instead of UPN. I had it in my head that it was a Fox show I was taping."

In August 1995 UPN launched its second season with nothing but drama programming. *Nowhere Man*, the most promising show, was *The Fugitive* with *X-Files* paranoia; *Deadly Games* was a cross between the 1960s *Batman* and the short-lived 1987 ABC show *Once a Hero*, and the underrated *Live Shot* was *ER* in a newsroom.

Fall 1995 was also when CBS, which went from first to third over the 1994–95 season, decided to go after a much-younger audience. The Tiffany network introduced the most new series (11) and moved the aging *Murder, She Wrote* up against NBC's *Friends*. Its most hyped attempt to gain younger viewers was *Central Park West* from *Melrose Place* creator Darren Star, which was referred to by many critics as "Melrose Place East."

"On certain nights our target audience will remain older, but on nights where we have nothing to lose, we're going to go younger than in the past," said David Poltrack of CBS in August 1995. He pointed out that CBS was dominant in the 25 to 54 demographic for several years in the early 1990s as a result of such Baby Boomer hits as *Murphy Brown* and *Northern Exposure*. "Through a series of missteps, we ended up losing that franchise and our no. 1 position," he said. "It's gotten to the point that we no longer have a viable franchise to protect. We got our-

Nielsen Ratings for the 1994–1995 TV Season

Households
1. *Seinfeld*
2. *ER*
3. *Home Improvement*
4. *Grace Under Fire*
5. *NFL Monday Night Football*
6. *60 Minutes*
7. *NYPD Blue*
8. *Friends*
9. *Roseanne* (tie)
   Murder, She Wrote

Ages 18–24
1. *Beverly Hills, 90210*
2. *Seinfeld*
3. *ER*
4. *Melrose Place*
5. *Home Improvement*
6. *Grace Under Fire*
7. *Friends*
8. *Roseanne*
9. *House of Buggin'* (tie)
   The Simpsons

Ages 18-34
1. *Seinfeld*
2. *ER*
3. *Friends*
4. *Home Improvement*
5. *Grace Under Fire*
6. *Beverly Hills, 90210*
7. *Ellen* (tie)
   Roseanne
9. *Madman of the People*
10. *Melrose Place*

selves into a position where there wasn't a lot of downside to being more aggressive and experimental and reaching down into that younger audience that has been so difficult for CBS to get in the past."

At the same time that CBS was going younger, Fox (under the leadership of former CBS executive John Matoian) was trying to go after older viewers. "We're still fighting a battle," said Charles Kennedy in March 1995. "We have shows that have an enormous appeal inherently to people age 35 to 40, but they don't tune in because they're not used to tuning into a Fox station or they think it's not for them. We haven't decided we're going to be old, we've just decided we're going to be more evenly balanced between 35 to 49 and 18 to 34 year olds and still a chunk of teens and kids."

I began this chapter with a survey of the shows Gen Xers remember watching most frequently as they were growing up. In the next chapter, I trace the history of Gen X programming in the 1990s. The shows Xers said they watched most frequently in 1995 were

1. *Seinfeld*
2. *Melrose Place*
3. *Friends*
4. *Beverly Hills, 90210*
5. *The Simpsons*
6. *ER*
7. *Mad About You*
8. *Star Trek: Voyager*
9. *The X-Files*
10. *Frasier*

This survey was conducted from February through April 1995 on the Internet and on paper among Xers in cities across America. It's interesting to see in this segment of the survey that a higher percentage was won by the top vote-getter than in the earlier poll on favorite TV shows as Xers were growing up. Whereas *The Brady Bunch* only received 20 percent of the nominations, *Seinfeld* got 34 percent of the vote. When I compare this poll to the Nielsen ratings for the 1994–95 season, six of the Top 10 in my survey are also in the

Nielsen Top 10 for ages 18 to 24, whereas five from my survey show up in the Nielsen Top 10 for ages 18 to 34. When I compare my results with the Nielsen statistics, it's clear that the survey I conducted skewed to the younger segment of Generation X. It's also clear that putting the survey on the Internet caused a bias, which explains how *Star Trek: Voyager* landed in the Top 10.

Other programs just outside the Top 10 in the survey included *Party of Five, My So-Called Life,* and *Roseanne. The Late Show with David Letterman,* reruns of *Star Trek: The Next Generation, New York Undercover, Northern Exposure, The Real World, NYPD Blue,* and *Married . . . with Children* also received nominations. There's also a dirty little secret among some Xers: they watched the original version of the Saturday morning teen sitcom *Saved by the Bell* and not just when their younger siblings had control of the remote.

Youth-quake

At 8:30 P.M. October 4, 1990, a
jolt on the TV landscape was felt that would eventually transform television. It began as a show once titled *Class of Beverly Hills* aired its premiere episode on Fox. Although certainly programs before *Beverly Hills, 90210* appealed to a young audience, this was the first that would really capture the attention of a maturing Generation X. When it premiered, no one knew what to make of a TV show that had a zip code as part of its title. In the *Los Angeles Times*, Howard Rosenberg called it "a zip code for stereotypes and stock characters." In an October 1990 review, Matt Roush of *USA Today* urged viewers to "be there or be . . . discriminating." Tom Shales of the *Washington Post* wrote that the show's producers "created a vacuum, a perfect void, a black hole in the already vast and empty TV schedule."

To go with Shales's black hole theory, that anomaly has a name—Aaron Spelling. Since the premiere of *90210*, Spelling's contribution to the nation's airwaves has increased dramatically, but its beginnings were modest. Spelling had been out of the media limelight during the late 1980s. Once *The Colbys* tanked (a UFO storyline?) and *Dynasty* ended, Spelling couldn't seem to get programs off the ground. *Nightingales,* a short-lived NBC soap (set at *Melrose Place's* Wilshire Memorial Hospital), lasted only a few months in early 1989 and drew fire from nurses' groups who protested the show's lack of realism. These nurses argued that in the real world nurses are more interested in healing their patients than sleeping with them. Even Spelling admitted during the 1992 TV critics press tour that he was in a slump. "We had a bad period," he told the *San Francisco Chronicle*. "Frankly, I don't know what would have happened after *Nightingales* if [former Fox Chairman] Barry Diller and Fox hadn't called and said, 'Would you like to do something about a high school?'"

When it was announced that Spelling was executive producing *90210* for Fox, no one stirred. TV is fickle. Despite Spelling's string of hits in the late 1970s and early 1980s, no one expected *90210* to be much of anything. "I think everyone was surprised, especially because there were several other shows

One of the first cast photos from *Beverly Hills, 90210*, this shot is probably from the pilot because Dylan (Luke Perry) and Donna (Tori Spelling) are nowhere to be seen. Gabrielle Carteris, Jason Priestley, Brian Austin Green, Carol Potter, Shannen Doherty, Ian Ziering, James Eckhouse, Jennie Garth, and Douglas Emerson were the original cast members. Emerson's character died during the show's second season. Fox Broadcasting.

about high school students introduced that year," said *Richmond Times-Dispatch* TV critic Douglas Durden. "Despite its exclusive zip code, *90210* began its TV career as a realistic look at teenagers from the perspective of teenagers. The fact that it was a semisoap opera for an audience weaned on *Dallas* and *Dynasty* didn't hurt either. And, unlike its predecessors of the 1980s, *90210* didn't try to appeal to a wide audience by including characters of several age groups. It created a world where its primary characters were all the same age, just as *Melrose Place* would do two years later."

Although Durden's original review of *90210* was fairly positive, most critics turned up their noses, figuring the show would disappear quickly and quietly. *Beverly Hills, 90210,* however, defied the critics. It didn't happen during the first season (when it aired opposite *Cheers*), but once new episodes turned up in the summer of 1991, stars Jason Priestley and Luke Perry became regular cover models for the teen magazines (despite the fact that the actors were much older than the characters they portrayed). Soon *90210* dolls and backpacks were flooding stores. They were followed by two soundtracks (one while the characters were in high school, another when they moved on to college), paperback novels, and unauthorized "tell-all" cast biographies.

"I think people felt kind of jazzed by the look and how they were talking and dressed," Matt Roush said. "The high hair and boys wearing earrings and stuff, whatever the fad was, you'd see it reflected or sometimes predicted on *90210.*" Sideburns, not popular with mainstream teens in decades, were suddenly hot again, thanks to the popularity of Perry and Priestley with female viewers. "I think we were kind of fortunate," said Charles Rosin, executive producer of *90210* during its first five seasons. "For the sideburns, the guys were trying to do something more individualistic than what was going on at the time. So Luke let his hair grow, and Jason followed suit. With the girls, we've had different costume supervisors. The one we've had the last three years basically tends to shop at stores that are trendy here in L. A. Our clothes are the West Coast version of what's going to be in K-Mart four months later. It will trickle down."

The backlash many shows experience somehow by-

Show Stats

Beverly Hills, 90210

Premiered: October 4, 1990, on Fox
Created by: Darren Star, an Aaron Spelling
    production

Primary cast:
Jason Priestley as Brandon Walsh
Shannen Doherty as Brenda Walsh (1990–94)
Luke Perry as Dylan McKay (1990–95)
Jennie Garth as Kelly Taylor
Ian Ziering as Steve Sanders
Brian Austin Green as David Silver
Tori Spelling as Donna Martin
Gabrielle Carteris as Andrea Zuckerman (1990–95)
Joe E. Tata as Nat Bussichio
Carol Potter as Cindy Walsh (1990–95)
James Eckhouse as Jim Walsh (1990–95)

Plot:
    The first youth ensemble drama, *90210* began as Brandon and Brenda moved with their family from Minneapolis to Beverly Hills when Jim was transferred. At first, the twins suffered from the familiar TV staple, the fish out of water syndrome. They couldn't relate to West Beverly High's valet parking or fellow students who'd had plastic surgery. Soon enough they found their places along with romantic entanglements, friends, and popularity.

    At the end of the 1992–93 season, the gang grad-

passed *90210* itself and was instead aimed squarely at one of its stars, Shannen Doherty. This trend, encouraged and bred in part by the tabloid press, even led to the publication of the *I Hate Brenda Newsletter,* a 'zine put out by two Los Angeles twentysomethings that eventually became The *'I Hate Brenda' Book: Shannen Doherty Exposed!* "It didn't make me feel bad," Rosin said. "It was not a slam against the show; it was against Shannen. Shannen used it as her defense too, saying, 'Well, I hate Brenda too.' Shannen is an extremely negative person, and she didn't work at all to preserve or to enshrine her talent; she didn't take care of herself."

Rosin was with *90210* as executive producer from June 1990 to May 1995. He left his job as a supervising producer on *Northern Exposure* to oversee the future of *90210* just after the show was put on the Fox fall schedule. Rosin recalled that the first night after he'd started work on *90210* he went home and watched MTV, a network he was unfamiliar with.

"I remember this dance show coming out of New York City, and they played a song called 'Get a Life,'" Rosin said. "The host of the show asked this pretty, young Manhattanite what the song meant. This young woman might as well have been Jennie Garth, and she said the song meant you must be working for various causes because if you're not doing something, you might as well go out and get a life." Rosin said that image didn't square with the "goal of getting a BMW" as reflected in the Reagan youth of the 1980s. Something else was happening. "There was this idealistic quality, a longing for ideals, stability, and values, that something is more important than what is ephemeral and disposable," Rosin said. "That in one way makes this generation have some connection to the ideals and hopes and longings of my generation which was in high school in the late 1960s and early 1970s."

uated from high school, and in the fall of 1993 they all signed up for classes at the fictional California University. During that season, the show confronted the usual collegiate issues from the Greek system to student government and the school newspaper. At the end of that year, Shannen Doherty was fired/quit, and Brenda went to London to study acting. During the 1994–95 season, the focus was less on college life and more on romantic melodrama as Donna dumped David and found love with an eventually abusive singing boyfriend, Ray Pruit (Jamie Walters). Valerie (Tiffani-Amber Thiessen) was brought in to be the new bad girl, moving into Brenda's vacated room. Andrea, now married to Jesse Vasquez (Mark D. Espinoza) and mother of a child, had an affair, reconciled with Jesse (who, it turns out, also had an affair), and then left the series (Carteris signed up to do a daytime talk show that lasted less than one year). Clare Arnold (Kathleen Robertson), daughter of CU's president, also became a full-time cast member and an occasional girlfriend for David before moving on to date Steve. At the end of the 1994–95 season, Jim and Cindy moved to Hong Kong, leaving Brandon and Valerie to share the Walsh home with new housemate Steve. The 1995–96 season also saw several new characters enter and exit through the *90210* revolving cast door. The most satisfying twist to many longtime viewers was the offscreen reunion of lovebirds Dylan and Brenda. While Perry and Doherty were gone, their characters got back together in London and sent letters to the Beverly Hills gang with the happy news.

So it came to pass that the idealistic Brandon and Brenda Walsh moved to Beverly Hills, a town more concerned than ever with all things ephemeral and disposable. Despite the expensive cars and clothes, *90210* managed to humanize its wealthy characters to a point where even people in the heartland could identify with their problems. Rosin said series creator Darren Star wanted *90210* to deal with the emotional lives of teens—to be a *teensomething*. Although *90210* did jump-start the whole youth ensemble drama trend, it wasn't until *My So-Called Life* that many teens felt their lives were portrayed accurately. Whereas *90210* was a hit with the popular crowd (cheerleaders, jocks, class presidents, etc.), *My So-Called Life* appealed more to those on the fringe. This is also one of the reasons *90210* was a hit and *Life* was not.

From teens dealing with divorced parents, suicide, AIDS, and breast cancer to choosing to have sex or to remain a virgin, *90210* covered plenty of issues during the years its characters were in high school. Plenty of time also was devoted to developing relationships among the characters. Although the characterizations were simple in the beginning (the rich bitch, the jock, the nerd), over time, the characters became more realistic. As true characters emerged from the stereotypes, *90210* became a lot more fun to watch. In early 1996 when Fox aired a look back at *The Best Moments of 'Beverly Hills, 90210'*, it was tough not to feel a little wistful and nostalgic. The gang from West Beverly really seemed like great friends, and they'd certainly been through a lot together. Nevermind that this was the same show that killed off a character (Scott Scanlon, played by Douglas Emerson) and dealt with the aftermath in a single episode. For all its shortcomings as a dramatic series, *Beverly Hills, 90210* still managed to touch and move its audience, even those who watched it as a joke.

Although the method of storytelling on *90210* was fairly conventional, Rosin said they were able to play with the format enough to make it appear new. "*90210* always was a mixture of social drama with personal melodrama, romance, character comedy, and sometimes high concepts—dreams, going back to the Old West, things out of the ordinary," Rosin said. "That said to the audience, you don't know what to expect; *90210* will not be the same old formula."

New and Improved, Year after Year

Unlike many shows, *90210* managed to successfully reinvent itself every year through the introduction of new characters and situations. In high school, the gang spent time socializing at the Peach Pit, but when they entered college, the 1950s diner hangout was dated. So they opened the Peach Pit after Dark nightclub next door. Whereas Brandon had always been the rock steady center of the show, many of the other characters have gone through changes. First Kelly was the rich snob, then she wasn't, then she was again. David was the geeky nerd, then he was the rapper. Okay, so he was still a geeky nerd when he rapped, but at least his character grew a little. Donna, although always the virgin and the only consistently nice character on the show, grew tremendously when the cast entered college. Once just a pretty adornment for Kelly and Brenda, Donna became the queen of diversity, befriending several black characters. Her character was used to tackle the issue of domestic violence when she landed in an abusive relationship with Ray Pruit.

The loss of two major characters (Brenda in 1994 and Dylan in 1995) would cripple many shows, but these situations reinvigorated *90210* as new characters were introduced who weren't carbon copies of those they replaced. Clare Arnold first appeared as a high school senior, the nymphomaniac daughter of California University's chancellor. Her sole aim was to land Brandon in bed when she was a recurring character, but once she joined the show as a regular cast member and became a college freshman, she became the resident brainiac (replacing Andrea, who was busy having a baby and then leaving the show), her hormones mellowed, and she dated David before moving on to Steve. When Brenda went off to London in May 1994, she was quickly replaced by Valerie. Whereas Brenda could be bitchy sometimes, Valerie was a true bad girl, smoking a joint in her first episode as she sat in Brenda's old bedroom. By her second season on the show, Valerie wasn't so much the bad girl as she was misunderstood and desperate for acceptance. Despite this remarkable chameleonlike ability, critics never cared for *90210*.

Will Smith starred as the title character in *The Fresh Prince of Bel Air.* © National Broadcasting Company, Inc.

"What was so wonderful was that the show was written off by critics [in the beginning], and Fox basically had no other shows to replace us with and had no money to develop other shows, so they had to stick with us," Rosin said. "We were left to our own devices without the glare and spotlight of the media. Once Brenda Walsh lost her virginity and didn't have remorse, people realized that they were seeing something on TV they hadn't seen before. It caught everybody by surprise. But it wasn't by trying to second guess what kids were doing. It was trying to anticipate what was all around."

At the same time in 1990, other TV programs also decided to go back to school. NBC's short-lived *Hull High* featured students and teachers who sang and danced. *Ferris Bueller,* a spin-off from the 1986 John Hughes film *Ferris Bueller's Day Off,* featured a pre-*Friends* Jennifer Aniston in the role Jennifer Grey created (TV karma saw to it that they appeared together in an episode of *Friends* in 1995), but the series lasted only until December 1990. More successful was Fox's *Parker Lewis Can't Lose* (later in its run the title was shortened to *Parker Lewis*), which made an impression with its amusing sound and video effects and strange camera angles. The only Gen X series from 1990 to come close to the longevity of *90210* was NBC's *Fresh Prince of Bel Air,* which ended its run in May 1996. Even though *Fresh Prince* got better Nielsen ratings, it never managed to reach the heights of cultural prominence bestowed upon *90210.*

"I've seen 95 percent of all *90210* episodes that have been on, but the truth is, I really don't know why I watch," said 23-year-old Joey Geiger of Madison, Wisconsin. "I guess it's funny to laugh at."

"I watch because it's so stupid," said Jennifer Cather, a 23-year-old living in Seattle, Washington. "And because it's not lifelike for most people. It's purely entertaining because it's so funny."

Alex Millar, 23, emphasized Rosin's point about how *90210* can change genres from week to week, although probably not in the same way Rosin would describe it. "I admit that *90210* is cheesy, but at least it is different cheese every week," Millar said.

"It's like what *The Brady Bunch* was to me growing up," said actress Jennifer Elise Cox. "It's like this comfort show, totally unrealistic, but you want to escape to their problems that seem so minor compared to your own."

Rosin would probably be happier with the following reasons people have given for watching *90210*. "My fave show now, by far, is *90210*," said Elyssa Komansky, 20, of Westport, Connecticut. "I like *90210* because I'm in college and the plots are really interesting."

"I would turn on *90210* during their high school years, and it was like watching an *Afterschool Special*," said Erin Smith. "Every episode had that same kind of weird moral learning stuff. The high school years were very realistic, especially Andrea Zuckerman. Every single [person] in my clique was Andrea."

"For one hour a week I can forget about my own problems and become involved in the lives of other people whom I can identify with," said student Joe Carreiro, 25, of Concord, New Hampshire.

That's an answer Rosin would love because trying to make the show realistic enough for viewers to identify with was something the producers had to fight for in the beginning. Rosin said he constantly had to stand up and remind those at the network, who were sometimes reluctant about some of the sentiments the show communicated, that Generation X was different because they were coming to terms with sex in an era of AIDS. "How do you deal with sexuality? Conventional wisdom is that a character should or should not be doing this kind of behavior. The TV world is divided between black and white, the girl is either a slut or a virgin, but in life there's only the middle ground; there's only contradictions, the ironies."

As the show aged so did much of its audience, which is why it had to change to fit the times. When many viewers were watching the high school years, they were in college, enjoying the memories of high school life. Now the same people have graduated to the real world and enjoy remembering their own collegiate years by watching the *90210* gang at California University. Not only the setting of *90210* changed as it aged. Social issues took a backseat to what Rosin called "romantic melodrama."

"I think you'll see fewer social issues, fewer high concepts," Rosin said in an interview at the end of the fifth season (May 1995) just before vacating the executive producer's chair. "It won't be a conventional soap, but it'll come pretty close to it. That's a reflection of maybe what the audience wants but also of certain people running the show and Aaron Spelling; that's what their orientation would be."

There's always been a fun streak to *90210* that yields more laughs for viewers who pay attention. What appears as a throw away line of dialogue to some becomes a great joke for others. "I have an English final tomorrow, and I still don't know who killed the damn mockingbird," complained Donna in one fifth-season episode.

Then there was this exchange:

"What's *Playhouse 90?*" David asked.

"I think it's on cable," Clare replied.

Erin Smith, although a bigger fan of *90210* in its high school years, said she likes it when the producers include such unexpected references. "The writing had weird stuff, weird jokes," Erin said, "like when Andrea was in a wheelchair and somebody called her 'old Ironsides.' Does anyone get that? There's a lot of payoffs for the people who pay attention. I always love stuff that's a lot more deep than people think."

Beverly Hills, 90210 is slated to run on Fox through the 1996–97 TV season, and although it's remained fresh, there's only so long any series can sustain itself. "It starts to feel more old hat," Rosin said. "Look at *L. A. Law* or *Northern Exposure.* I hope it can stay fresh and vibrant until the end, but that remains to be seen. The run we had was terrific, particularly the years we were in sync with the younger audience who grew up to be Generation Xers."

After the fall 1990 premiere, Fox followed-up *90210* in the spring of 1991 with a show that tried to cash in on the "reality-based" TV trend. *Yearbook* was the Gen X answer to *Cops* and *Rescue 911,* which were both riding high in the Nielsen ratings. Unlike MTV's *Real World,* which would follow just one year later, *Yearbook* was more in line with a true documentary because it didn't involve forcing strangers to live together. Instead, camera crews followed students (mostly seniors) around Glenbard West High School in a middle-class Chicago suburb. Episodes dealt with teen pregnancy, naming the homecoming queen, the Gulf War, a star quarterback's attempts to get into an Ivy League college, and a student whose guidance counselor mother was diagnosed with leukemia.

Copycats

Although *Yearbook* didn't last, *90210* caught on when Fox aired original episodes during a special 1991 summer season. Soon *90210* was on its way to becoming the first hit drama for the Fox network. When executives at the other networks saw the success at bringing in an audience advertisers desired, it became time to send in the clones. Aaron Spelling, credited with the original, was only too eager to copy himself. In the summer of 1992, *Melrose Place* was spun off from *90210* with much fanfare from Fox. Although the network sent out no preview tapes to critics (never a good sign), Matt Roush weighed in with his opinion in *USA Today* the day after the show's premiere. "*Melrose*, the summer's most hyped new series, has the odor of cloned creative stalemate," Roush wrote. "Put it this way: If you love *Beverly Hills, 90210*, you probably deserve *Melrose*."

Although the ratings were high at first, people soon tuned out in droves as the dull lives of these earnest twentysomethings bored them to tears. Of course, that all changed with the addition of Heather Locklear and the change in the show's direction in early 1993.

In the summer of 1992, CBS rolled out two youth series of its own. *Freshman Dorm* more closely resembled *90210* (set in college instead of high school), but Spelling's *2000 Malibu Road* received more press as a result of its slightly older and sexier cast, which included Drew Barrymore and *Flashdance* star Jennifer Beals. This time it wasn't only the critics who rejected the shows.

"I used to watch *Freshman Dorm*. . . . I also watched the few episodes of *2000 Malibu Road*," wrote Chris Knight, a 25-year-old aerospace engineer in Lancaster, California, in an e-mail message. "You have to understand though, that I have a craving for bad television. I'm the first to admit that *Freshman Dorm* was a terrible show, but I enjoyed it

Show Stats

Freshman Dorm
Premiered: August 11, 1992, on CBS
Created by: Steve Tisch

Primary cast:
Robyn Lively as Molly Flynn
Paige French as Lulu Ambercrombie
Arlene Taylor as K. C. Richards
Casper Van Dien as Zack Taylor
Kevin Mambo as Alex Woods
Matthew Fox as Danny Foley

Plot:
Right on the heels of *Class of '96*, this short-lived summer series was set at the fictional Western Pacific University, which some critics claimed was based on life at Malibu's Pepperdine University, where, in fact, *Freshman Dorm* was filmed. At the center of the show were three roommates. Molly was a theater major from Milwaukee whose boyfriend, Danny, was on an athletic scholarship and managed to deflower her during the first episode. K. C. (short for Kamala Consuelo) was embarrassed about her Hispanic background, and Lulu was a New York tart who hit on her philosophy professor. Other regulars included Zack, the surfing dude, who roomed with Alex, the show's token black character.

anyway. I'm kinda mad at *2000 Malibu Road* because they never wrapped up all the plot lines before it was canceled. I think a lot of these shows flopped because the producers were more interested in trying to copy existing 'formulas,' that is, *90120, Melrose Place*, and so forth, than in trying to create original and fresh programming. To be an enjoyable show (even if the writing, characters, and plot are terrible) a viewer must either experience something new through the characters or really be able to identify deeply with the characters and situations."

Tom Shales of the *Washington Post* called *Freshman Dorm* a "limited-run and limited-mentality summer series with 'Fox' written all over it. In crayon, of course."

The Spelling-produced series *2000 Malibu Road* also received the critics' wrath. From *L. A. Law* cocreator Terry Louise Fisher, it was a much sexier affair about a group of women living at a beach house. The pilot episode alone featured murder, blackmail, attempted rape, and Lisa Hartman Black as a former prostitute named Jade. Despite cloning success and adding even more titillation, the household ratings were poor for both shows. By the time *Freshman Dorm* and *2000 Malibu Road* debuted, it was already late summer, and there was nothing to stop more doomed youth series from languishing in the ratings once the networks rolled out their fall lineups.

Fox ratings sank to the depths with Spelling's *The Heights*, a one-hour ensemble drama about a garage band made up of blue collar grunge kids who sang Top 40 music. Although Jamie Walters's "How Do You Talk to an Angel?" shot to the top of the music charts (and then became the show's theme song), *The Heights* never attracted a large audience, lasting only 13 episodes.

Spelling's contribution to NBC was an equally lackluster drama, *The Round Table*, about a group of attractive twentysomethings who gathered in Washington's Georgetown section to socialize. The most notable thing about this series was its use of Spelling's acting stable. Roxann Biggs, who appeared

---

Show Stats

2000 Malibu Road

Premiered: August 23, 1992, on CBS
Created by: Terry Louise Fisher, an Aaron Spelling production, pilot directed by Joel Schumacher

Primary cast:
Lisa Hartman Black as Jade O'Keefe
Jennifer Beals as Perry Quinn
Drew Barrymore as Lindsay Rule
Tuesday Knight as Joy Rule

Plot:
Four women shared a home at 2000 Malibu Road, including Jade, a $3,000 a night hooker who was looking for a new job; Perry was a lawyer with memories of her slain fiancée police officer and a serious drinking problem; Lindsay was a wannabe actress; and her doting sister, Joy, was an overweight, overprotective loon.

Show Stats

The Heights

Premiered: August 27, 1992, on Fox
Created by: Eric Roth and Tony Spiridakis, an Aaron Spelling production

Primary cast:
Alex Desert as Stan Lee
Ken Garito as Arthur "Dizzy" Mazelli
Cheryl Pollak as Rita MacDougal
Charlotte Ross as Hope Linden
Shawn Thompson as J. T. Banks
Zachary Throne as Lenny Wieckowski
Jamie Walters as Alex O'Brien
Tasia Valenza as Jodie Abramowitz
Ray Aranha as Mr. Mike

Plot:

Just as a garage band from Seattle was climbing the charts, this TV series also tried to reach ratings nirvana, but failed. Alex was the new kid on the grunge block, a singer/songwriter who had the hots for Rita, the sax player who worked as a dispatcher for a beer distribution company. J. T. was the lead singer and garage mechanic; Hope was the guitarist and resident rich kid; Stan was the bass player who ran a pool hall with his dad, Mr. Mike. Dizzy was the drummer who was preoccupied with his pregnant girlfriend, Jodie.

as a token Hispanic nurse on *Nightingales,* returned to play a token Hispanic lawyer in *The Round Table.* She escaped the Spelling fold and landed the part of the half-human, half-Klingon chief engineer on *Star Trek: Voyager.* Another Spelling regular, Wayne Tippit, played the father of one of the *Round Table's* main characters. Tippit went on to play Palmer Woodward, father of Heather Locklear's Amanda, on *Melrose Place.* Other examples of the Spelling ensemble include Jamie Walters, who starred in *The Heights* before moving on to romance (and, subsequently, to abuse) Tori Spelling's character on *90210.* James Wilder got harpooned by Daphne Zuniga on *Melrose Place* before showing up on *Models, Inc.* where he tangled with Emma Samms, an alumna of Spelling's *Dynasty.* Stanley Kamel played Amanda's boss at D&D Advertising on *Melrose Place* before arriving on *90210* in September 1995 to play the man who murdered Dylan's father (and, later, Dylan's wife). Teresa Hill of *Models, Inc.* later turned up on *Melrose Place* as did Lonnie Schulyer, who also appeared in the failed Spelling pilot *Pier 66.* David Gail almost married Brenda on *90210* before romancing a southern belle on *Savannah.*

Spelling also makes consistent use of stock footage. *Melrose Place* and *90210* frequently have the same Los Angeles shots appear during their weekly guest star credits. Matt from *Melrose Place* found himself in the same prison as Lucille from *Savannah* despite a continent between them. And is it coincidence that Hong Kong footage from *Dynasty* turned up when Alison was assigned there on *Melrose Place?* Or that *90210's* Walsh parents moved to Hong Kong perhaps in anticipation that the producers might want to again recycle the same footage?

Other shows that emerged in fall 1992, dubbed "The Year of the Young and the Shirtless" by the *Toronto Star,* included Malcolm-Jamal Warner's *Here and Now* about a graduate student who worked at a youth center; a sketch comedy series called *The Edge* (featuring a pre-*Friends* Jennifer Aniston), another sketch comedy called *The Ben Stiller Show* (starring a pre-*Reality Bites* Jerry Stiller and Janeane Garofalo); *Flying Blind*, a Fox sitcom starring Corey Parker and Tea Leoni that most critics liked. All those shows flopped, lasting one season or less. The only other shows to debut in 1992 that held any interest for Generation X were the long-running *Mad About You* (NBC) and *Martin* (Fox). Both shows began their tenures on Thursday nights in different time slots, but they soon were forced to do battle in the Nielsen ratings, splitting the Gen X audience along racial lines.

Nervous Network Casualties

One decidedly un-Gen X show at first glance was ABC's *Homefront*, which aired from 1991 to 1993. Set in post–World War II Ohio, *Homefront* would seem an unlikely candidate for inclusion in a book about Generation X and TV, but given its young cast and serialized nature, this drama series actually attracted a small but loyal following among the 18 to 49 demographic instead of the 55 plus audience ABC expected. "When we produced the pilot, everybody said, 'How in the world are you going to get young people to watch that show?' The problem is we haven't been able to get anybody else but young people to watch the show," said *Homefront* executive producer David Jacobs in a 1993 interview with *Daily Variety*. During its first months on the air, 37 percent of *Homefront*'s audience was in the advertiser-friendly women 18 to 49 demographic.

Homefront also fit the Gen X mold because it was different in its period setting and music. It's also my all-time favorite TV show. *Homefront* was beautifully produced, written, directed, and acted. Unfortunately, the show came at a time when nostalgia was least in demand, and ABC didn't see the show's

Show Stats

The Round Table
Premiered: September 18, 1992, on NBC
Created by: Nancy Miller, an Aaron Spelling production

Primary cast:
Stacy Haiduk as Rhea McPherson
Roxann Biggs as Jennifer Clemente
David Gail as Danny Burke
Thomas Breznahan as Mitchell Clark
Pepper Sweeney as Deveraux Jones
Eric King as Wade Carter

Plot:
These twentysomethings spent their down time in Washington, D.C.'s, trendy Georgetown in a fictional bar called The Round Table. Because they spent so much time there, the group christened themselves the Knights. Rhea quit her job as a newspaper reporter to become an FBI agent; Jennifer worked as a prosecutor in the U.S. Attorney's office; Danny was the bartender and Jennifer's beau; Mitchell was a Justice Department attorney; Devereaux was a Texan turned Secret Service agent; and Wade was a rookie cop.

potential. The network didn't give *Homefront* time to grow in a decent time slot, and many critics didn't speak up in support of the show because they were too busy fawning over politically correct, "serious" fare such as *I'll Fly Away* and *Brooklyn Bridge*. Both were excellent programs, but some critics unfairly dismissed *Homefront* because it balanced its serious social issue storylines with comedy, singing, and dancing.

Despite lasting only two seasons, *Homefront* was not a failure. It exemplified all the good things about television. Most of the time TV is a passive, sedentary experience that doesn't engage the viewer. *Homefront* introduced audiences to memorable, realistic characters and offered minihistory lessons, with each episode serving as a new chapter in a great novel. Despite its period setting, if the show had been handled more carefully by ABC management, *Homefront* could have been a Gen X hit in spite of itself.

In January 1993, Fox launched *Class of '96* as its Tuesday, 8:00 P.M. entry. Although this tale of college freshman at the fictional Ivy League Havenhurst College was another ensemble youth drama, it transcended its predecessors in almost every way. The acting, writing, and overall execution were of a much higher caliber.

"It was the last of those ensemble shows to be launched," said Robert Greenblatt, Fox executive vice-president of comedy and drama development. "We brought it out in midseason, but I think what really killed it was that it was part of our Tuesday night lineup, which at the time, was a brand new night for us. We hadn't been programming Tuesdays [before] that. I don't think anything could have succeeded in that time period."

Class of '96, was able to rise above its fellow Fox programs, but it only lasted until the end of the characters' freshman year. "We had an executive producer/creator [John Romano] who is pretty good at developing three-dimensional characters," Greenblatt recalled. "That show was really about that time in your life when you're in college and coming alive and all that kind of thing, and I

Show Stats

Class of '96
Premiered: January 19, 1993, on Fox
Created by: John Romano

Primary cast:
Jason Gedrick as David Morrissey
Brandon Douglas as Whitney Reed
Gale Hansen as Samuel "Stroke" Dexter
Perry Moore as Antonio Hopkins
Lisa Dean Ryan as Jessica Cohen
Megan Ward as Patty Horvath
Kari Wuhrer as Robin Farr

Plot:
   Youth ensemble drama about first-year students at the fictional Havenhurst College, located in the Northeast. David came from blue collar roots and was the first in his family to attend college; Jessica was wealthy; Antonio was from the ghetto; Whitney was a rich preppy; Robin was a redheaded bombshell; Patty was an aspiring actress; and Stroke was a money-grubbing nerd.

think it could have caught on. We only did 17 episodes, and it was over. It was really well done; we had really good casting; we didn't give it enough time."

Cancellations of programs with potential, such as *Class of '96*, have taught network executives that dramas usually take time to acquire a large audience. Often it takes two full seasons before a show can be declared a hit. "I have yet to have a drama work very quickly," Greenblatt said in a 1995 interview. "Except for *ER,* which is a fluke, and *NYPD Blue,* which had a year's worth of publicity because of the nudity, it just doesn't happen. Look at *Homicide;* it's in its fourth season, and every year they do six episodes and then [NBC] gets tired of it or scared of it and they take it off. Finally now, it's starting to take off. With *Class of '96* we only had 17 episodes, a bad night, and we [reached] a saturation point of those [youth] shows. We just couldn't make it work."

Seeking Young, Black Viewers

After the networks' experiences with these Gen X failures, they took some time off. The fall season in 1993 consisted of programs with a broader appeal, including *Lois & Clark: The New Adventures of Superman, NYPD Blue, seaQuest DSV, Grace Under Fire, Dave's World, The Nanny, Frasier,* and *The X-Files,* which did acquire a large following among Gen Xers. One show that premiered in fall 1993 that was aimed at and starred Xers was Fox's *Living Single* (originally titled *My Girls*). When it premiered, *Living Single* wasn't tagged with the Generation X label; instead it was called "a black *Designing Women*" or "a young, black *Golden Girls*." One year later, *Living Single* aired opposite *Friends,* which did get the X label. Both shows feature twentysomethings who live in New York and deal with romance, jobs, and friendship. *Living Single* creator Yvette Lee Bowser said she was neither sur-

Show Stats

Living Single
Premiered: August 22, 1993, on Fox
Created by: Yvette Lee Bowser

Primary cast:
Queen Latifah as Khadijah James
Kim Coles as Synclaire James
Erika Alexander as Maxine Shaw
T. C. Carson as Kyle Barker
John Henton as Overton Wakefield Jones
Kim Fields as Regine Hunter

Plot:
Six twentysomethings living in New York deal with love and friendship. Three of the women share a brownstone; the guys are their neighbors. Khadijah founded *Flavor,* an urban magazine with a woman's point of view. Her cousin, Synclaire, works there too; their third housemate, Regine, climbs social ladders in an ongoing attempt to marry a rich man. Maxine, Khadijah's college roommate, is a divorce attorney who visits the girls frequently. The guys include Kyle, a ladies' man and stockbroker, and his roommate, Overton, the building's Mr. Fix It.

One year before *Friends* became a hit, *Living Single* staked a claim on the "twentysomething friends living in New York" concept. Queen Latifah, Kim Fields, John Henton, Erika Alexander, T. C. Carson, and Kim Coles (on floor) star in the sitcom. Fox Broadcasting.

prised nor disappointed that her show didn't receive the Gen X label, even though she feels it's definitely a Generation X show.

"The concept was a distinctly African-American female point of view, but from the pilot my intention was always to [depict] this group of very close-knit friends," Bowser said. "Like anything else, to become successful a show has to have a point of view. This show comes more from a female point of view, and *Friends* comes from more of a generational point of view."

In *USA Today*, Alan Bash compared the two shows, both produced by Warner Bros., in fall 1994 and found that although only 3 percent of black homes were tuned to *Friends*, 48 percent watched *Living Single*. "But I wouldn't dare say that only African-Americans watch *Living Single* and only Caucasians are watching *Friends*, given what we know about how Nielsen distributes their boxes," Bowser said. "If no Caucasians were watching, we would not be on the air, and if no African-Americans were watching *Friends*, they would not have the numbers they do."

The ad agency BBDO's 1994–95 report on black television viewing found that Fox's *Living Single* and *Martin* were the no. 1 and no. 2 shows among blacks in the 18 to 34 age group. But other shows generally associated with the white Gen X stereotype also made the Top 20, including *The Simpsons, Beverly Hills, 90210, Married . . . with Children, Models Inc.,* and *Roseanne.*

The survey also found that the younger the audience, the more likely these "black shows" are to be watched by nonblack audiences. Within the Top 20 shows for black teens 12 to 17, there are 15 shows that are also in the Top 20 for total teens 12 to 17, the report stated. Among black viewers 18 to 24, eight of the Top 20 shows are also the most popular with total viewers 18 to 24, and for those 18 to 34, seven shows are common on both lists.

Black and white viewers went their separate ways until age 50-plus, when they shared 10 of the Top 20 programs. Programs generally associated with drawing large numbers of Generation X viewers but not black viewers (in total households[HHs]) included *Seinfeld* (2d in total HHs, 109th in black HHs), *Mad About You* (14th compared to 110th), *Frasier* (12th compared to 87th) and *Friends* (18th compared to 114th). The last statistic is not a surprise because at the time this survey was conducted, *Friends* and *Living Single* occupied the same time slot.

Show Stats

New York Undercover
Premiered: September 8, 1994, on Fox
Created by: Dick Wolf and Kevin Arkadie

Primary cast:
Malik Yoba as J. C. Williams
Michael DeLorenzo as Eddie Torres
Patti D'Arbanville-Quinn as Lt. Virginia Cooper
Fatima Faloye as Chantal Tierney
George Gore II as Gregory "G" Williams
Lauren Velez as Nina Moreno (1995–)
Michael Michele as Sandra Gill (1994–95)

Plot:
    Filmed on location in New York, this police drama features a squad of young urban detectives who work the streets undercover. Each episode opens with a musical sequence, and music is featured throughout. J. C. had to deal with the murder of his fiancée in 1995; Eddie fell for the new girl in the squad room at the start of the 1995 season. Chantal is the mother of J. C.'s son, G, and Lt. Cooper is the no-nonsense squad leader.

During the 1995–96 TV season, the BBDO survey found similar statistics, the top five programs in black households were *New York Undercover, Living Single, The Crew, In the House* and *Fresh Prince of Bel Air.* Among the 18 to 34 age group, the top two programs were *New York Undercover* and *Martin.*

"I do think there's something calculated in terms of devising shows for [a certain] audience," said Matt Roush of *USA Today* in an interview. "There's something odd here in this stage of things in terms of how segregated we tend to be, in terms of how white bread the white bread shows tend to be. Even on *My So-Called Life*, there wasn't a black presence and nobody on *Party of Five* that I can remember. And the Spelling shows are hugely white. On *Models Inc.* they [introduced a black character], but everyone turned out being the same shade of plastic really."

Bowser agreed that it's unfortunate American TV remains, in many ways, a segregated medium. "I would love to create a show that was much more integrated, but I quite honestly have concerns about whether people are ready to watch that," she said. "*The John Laroquette Show* has two black characters and six caucasian characters, but that isn't what I'm talking about. But I'm also not talking about bogus attempts at rainbow coalition shows that are not realistic or relatable. We'll keep pushing as creators of shows, but I also have to keep in mind not only what my personal desires are but what people want to see and what they will watch—what's going to sell—without me selling out as an African-American woman. That's always on my mind."

Rose Catherine Pinkney, 30, was television vice-president for Uptown Entertainment, which coproduced the first season of *New York Undercover* along with Dick Wolf and Universal Television. *New York Undercover* (originally titled *Uptown Undercover*) premiered in fall 1994 and features a pair of young cops who happen to be black. Like *Living Single, New York Undercover* was never given the Gen X tag.

Michael DeLorenzo and Malik Yoba star as detectives in *New York Undercover*.
Fox Broadcasting.

"Yes, it's got young people and it's also got people of color and it's also very urban," she said. "In any given sentence it could be put into any of those categories, but I think because in America race is generally the most obvious thing, it's become a black show, just like *Living Single* becomes a black show. Before anyone looks at age, race just stands out first."

Pinkney recalled the day she went to pitch an ensemble show to two white writers. Pinkney suggested that one of the characters, who would be equal in stature to the four other white characters, be black. "Simply because I was a black executive bringing in a show and suggesting one black character, they presumed it was to be a black show," Pinkney said. "The white writer was confused, and it was funny to me that again race supersedes everything else, which is sometimes positive and sometimes negative."

There are exceptions, such as NBC's *The Cosby Mysteries,* which escaped the black show label and was lumped in with *Matlock, Murder, She Wrote,* and other mystery shows that are watched by a predominantly older audience. Pinkney said she thinks labeling often comes down to whatever is the most easily definable thing that a show has in common with another major group. "My parents watch older shows before black shows because [for them], the senior problems are more prevalent than the black problems may be."

Pinkney said she doesn't generally hear her peers referring to themselves as Generation X. "We don't think we're included in that set of people," she said. "When all the articles started coming out about it, just for whatever reason, people I know did not quickly identify with Gen X, even my white friends. I don't know if that's because I'm at the older end or whether it was a black thing. Even with *New York Undercover,* we do more the urban side of pop culture, but people don't think of them as Generation X. But they're so obviously Generation X, more so than the *Friends* are to me."

Although one could fault the networks for fostering separatism by creating programs for specific audiences (and in the case of *Living Single* and *Friends,* putting them on opposite one another in both fall 1994 and 1995), Pinkney said the reality of it is simply business. "Whenever you're programming, you choose the best show for audience flows, whether it's an action show after football, black shows with black shows, women's shows with women's shows," Pinkney said. "Look at [the ABC] TGIF [Friday night lineup of family shows]; it's two hours of family [shows] and it really works."

As for the absence of minority characters on Gen X dramas, Pinkney said it probably correlates with the lack of minority writers on the staffs of those programs. Often there's nobody there to give the characters honesty and genuineness in being, Pinkney said. "You end up with characters who are not as complex as real people. You get the angry black man, the crack addict daughter, the overly buppiefied character; all the stereotypes are introduced, and that's not appealing in any kind of character. There often aren't people who can plead the cases of these characters."

Pinkney said that when she worked for Fox's 20th Television division, there were producers pitching an idea for a show about an Asian-American family, and they wanted to have several generations in the same house. The executives, including Pinkney, thought this premise was contrived. They later learned that in Asian culture such an arrangement is normal. "Simply because there was not that person in the room, this thing that would have been a given just didn't go any farther. It's having a perspective in the room, a new way of thinking."

Get Me a Hit Drama, STAT!

Fall 1994 saw another resurgence of X programs with *Friends* on NBC, *Blue Skies* on ABC, and *Wild Oats* on Fox. Only *Friends* survived past Christmas, although *Blue Skies* was retooled and brought back in early 1995 as *A Whole New Ballgame,* which also flopped. *ER* became a huge hit across all the desired demographics, but it was also the first conventional drama to capture the attention of a large segment of Generation X TV viewers in many years. At the end of the 1994–95 season, *ER* was no. 2 in both households and the 18 to 34 demographic and no. 3 in the 18 to 24 demographic. Granted, *L. A. Law* had similarly successfully sitcoms as its lead-in, but during the 1993–94 season, it didn't generate ratings anywhere near those of *ER*. So why was *ER* able to attract short-attention-span Xers to sit in front of the tube for an hour—because it combined the intelligence and characterization of *St. Elsewhere* with an MTV pace. "The trick with *ER* is that it comes already on fast forward," said *New York Daily News* TV critic David Bianculli.

"Sometimes I've forgotten half of what I watched," said Matt Roush of *USA Today.* "Sometimes an entire scene is played for you at such a pace that you just sort of scratch your head, and you just know it was a riveting moment; you're not really sure what you saw, but you just know it was kind of visceral."

When *ER* premiered against *Chicago Hope* in fall 1994, many thought *ER* would be the underdog given the big names behind *Chicago Hope* (stars Mandy Patinkin, Hector Elizondo, Adam Arkin, creator David E. Kelley). Instead, *ER* became the smash success, sending *Chicago Hope* to a new time slot.

"*ER* is at least as emotional as *Chicago Hope* in terms of giving you the payoff, and it's not nearly as contrived a show," Roush said. "*ER* has a realism to it that I think this new generation probably wants. They're a very demanding generation because they've seen so much and have so much to see. What they will swallow and accept on a mainstream mass level is always going to be a difficult thing to predict."

ER executive producer John Wells said his staff doesn't write down to the audience. Instead, they assume viewers are extremely video literate and have a lot of experience watching TV. "That allows us to jump around, and people follow because they've seen a lot of television and films in their lives," Wells said in a 1995 phone interview. "The last couple of generations are the first literally raised on TV and are very familiar with all these forms, which allows us to do some shorthand and keep the pace up and have lots of stories going, and people really follow it."

Jacob Palm, a 22-year-old senior at Cornell University, said *ER* is his favorite show because it depicts a realistic world that alternately looks better and worse than the real world. "It's an exciting and fast-paced life I'll never have," he said. "I feel as if I personally know the characters, both envying and feeling sorry for them at the same time."

Wells said that when he and creator Michael Crichton developed *ER*, the fast pace came more from realism than from a desire to attract MTV viewers. "It was certainly a conscious effort not to do the type of medical show that had been done in the past because we felt that story form was very tired," Wells said. "The pace of the show [came about] because we wanted to be true to the real emergency room experience. So when we made the show realistic, that cranked the pace up. This is really what emergency rooms are like. You don't follow a patient through entire days like we saw in traditional medical shows."

Wells said *ER* has been described as the first dramatic TV show created for the age of the remote control. There's no reason to channel surf if you tune in and don't like what you see because people know they can stick around to see what else is thrown in. *ER* also represents the pace most people live now as they try to balance their personal and professional lives. Wells said the success of *ER* with Gen X hasn't surprised him as much as its appeal to older viewers. "There was a concern at the network that the show moved so quickly, that it didn't follow a standard linear storytelling, that it would be limited to a younger audience," Wells said. "The younger audience is bored with the old form, which everyone sort of accepts, but it turned out the older audience is bored with the old form too, and they were willing to come to something new."

Through its first season, *ER*'s pace slowed and more time was spent developing the various main characters. By this time, Xers were already hooked, so even though the pace was less breakneck, they kept coming back to the emergency room. Of course, it didn't hurt that Quentin Tarantino (who at the time was the most worshipped of Gen X directors because of *Pulp Fiction*) was hired to direct a late-season episode. Other X shows in 1994 included *Party of Five* on Fox and *My So-Called Life* on ABC.

A Soap Comes Back from the Dead

In late 1992, most people thought *Melrose Place* was doomed because of continually dropping ratings, but at the end of the 1992–93 season, things had turned around. By the end of the 1993–94 season, *Melrose Place* was television's most talked-about address. "No one expected *90210* to break out like it did, and I think it was doing it just by taking itself seriously," said *USA Today* TV critic Matt Roush. "*90210* was *Dallas*, *Melrose Place* is *Dynasty*,

Show Stats

Melrose Place
Premiered: July 8, 1992, on Fox
Created by: Darren Star, an Aaron Spelling production

Primary cast:
Josie Bissett as Jane Mancini
Thomas Calabro as Michael Mancini
Marcia Cross as Dr. Kimberly Shaw
Kristin Davis as Brooke Armstrong Campbell (1995–96)
Laura Leighton as Sydney Andrews (1993–)
Doug Savant as Matt Fielding
Grant Show as Jake Hanson
Andrew Shue as Billy Campbell
Courtney Thorne-Smith as Alison Parker
Daphne Zuniga as Jo Reynolds (1992–96)
Heather Locklear as Amanda Woodward (1993–)
Amy Locane as Sandy Louise Harling (1992)
Vanessa Williams as Rhonda Blair (1992–93)

Plot:
    This spin-off of *Beverly Hills, 90210* began as an earnest twentysomething drama and evolved into a wickedly funny soap. In the beginning, Jane and Michael were newlyweds, but by the end of the second season, Michael was sleeping with Jane's sister, Sydney. Billy and Alison began as roommates, became lovers, and were *thisclose* to being married at the end of the second season, but then Alison had memories of being molested as a child by her father (Monte Markham!). At the end of season three, Billy married the conniving Brooke while Alison fell off the wagon. Amanda was introduced in early 1993 to save the show, and save it she did, becoming the

most loved/hated character. Since then, she's had Billy, Jake, and just about anyone or anything else she's wanted. Matt is the gay social worker (a remnant from the show's idealistic days) who is forever in search of a storyline. Jo, a photographer, is Jake's one true love, but they never seem to stay together for long (like anyone else on this show does either). Kimberly is the third Mrs. Michael Mancini (after Jane and then Sydney), but she went nuts after a brain injury and stalked various characters before blowing up the apartment complex. Sandy was Jake's former flame and a waitress at Shooters, the local bar where the gang hangs out. She left after only a few months into the series for a career in New York. Rhonda was the show's token minority character, but she left Melrose Place when she got married at the end of the first season.

Trivia note: Andrew Shue was not the first actor to play Billy. Canadian actor Stephen Fanning was originally cast in the part but quit/was fired over "creative differences" just a few days into filming the pilot. Another bit of trivia can be found each week in the exterior establishing shot of D&D Advertising. The building used for D&D is part of the same complex in which Spelling Entertainment is located on Wilshire Boulevard in Los Angeles. The D&D sign itself contains an inside joke. Beneath D&D Advertising the sign reads "Johnson, Mendelsohn & Associates." Dee Johnson is the show's coproducer; Carol Mendelsohn is a coexecutive producer. Below that the sign reads "Correll Institute," presumably a misspelled tribute to Charles Correl, who directs many *Melrose Place* episodes. The El Pueblo apartment complex used for the exterior establishing shots of Melrose Place is located at 4616 Greenwood Place in the Los Feliz district of Los Angeles. The Melrose Place street sign is located at the corner of Melrose Place and La Cienga Boulevard.

that seems kind of clear. *Dallas* seemed to be more moralistic and *Dynasty* was more anything goes, and *Melrose Place* is definitely that."

One gauge of the show's popularity can be found in a *Los Angeles Times* article from December 1994 that showed *Melrose Place* to be the TV show that generated the greatest number of pizza orders (calculated by comparing orders during its time slot with weeks when the show didn't air) for Domino's Pizza. *Melrose Place* also ranked no. 1 for orders of vegetable-topped pizzas. (In the stats the number of crank calls to Domino's went up 16 percent when *The Simpsons* was on the air.) *Melrose Place* probably wasn't at the top of the Domino's list when it began in the summer of 1992. After all, it started as a supposedly realistic look at twentysomething life. When Fox rebroadcast the premiere in 1995, the announcer even made fun of its humble beginnings.

"Remember when Alison and Billy were roommates and Michael was a nice guy?" the 1995 promo gushed.

Things were different then—and a lot less fun.

"Alison, this is real life; you can't just stall on the rent," lectured Michael, who was then the apartment manager.

Life lessons were the order of the day, but few viewers cared. After a strong start, the ratings began to trend downward. From those early episodes, (which everyone with cable was able to see when E! Entertainment Television began airing reruns in August 1996) the beginnings of the "good" *Melrose Place* emerged, even though at the time the writers didn't know it would end up where it has.

"Natalie is gone," Alison whined in the pilot when her roommate snuck out in the middle of the night. "She and all of her things have disappeared."

"Maybe she got kidnapped," Matt replied.

"Come on, Matt. Who would want Natalie?"

In a little-seen cast photo from *Melrose Place* that was taken before filming on the pilot began, actor Stephen Fanning (*seated on the bottom step*) was cast as Billy Campbell but was replaced after only a few days by Andrew Shue. Other first-season cast members included (*top row*) Courtney Thorne-Smith, Josie Bissett, Thomas Calabro, (*middle row*) Amy Locane, Grant Show, Doug Savant, and Vanessa Williams. Fox Broadcasting.

Aaron Spelling's Parallel Universe Life sure is strange in

that alternate reality where *Melrose Place* and *Beverly Hills, 90210* take place. The same things happen to characters on both shows and, frequently, within just a few weeks of one another. Granted, *Melrose* is a *90210* spin-off, but the number of similar plots is astounding. Is there some hidden agenda or just a lack of imagination?

Melrose Place	*Beverly Hills, 90210*
Jane dates Chris Marchette	Dylan dates Toni Marchette
Alison goes to rehab	Dylan goes to rehab
Sydney joins a cult	Kelly joins a cult
Kimberly in sweat tent	Brandon and Dylan in sweat tent
Alison moves to Hong Kong	Jim and Cindy move to Hong Kong
Jo gets beaten up by Jess	Donna gets thrown down the stairs by Ray
Man in mirror talks to Kimberly	Jim and Cindy in mirror talk to Brandon
Kimberly gets electro-shock treatments	David's mom gets shock treaments
Amanda's involved with the mob	Dylan's involved with the mob

"Space aliens," Matt joked. "You read about it all the time."

When *Melrose* started, no one was getting kidnapped. How things changed. "In the first five or six episodes, it was not a continuing story," recalled executive producer E. Duke Vincent during a panel discussion at the 1995 TV Festival of the Museum of Television & Radio (MT&R) in Los Angeles. "When we addressed that problem, the answer was, we think it will work if we turn it into a soap, meaning it would be a continuing story. The minute that happened, it began to turn around."

Creator Darren Star put it more bluntly: "It was a desperate bid for ratings actually," he said at the MT&R festival. "It was boring at the beginning. . . . We found [that] the audience wasn't interested in seeing these self-contained episodes. They didn't buy it."

Naturally this came as a disappointing shock to Fox. Researcher Charles Kennedy said he had mountains of data about the original concept—twentysomethings going through life and the real issues they face—but it all became useless once the show's direction changed. Further research showed that "every time we went to the Billy-Alison storyline and the soap part of it, [the interest level] bumped up. We saw it in the ratings; we saw it in the way people responded. The introduction of the villain with Amanda just sent it over the edge. *Melrose Place* went through a whole transition and became a different show."

That introduction proved to be the show's turning point. "There was a telephone call made to a certain blond actress whose name shall go unmentioned," Vincent joked as he shared the stage at the MT&R seminar with the unnamed Heather Locklear. "And, of course, that was an enormous lift for us."

With the addition of Locklear in early 1993, a move that was only supposed to last a few episodes, *Melrose Place* began to come out of its funk. The ratings started going up, and more people seemed to talk about it. Even though Locklear is still listed in the opening credits as a "special guest star" (at this point, that, too, is comical but makes Locklear stand out from the rest of the cast), she is clearly the show's true star. The addition of other characters, such as Laura Leighton's Sydney and Marcia Cross as Dr. Kimberly Shaw, also helped move things into a higher gear. The successful introductions of Locklear, Leighton, and Cross led to what seems to be a new celebrity/character appearing with every new story arc although they usually don't last beyond that. Blink-and-you'll-miss-them stars featured in brief stints on *Melrose Place* include Kathy Ireland, James Wilder, Mackenzie Phillips, Traci Lords, Jasmine Guy, Dan Cortese, Morgan Brittany, Antonio Sabato, Jr., Priscilla Presley, and Loni Anderson. Although these actors may not all be household names, they are names Xers know. By rotating in fresh faces, Fox is able to generate new publicity continually for the show.

Melrose Place producer Kimberly Costello, who worked on the series during the second through fourth seasons, points to the beginning of the show's second season as a turning point. "The first season took itself so seriously, so we said this is really very funny, and without making it a lampoon of night time drama, we decided to play with it," Costello said. "When Michael turned at the end of season one and became kind of cynical and all of a sudden he was able to have a quicker wit and a more cynical edge to him, that's where his one-liners started coming in."

Melrose Place Episode Titles Although the individual

episode titles are never shown at the beginning of *Melrose Place,* each one-hour show does have a name. Sometimes newspaper TV grids will list the title, but often it doesn't even appear there. "We have a lot of fun writing them," said Kimberly Costello, the show's producer. "They're kind of our inside joke."

Some examples are
"I Am Curious Melrose" 9/12/94
"The Cook, the Creep, His Lover, and Her Sister" 10/24/94
"They Shoot Mothers, Don't They?" 10/16/94
"To Live and Die in Malibu" 3/20/95
"All about Brooke" 4/3/95
"Melrose Impossible" 4/10/95
"Framing of the Shrews" 5/15/95
"Post Mortem Madness" 9/11/95
"Melrose Is Like a Box of Chocolates" 9/18/95
"Amanda Unplugged" 10/30/95
"El Syd" 11/6/95
"The Brooke Stops Here" 1/8/96
"The Bobby Trap" 1/22/96
"Devil in a Wet Dress" 2/12/96
"True Fibs" 4/15/96

Costello, who wrote for the show *Sisters* before coming to *Melrose Place*, said the writers of *Melrose* have no shame about making a prime time soap.

"When I worked on *Sisters,* I just remember our story meetings where we were constantly told, 'This is not a night time soap but a continuing storyline of several characters.' There's nothing wrong with being a soap. They're intriguing and fun and pull people in for a length of time, not just one episode. The S-word isn't necessarily negative, and we kind of embraced it at one point. So we started playing with the story to make it more surreal."

And faster-paced. Part of the *Melrose Place* formula is to go through storylines faster than any other prime time drama does. Costello said the show is plotted at the beginning of each season in six-episode story arcs, and by mid-season the creative team knows what will be the end of the season cliff-hanger. Still, sometimes things don't always go as planned. "Amanda's cancer was supposed to be the cliff-hanger [for season three], and it wound up being played in the middle of the season," Costello said. "We chew up story so fast that what we think will happen at the end of the season ends up happening sooner."

From Bad "Bad" to Good "Bad"

In spring 1994, the media finally caught on that *Melrose Place* was a pop culture phenomenon after the resurrection of Kimberly, who had been "killed" when a drunken Michael crashed their car in late 1993. Turns out she was still alive and when she returned—new, improved, and nuts—the audience went wild, especially when she'd take off her wig to reveal a nasty scar on her head from the accident. This was the beginning of the third incarnation of *Melrose Place*. From realistic twentysomething drama to cheesy soap to over-the-top, self-conscious farce, *Melrose Place* morphed into three different types of shows in just three seasons. Ginia Bellafante wrote in *Time* in May 1996 that *Melrose Place,* during its second season, became "a dumb-brilliant parody of the soap universe, a show in which women dressed for work as though life were a continual audition for the *Howard Stern Show*." Gen X loves programs like *Melrose Place* because they can feel superior in that sarcastic, cynical way that has become the generation's trademark. Although no one would argue that *Melrose Place* deserves a place in the quality TV hall of fame, it does deserve recognition as a program so outrageous that it's more than just "bad TV." In the book *Bad TV*, author Craig Nelson explains the difference between bad TV and *bad* TV. "Bad TV is just boring and amateurish; something you banish with a quick flick of that remote control. *Bad* TV, however, is something truly amazing, enriching, and compelling—TV so bad, it's in a class all by itself." Nelson says that whereas bad TV is merely "dull, meretricious, sickening, and poorly done;" *bad* TV is "amazingly, stupefyingly, remarkably 'I can't believe they did this!' television. Whereas bad TV is to be avoided, *bad* TV should be watched as often as possible." So it is that *Melrose Place* is frequently the epitome of *bad* TV.

"I think all the characters have gotten pretty far out there," said producer Chip Hayes at the MT&R festival. "But I think Kimberly's got the prize right now." The outrageous plots aren't limited to Kimberly. Sydney has been a hooker, an exotic dancer, and a drug addict. Jo harpooned Reed, the father of her child, then Kimberly kidnapped the kid, forcing Jo to go to the authorities, who put the child up for adoption so neither one would have it. Matt was framed for the murder of his lover at the end of the third season; Jake pushed his half-brother off a building; and Alison became an alcoholic, went into recovery, and then fell off the wagon again before temporarily going blind in the 1995 explosion (courtesy of Kimberly) that blew the apartment complex to bits. Previously, Alison rose from receptionist to president of D&D Advertising in a little more than two years.

"I think it makes perfect sense myself," said actress Courtney Thorne-Smith at the MT&R festival. "I only slept with a few clients. I was only drunk at work a few times. I think my skirts could have been a little shorter. So I think it makes perfect sense."

When actor Jack Wagner appeared on *Late Night with Conan O'Brien* to chat about *Melrose Place* in the summer of 1995, the host echoed the sentiments of those who take the show at face value and can't see that it's all a goof. "What's so fascinating about these [prime time soap] shows is that all the characters hate each other," O'Brien said. "They have all slept with each other, betrayed each other, and tried to kill each other, yet they refuse to live separately."

It's that ridiculousness that makes the show so enjoyable for its fans.

Whereas Brandon of *90210* called his pyromaniac girlfriend, Emily Valentine, a "borderline personality," Michael of *Melrose* simply called Kimberly "that crazy bitch." That's the difference between these two shows. *90210* isn't much more than the sum of its parts, but *Melrose Place* actually works on many different levels. For some people, it's a steamy soap to get caught up in; for others, it's a self-aware comedy strewn with in-jokes. For example, Amanda's way with words delights some viewers.

"She'd say, 'Oh, I liked your hair better the other way' rather than 'I hated your hair,'" Costello said, "or, 'That was an interesting choice for a dress.' Her lines have always been fun. I wrote a line for Amanda after Syd had told one of her secrets, and when Amanda found out, she said, 'Her mouth is as loose as her scruples,' which is true. She's stating the truth in a funny way. Amanda's not going for the joke, she's just being obvious."

After being stalked and giving birth to a child that Kimberly kidnapped, Jo held a gun to a psycho cop and bellowed, "I am tired of being the victim!"

"We just made it apparent to all that this is the sixth time she's been in dilemmaville in the past two months," Costello said. "We just put the obvious out there, saying the same thing we know the audience is asking."

There's enough crazy behavior on *Melrose Place* to warrant the publication of a guidebook, *Life Lessons from Melrose Pl.* by Anthony Rubino, Jr., who also wrote *Life Lessons from The Bradys*. In his index card–size *Melrose* book, Rubino comes up with such gems as "It's difficult to deny blowing up a building when, like, 10 people saw you do it" (referring to Kimberly bombing the apartment complex) and "Being a regular member of a community for a prolonged period of time may help keep you from harm in the event of an explosion. If you've only been around for a few weeks, your chances of being killed increase significantly" (regular cast members survive, guest stars die).

Then there are inside jokes on the show itself, such as the name that appeared toward the end of season three on the door of the hospital chief of staff: Calvin Hobbs, M.D. At the same time that *Melrose Place* is over-the-top, there is some basis in reality as a result of the show's less-soapy beginnings.

"The thing is, we all know people who do [some of] these things," Costello said. "And the reason they enjoy *Melrose* is because there is some grounding in relationships and community. Every one of these people is searching for love and affection. Even in the episode [at the beginning of the third season] where Michael gets his memory back, he says to Kimberly, 'Kill me or love me, make up your damn mind'."

The sense of some sort of loose-knit family of friends (and, frequently, enemies) also exists in *Melrose Place* as it does in all the other Gen X shows. Costello said the writers and producers wanted to solidify that even more at the start of the second season, which is why Billy lost his job at *Escapade* magazine and wound up working with Alison and Amanda at D&D Advertising and Matt got a job at the hospital where Kimberly and Michael work. "It made it so it was not just about the apartment building," Costello said. "It crossed their lives in a couple of different places, which meant we got to see them interact as people at different levels. Before, Billy wouldn't have known what Alison's face was at work, but [by bringing him into D&D] it gave them an opportunity to interact on business and social levels without it always having to be about the apartment. You can have Billy at *Escapade*, but it's Billy and some third party who doesn't really mean much to us. So on an emotional storytelling level, it made things fun and gave us more points to work off of and places to go. How many people bring work home and have Amanda constantly knocking on their door needing a report at 8:00 instead of 9:00?"

The fact that anyone can feel sorry for Alison, who never met a secret she could keep, is testimony to the fact that even while viewers laugh at *Melrose*, they also identify with it, at least sometimes. One aspect of *Melrose Place* that has no basis in reality is its yearly season finale cliff-hanger episode. The cliff-hangers at the end of seasons two and three even managed to stir up publicity because of controversy. For the third season finale, Spelling and Fox found themselves forced into a public spectacle when real life interfered with fiction. The plot for the finale, leaked by *TV Guide* months in advance, was to have the episode end with crazy Kimberly blowing up the apartment complex. After the season finale was filmed and the actors had gone on hiatus, the Federal Building in Oklahoma City was bombed.

At first, Spelling and Fox said they'd decide what to do within one week.

At the end of that week, they decided not to say anything, thus tantalizing viewers to tune in to see what would happen. The building didn't blow; instead the last image was a freeze frame of Kimberly pushing the button. This gave Fox the opportunity to tout the "explosive" fall 1995 season premiere wherein the bomb finally went off. In the end, the Oklahoma tragedy worked in favor of the show by heightening awareness for both the cliff-hanger and the season premiere.

The show's second season finale featured Matt kissing another guy, but it was shown in slow motion with camera angles that made it impossible to see exactly what was going on. This scene can be viewed as either a cheap stunt to get publicity or a genuine effort on the part of producers to give Matt a storyline. The kiss was never followed by a storyline between Matt and this guest character the next season, but at the Museum of Television & Radio festival, actor Doug Savant, who plays Matt, defended the show's efforts to depict his character.

"We've been able to push the envelope to a certain degree," Savant said. "I think the show should be supported for that and appreciated for that. I would be remiss if I didn't say we'd like to see it go further, just with simple things like handholding, just gentle human-to-human relationships that are loving, to show what is in our common humanity that crosses over barriers of sexuality. I don't think there's ever any intention to be offensive or scare anybody; that would be counterproductive to what we hope to achieve here and that would be breaking down barriers of homophobia."

Melrose Place as a forum to break down social barriers? Perhaps, but that's not why the audience is watching. "I find it appealing because it's so outrageous," said Jennifer Hale, 25. "The people have crazy problems and often show no sane judgment in their actions. I'd have to say my favorite thing about the Spelling shows, including *90210,* is the camaraderie they help create. Every once in a while, a show will be really outrageous, and at the end of each segment, when the commercials start, my phone will ring—one of my friends calling to yell about what the characters just did. It's like audience participation."

"It's a social thing, really," said Tena Walters, a 22-year-old student at Pacific Lutheran University in Tacoma, Washington. "It's a time when roommates and others can forget classes and laugh at somebody else's life."

"It's great because it allows viewers to live vicariously through characters they can really relate to," said Steve Sebelius, a 29-year-old newspaper reporter in Las Vegas. "They do things people could never do in real life."

"I like to see how far they'll go," said Petra Renée Wicklund, a 24-year-old law student at Yale. "I like to yell 'Bitch!' at the TV screen."

"*Melrose* is downright dirt—and we like it!" said Benjamin Bryant, 19. "We are the generation that grew up with the TV greats of *Dallas, Knot's Landing,* and *Dynasty,* and then nighttime soaps disappeared. Now that there's one again, we're lapping it up and loving every decadent minute."

Perhaps one of the most recognized *Melrose Place* fans on the Internet is Ian Ferrell, a 25-year-old program manager at Microsoft, who sent out a weekly "Melrose Place Update" via e-mail for several months. "When I was doing it, *Melrose Place* was kind of cool," Ferrell said, sounding disillusioned. "They weren't aware they were such a cliché, and it was really campy. Now they're playing it up, and it's kind of depressing."

Ferrell points to the beginning of the second season as the time when the show headed into self-awareness overdrive. "They had a cool cliff-hanger, and then when they came back, they were really self-aware," he said. "Now it's like the first *Star Trek* series, any guy in a red shirt would get totally nuked [like a *Melrose Place* guest star]. The characters now either turn out to be psycho or they get killed. But they've killed off so many characters, there's no shock value in killing anyone. They've gone through storylines so fast, the only thing they can do is have an alien landing or otherworldly experience."

As the fourth season began, Costello said some of the craziness was being toned down. "There were

"Placemats" Join to Watch *Melrose* En Masse

From the *Richmond Times-Dispatch,* Mar. 26, 1995, J1.

Television was never designed to be watched in packs. But every few years a program comes along that encourages such communal gatherings. *Melrose Place* is such a TV show. In college dorm rooms across the country, Placemats (as some fans call themselves) gather weekly to watch the sexy and sinister doings of Amanda (Heather Locklear) and company on this trashy Fox soap. When *Monday Night Football* ends for the year, some bars also become popular sites for *Melrose* watching en masse. In Richmond, Virginia, the local Fox affiliate teamed with a Top 40 radio station in the spring of 1995 to sponsor "Melrose Mondays" at a local restaurant/bar, Renegades.

On a Monday in late March 1995 more than 60 people gathered to watch as the evil Dr. Michael Mancini (Thomas Calabro) chose a particularly cruel way to file for divorce from his psycho back-from-the-dead wife, Dr. Kimberly Shaw (Marcia Cross). "I've wanted to do this ever since you walked back into my life like a refugee from *Night of the Living Dead*," Mancini told a crushed Kimberly as he served her divorce papers. The crowd at Renegades broke into applause and laughter.

"But how can she be pulling on her hair like that if it's a wig?" asked Trish Tyler, 26. Kimberly "died" in a car accident in 1993 then showed up again in 1994 wearing a wig to cover scars on her head. Every now and then references are made to the wig; on a really good episode the wig is torn from her head. "The wig jokes are great," Tyler said. She and her friend, Rachel Alexander, 23, are regulars at "Melrose Mondays," along with Rachel's roommate, Greg Street, 27, and her boyfriend, Richard Semmen, 27.

"It's more fun seeing it here," Tyler said. "It's like seeing a funny movie in a theater. That group reaction really nails it."

"It's like a big event everybody looks forward to," Alexander added.

"I like the overall bitchiness of it," Tyler said. "It's a riot. This is the only thing I watch regularly. It's an addiction."

Not everyone wants to admit to that addiction, especially men, who make up a smaller percentage of the *Melrose* viewership. "I'm more of a closet fan," Street said. "It's a soap kind of thing. It's not too macho."

"You can't go to work and tell people you watch it," Semmen agreed.

Then why do some guys watch *Melrose*?

"Heather Locklear," Semmen said.

"It was great that (former porn star) Traci Lords was on there," Street added.

"She's gone now," Alexander replied.

"No, she's supposed to come back and get (Sydney)," Street said with hope in his voice.

Another thing that appeals to fans of both sexes is the "cheese" factor. On the episode they watched, D&D Advertising intern, Brooke (Kristin Davis), tried to seduce her coworker, Billy Campbell (Andrew Shue). "This is a very special place," Brooke cooed as she stood near a bench outside her father's house. "This is where I lost my virginity."

"A month ago Michael and Amanda hated each other, and now they're in each other's arms," Street said. "If it was too serious and not as cheesy, I wouldn't watch."

Although they tune in for *Melrose* and *90210*, their worship of Aaron Spelling programs did not extend to *Models Inc.* "It just looks stupid," Alexander said. "It was something I could never get into. I don't care to watch a bunch of models."

"It was beyond the realm of my reality," Tyler explained. "You're a bunch of models, suck it up and take it."

Although Renegades was just as noisy as any other bar until 8:00 P.M., as soon as *Melrose* came on, the sound level dropped and few people dared to speak loudly. During commercials, prizes were given away, and the evening's hosts checked in on the progress of Joyce Hart, 24, who had volunteered to have her hair dyed red so she could look more like one of the *Melrose* vixens, Sydney (Laura Leighton). "Sydney's the underdog and my favorite character," Hart said. "And this is going to sound corny, but I've always wanted to have red hair."

Roommates Rick Arthur, 22, and Brian White, 23, said they watch the show "religiously."

"I'm not ashamed to admit it," Arthur said. "At Clemson the whole campus shut down, and we used to watch. Plus, it was a good way to meet girls, and it's always good conversation."

definitely antics, but part of it was just a natural process for some of our more eccentric characters to go through," she said. "This year, we're concentrating back on relationships because the real root of the emotional power of the show is the relationships people have with each other rather than on the storyline counting on hijinks all the time. We're turning back to stories from more organic places, personal relationships, and misconceptions, rather than have the hijinks move the story forward."

Executive producer Frank South echoed those comments in a July 1995 *TV Guide* interview with writer Mark Schwed: "We've gotten ourselves into quite a box. We didn't want them to go through this trauma [of the apartment blowing up], then just stand up, dust themselves off, and say, 'Who are we gonna sleep with next?' The only way out of that isn't for some magic to happen. This year we're going to be more honest. We're going to dig into these characters more and find out more about them."

That kind of promise sounded like more of a curse to at least one *Melrose Place* fan who posted a note to the show's newsgroup. "Allow me to be the first to sound the alarm: Hey! I like camp trash! I want my smut!" wrote Mike Mason, 28, public affairs director for the American Maritime Congress by day, law school student by night. "Am I alone in feeling this way? I like *MP* precisely *because* it's campy and trashy, and it's *unapologetic* about it. Who wants this 'dig into these characters'-type of syrupy, gooey daytime-soap-opera stuff? This South guy thinks he's some kind of *artist*??? Hey, Frank, give me my Amanda in a short, tight dress pulling people's hearts out and stomping on them . . . or I'm going right back to watching *Monday Night Matchup* on ESPN!"

At this writing, *Melrose Place* has concluded its fourth season, and the show has deteriorated quickly. Posters to the Internet are already declaring it as good as dead. A May 1996 *TV Guide* reader's survey included the show in a multiple choice list of programs that "are most ready for cancellation." The self-consciousness of the third season gave way to generic soap opera plots and boring relationship melodrama in year four. Amanda's love affair with Bobby Parezi (John Enos III), the brother of her dead ex-husband, Jack (Antonio Sabato, Jr.), rendered Amanda much less in control. Sydney sashayed about in a 1960s hairdo and poodle skirts that made her a cartoon; Kimberly became sane, lost it again, and then almost died in the season finale; Brooke died; and Jane just argued with Jo and Richard (Patrick Muldoon) each week. At the beach wedding celebrating the renewal of vows between Kimberly and Michael, no one even kicked sand in anyone else's face. Boring. Even the season finale, in which Jane and Syd killed and buried Richard (only for his hand to come shooting out of the ground like a scene from a *Friday the 13th* movie) was lame. *Melrose Place* was at its best when Kimberly ripped off her wig, when Syd got thrown into a hole in the ground, when Alison got drunk, when Amanda was in charge, when Jo harpooned Reed, when the stunt casting involved cheesy former porn star Traci Lords instead of cheesy tabloid veteran Loni Anderson. Luckily, the *Melrose* producers are adept at switching gears, so these doldrums could be short-lived. But even *90210* managed to remain fresh and vibrant much longer before viewers started writing its obituary.

A Show That Couldn't Be Saved

Although *Melrose Place* slowly grew up to be a hit, that wasn't the case with *Models Inc.*, the *Melrose Place* spin-off that starred Linda Gray as Hillary Michaels (mother of *Melrose*'s Amanda), owner of a modeling agency. *Models Inc.* premiered in the summer of 1994 after several characters appeared in episodes of *Melrose* that spring. Like *Melrose,* it began with tolerable ratings but soon found itself at the bottom of the weekly Nielsen list. Whereas *Melrose* began as a drama about realistic people facing normal problems, *Models* proclaimed itself a soap about "beautiful people with big problems," something audiences couldn't relate to or didn't want to hear about. So what if the youngest model lost her virginity in the second episode and went on to become an alcoholic, she had tons of money. At least Alison of *Melrose* had relatable problems in the beginning, such as paying the rent. *Models Inc.* took itself too seriously. Whereas *Melrose* featured jokes at its characters' expense, *Models* was frequently no fun at all. "For my money, I never found a character I liked," Costello said. "And you have to like who they are in the beginning. I couldn't get it even though I really wanted it to work for them."

Of course, TV critics were never fond of the show, nicknaming it *Models Stink* and *Models Sink*. Matt Roush of *USA Today* called it "the fake vomit of junk-food TV" in his review of the premiere episode in June 1994. "After a while, you begin to pine for the intellectual heights of *Melrose*, the maturity of *90210*," Roush wrote. "*Models Inc.* may have sex on the beach, deceit on the job, sisters who slap each other by the hot tub. What it ain't got is fun."

Charles Kennedy, vice-president of Fox program research, said the problem with *Models Inc.* was that it began as a soap opera with too many things happening. "People didn't have the time to invest in the characters first to care what happened," Kennedy said. "We started too soon with the show in the point that we picked. Already, too many big things were happening, and you weren't invested in the characters. Also, *Models Inc.* lacks an element *Melrose Place* has and that's the element of friendship. On *Melrose Place* there are real friendships and they go back and forth and they change and people become attracted to different people. *Models Inc.* doesn't have that element, and we know that friendship is one of the most important things in appealing to Generation X. Look at *Friends*; it even has it in the name."

In an effort to save *Models Inc.*, several new characters were introduced midway through the 1994–95 season, including Emma Samms in the Heather Locklear role. "There's a lot of experimentation that goes on early in a show with the characters," said Fox's Robert Greenblatt in a 1995 interview before the cancellation of *Models*. "We changed a bunch of the characters in the first 10 episodes of *Melrose*; we did the same thing on *Models*, but we still didn't have that experienced actress that could work things up into a frenzy. We came up with this character, Grayson (Samms), and we decided to see if we could do the same thing we did with Heather. No one really thought it would be able to turn around like it did on

---

Show Stats

Models Inc.
Premiered: June 29, 1994, on Fox
Created by: Charles Pratt, Jr., and Frank South, an
  Aaron Spelling production

Primary cast:
Linda Gray as Hillary Michaels
Kylie Travis as Julie Dante
Cassidy Rae as Sarah Owens
Teresa Hill as Linda Holden
Carrie-Anne Moss as Carrie Spencer
Stephanie Romanov as Teri Spencer/Monique Duran
Garcelle Beauvais as Cynthia Nichols
Cameron Daddo as Brian Petersen
Brain Gaskill as David Michaels (1994)
David Goldsmith as Eric Dearborn
Don Michael Paul as Craig
James Wilder as Adam Louder
Emma Samms as Grayson Louder

Plot:
   This spin-off featured the mother of *Melrose Place*'s Amanda Woodward, Hillary Michaels, as owner of Models Inc., a boutique modeling agency. Julie was the bitch; Sarah, the virginal ingénue (although not for long); Linda, the waif with a porn movie in her past; Carrie, the aging beauty with a psychotic streak; Teri, the airborne model who was pushed to her death from a balcony in the pilot; Monique, the Teri look-alike who fell in love with club owner Adam; Cynthia, the token minority

model added to the cast in the fifth episode after complaints that the show needed diversity. Cameron was the photographer with an obsession; Eric was Linda's obsessive boyfriend; David (a Brad Pitt wannabe) was Hillary's son, whom she sent on an assignment to Europe (for acting lessons, perhaps?) and never returned. Craig was a surfer who lived next-door to the models' beach house, and Grayson was Adam's thought-to-be-dead wife who returned, with their child, to ruin Adam's engagement to Monique and boost ratings. She failed on both counts.

Melrose. That was just a lucky break. With *Models*, we've tried a lot of things over the past 25 episodes this year. We've tried different characters, different relationships; we've tried a lot of variations within that world, and we feel that the potential has sort of been tapped and there's not much potential to grow."

Watching Us Watching Ourselves

Friends **story editors**

Adam Chase and Ira Ungerleider (both 26 during the first season of *Friends*) grew up in Morristown, New Jersey, but they never met until 1986 when both attended Northwestern University. "Our mothers knew each other through the local synagogue," Ungerleider said while sitting at the kitchen table in Monica's apartment on the *Friends* set. "They insisted that we meet because we were both nice Jewish boys from Morristown, so, of course, we had to get to know each other."

Although they met during their freshman year, they didn't start writing together until their junior year. "It took two years to bounce back from our mothers having introduced us," Chase said. While Ungerleider studied television, radio, and film, Chase toiled in the theater department. "I didn't get into writing until college when I started doing student television stuff at Northwestern," Ungerleider recalled. "I did everything, learning to use the cameras, writing sketches, performing in sketches, directing television shows. I did every job in a television studio."

At the same time, Chase majored in performance studies, a combination of acting, directing, and writing. "You kind of got to do everything and that's what really started to light my fire," Chase said. After graduating in 1990, they drove out to Los Angeles but didn't start writing together for another year or two. During that time, Chase worked for an agent where he saw plenty of TV show scripts.

"I was like, 'Jesus, these suck, these do not make me laugh,'" Chase said. "And that's when we started to talk about [writing]."

They started working on a script for *The Simpsons*, which never came together. On their next try, they wrote a spec script for *Seinfeld*. Although the episode never sold, it did get them an agent, which led to a one-episode deal with Gracie Films' short-lived *Phenom* (1993–94, ABC). The powers that be on this James L. Brooks executive-produced sitcom liked what they saw

4

and signed the pair to a three-year deal. After *Phenom* was canceled, the deal was renegotiated, allowing them to work on *Friends* in exchange for writing a pilot for Brooks's company.

Just as *thirtysomething* was a favorite program for many Baby Boomers, *Friends* (originally titled *Friends Like Us* and then *Six of One*) has become must-see-TV for Xers. Just don't utter the term *Generation X* anywhere near the show's producers or stars. "There is hesitation about referring to ourselves as a Generation X show," said Marta Kauffman, the show's Baby Boomer cocreator and executive producer, in March 1995. "I think the label is unfortunate and unfair. It implies a certain group of people within a certain generation, and it's not the entire generation. Before we did the show, we interviewed everybody we knew who was in that age group, and they were all highly motivated. Many of them were people who had worked since high school, supporting themselves, putting themselves through college."

Kauffman's definition of Generation X makes *Gen X* synonymous with *slacker*. But there's another reason the *Friends* creator doesn't like the term: it excludes many of the *Friends* audience, which Kauffman estimated to be aged 18 to 45. Before *Friends* broke out to become a runaway hit, the producers were afraid the Gen X label would scare off older viewers and, thus, bring down the ratings. "The reason they object to it here is because they want the show to appeal to as many people as possible, and we think that it can and it does," said Chase. "So when reporters say 'Generation X,' it could be detrimental to the show. Our contention is that the stuff [the characters are] experiencing is universal."

Kauffman said *Friends* is about people whose lives are in front of them, whose choices aren't made yet. These characters are also a little confused, Kauffman said. "They want love and commitment, they're afraid of love and

Show Stats

Friends

Premiered: September 22, 1994, on NBC
Created by: Marta Kauffman and David Crane

Primary cast:
Jennifer Aniston as Rachel Green
Courteney Cox as Monica Geller
Lisa Kudrow as Phoebe Buffay
Matt LeBlanc as Joey Tribbiani
Matthew Perry as Chandler Bing
David Schwimmer as Ross Geller

Plot:

Six twentysomethings living in New York deal with love and friendship. Rachel Green (Aniston) left her husband-to-be at the alter and moved in with Monica Geller (Cox), a friend from high school. Monica's brother, Ross (Schwimmer), went through a divorce when his wife, Carol (frequent guest star Jane Sibbett), left him for another woman, Susan (frequent guest star Jessica Hecht). At the end of the first season, Carol gave birth to Ross's son, Ben. Joey Tribbiani (LeBlanc), a dim-witted actor, and Chandler Bing (Perry), the resident smart ass, live in an apartment across the hall from Monica and Rachel. Phoebe Buffay (Kudrow), a ditzy masseuse who lives with her grandmother, is the final friend who hangs with the group at the Central Perk coffee house (where Rachel works as a waitress).

commitment. Some of them have made career choices, some of them haven't. The most important thing is that their emotional situations are, we hope, universal, not just something that happens to someone in his or her twenties."

One thing the *Friends* staff strives to avoid is anything overly mushy. When Ross announced that he had to give up his pet monkey, Marcel, in "The One with Fake Monica," the studio audience heaved a collective "Awww." This caused former supervising producer Jeff Greenstein, 31, and others on the show's staff to cringe. "It's so TV," Greenstein explained. "Even if you get that as a legitimate reaction, there's something kind of clammy about it. If we have that 'awww' on the soundtrack, that means we're expecting 'awww' from folks at home, but those kinds of things should speak for themselves. We shouldn't have to say, 'Hey audience, this is a moment where you're supposed to be moved'."

Consequently, the "awww" was taken out in postproduction and was never heard on TV when the episode aired. Along the same lines, a joke made on *Friends* came back to haunt the production team. One of the first-season Chandlerisms was his quote of a TV announcer saying, "Tonight . . . on a very special *Blossom*." When it came time for the birth of Ross's son, NBC promoted the episode in the same tone of voice, with the announcer saying, "on a very special *Friends*."

"That's just mortifying to us," Greenstein said. "That acts as a catch phrase we use to identify an episode we don't want to do: 'Chandler loses a parent, on a very special *Friends*.' That's something we strive to avoid."

The producers of *Friends* prefer that each episode has three storylines, which differs from most sitcoms that feature just two stories. Because of this decision, there are more scenes, but they're shorter just like *ER, Friends*'s Thursday night companion. By using shorter scenes and telling more stories per episode, *Friends* is able to use its ensemble cast to the fullest extent and at the same time maintain the interest of even the most die-hard channel surfers. Kauffman said realism is important on *Friends,* so each episode should end with no lessons learned, no morals. Coincidences are another pitfall, she said.

"Television is filled with coincidences, and I find them fakey," Kauffman said. "*Seinfeld* is a funny, wonderful show filled with coincidences. For me, we're trying to have a show filled with characters you can invest in and care about, and I think a lot of television's tricks and gimmicks get in the way of connecting with the characters. They distance you because they always make you realize this is a TV show. For us, it's really important that the writing remains real at all times so that you can connect and be with them and feel for them and laugh at them. You can't be afraid of drama in comedy. I don't think it can replace comedy, but I think it's really important to allow the characters to have feelings."

Ever since *Roseanne,* more sitcoms have started including serialized storylines. This is especially true on *Friends.* "Maybe it's because it's more like life," Kauffman said. "Life doesn't start and end in 30-minute stories; things continue while other things begin. It's more realistic. I think it keeps people watching when there's something to invest in that doesn't end at the end of a half-hour. It makes you want to come back next week and sometimes stories are too big to tell in 22 minutes."

Although *Friends* has become a phenomenal success, Kauffman said NBC was initially wary of a sitcom that featured only young people. Would anyone over 35 watch? Kauffman said the first thing NBC wanted the producers to do was add a fortysomething character to bring in the older audience. A half-hearted attempt was made, Kauffman said, "but we kept saying, if the stories are compelling, the people will watch, and it began to be true, so they stopped asking for their older character." NBC eventually got the older character it wanted with the addition of Tom Selleck as a recurring boyfriend for Monica during the 1995–96 season. By that point, the show was such a huge hit that it's doubtful Selleck's addition was as much network-influenced as it was a decision by the show's producers to tell an older man-younger woman story.

As much as the producers tried to avoid the X label during the show's first season, *Friends* is a Gen X show through and through. Its success also proves that just because a show focuses on the lives of Xers, it can still appeal to a mass audience, which *Friends* obviously does. When the series premiered in September 1994 at 8:30 P.M. Thursday, many critics said it would be a success only because of its time slot (tucked between *Mad About You* and *Seinfeld*). Few TV insiders thought this ensemble comedy would be beating

Seinfeld by the time May 1995 sweeps rolled around. "If the series is to have legs, funnier writing is needed," wrote Tony Scott in *Daily Variety*. "Concept is okay, but the humor is less sophisticated than expected."

"Whether Generation X is a genuine social phenomenon or a marketing concoction, it's the motivating principal behind NBC's *Friends*," wrote Ginny Holbert in the *Chicago Sun-Times*.

"If NBC's new sitcom *Friends* were a math equation, it would look like this: *Friends* = *The Mary Tyler Moore Show* + *Seinfeld* x *The Real World* / the Budweiser slacker commercials," wrote Joyce Millman in the *San Francisco Examiner*. By using other TV shows to describe *Friends*, this review shows how media savvy the intended *Friends* audience is, not to mention the expected readers of this review. Critics reduced *Friends* to a formula show, but that formula became the building block for almost every sitcom in fall 1995. *Friends* is truly more than the sum of its parts. It is the most positive and realistic portrayal of Generation X yet, making twentysomethings likable and fun to watch, instead of constantly angst-ridden and depressed. Even Baby Boomers (like the show's creators) love watching *Friends*, probably to recapture memories of their youth. Beyond a positive portrayal of Gen X, *Friends* is filled with characters everyone can relate to. Although it may be easy to label them—the dunce (Joey), the smart ass (Chandler), the ditz (Phoebe)—viewers discovered that these characters have more depth than a stereotype. Joey may be dense, but he's also a sweet, caring guy. Chandler may joke around, but it's to cover his insecurities. Phoebe may be a bit spacey, but, well, she's spacey but still intelligent. Bottom line: *Friends* works because of the realistic characters and dialogue, the real-life situations, and great chemistry among the attractive and talented cast.

Black and White and Gen X All Over

"I'd like y'all to get a black friend, then I can stop by," said talk show host Oprah Winfrey to the *Friends* cast when they appeared on her show March 29, 1995. This wasn't the first time *Friends* (along with the rest of NBC's Thursday night lineup) had been viewed as something of a whitewash. Two weeks after the cast of *Friends* appeared on the cover of *Entertainment Weekly* in late January 1995, a letter to the editor accused the show of lacking diversity. Ironically, the complaint was about a lack of Asian-American characters on NBC's Thursday night shows, a shortcoming that would soon be rectified with the introduction of Ming-Na Wen on *ER* (and, later, on *The Single Guy*) and Lauren Tom as Ross's girlfriend on several episodes of *Friends*.

Complaints about a lack of African-American characters popped up even earlier in the *Friends* newsgroup, and *Friends* executive producer Marta Kauffman said she doesn't disagree. "I don't really know what to do about it," she said. "We try whenever we can to cast around our characters multiracially. When we cast the show, we did not say 'no black people, no Asians.' We auditioned Asians, we auditioned African-Americans, we auditioned Hispanic people, but these were the best people for these roles, and I don't apologize for that because I think it was the right choice. I certainly understand how people have that perception; then I think to myself, just to get sort of annoyed, *Seinfeld* is that way, *Mad About You* is that way. I'm not sure why we got singled out."

Yvette Lee Bowser, executive producer of *Living Single,* was understanding. "I think they need whatever the creators feel they can make into a good show, so I wouldn't criticize the show on that basis," Bowser said. "I have seen a black woman on *Friends,* actress Jenifer Lewis."

At the same time that people cite *Friends,* they could just as easily say the opposite of Fox's Thursday night shows, which during the 1994–95 season featured predominantly black characters. "*Martin* and *Living Single* could not be more sheltered in that regard just like *Friends* seems to be in its regard," *USA Today* TV critic Matt Roush said in an interview. "*The Cosby Show* [characters], although they had African art on the wall, didn't present themselves in a way that typified them. The characters on the Fox shows are types; they are knowing exaggerations of ethnic stereotypes. Bill Cosby has been the most outspoken person to call them minstrel shows. *In Living Color* set that groundwork by skewering the whole notion. They turned all those old clichés on their heads even at the same time that they indulged them."

It's also a 1990s phenomenon that shows will feature members of predominantly just one race instead of a melting-pot cast as was common in the 1980s. "You don't see a lot of mixture on these shows at all, and it might have to do with this whole notion that the audience won't be condescended to," Roush said. "They might sneer at something that looks like it's trying to sell itself to a rainbow coalition viewer-

ship. I think maybe people feel comfortable in the segregation of these shows. And doesn't that say something about the way TV works, the way we work, that it isn't willing to integrate?"

An aberration to this trend was the 1995 Fox sitcom *The Crew* about a group of Miami-based flight attendants. In the show's original pilot, it featured two female characters who were roommates, one white and one black. The white character was clearly the lead. After Fox scheduled the show to air after *Living Single,* the first episode was reshot, a new black male character was added, and the black female roommate became the lead. It remained one of the few integrated sitcoms in prime time until spring 1996 with the debut of ABC's *Buddies* and Fox's *The Show. Buddies* was a lame sitcom from the producers of *Home Improvement* with the premise of a twentysomething white guy and a twentysomething black guy who start a video production business together. The show was so blatant and tired that it treated its plot as if it were radical. Sadly, in the world of 1990 segregated sitcoms, it was. The show's humor was predictable and trite, and ABC pulled *Buddies* from the schedule after only a few weeks.

Far more interesting a concept, *The Show* was about a white writer working on a black variety show. *The Show* was created by John Bowman and premiered to good reviews but low ratings, frequently losing one-third of the viewers who tuned in to watch *The Simpsons* just before *The Show.* One of the characters even referred to the whiteness of *Friends* in *The Show* pilot: "They could find a monkey in New York City, but they can't find a single brother to hang out with? What's that all about?"

Bowser said the production of *Friends* one year after *Living Single* by the same studio, Warner Bros., was no coincidence. "When something works . . ."

she said. "We were compared to *Designing Women* and *The Golden Girls*. I only hope that someday people will be referring to something else as an 'old, white *Living Single*.'"

Although all the fall 1995 sitcoms were called *Friends* ripoffs by the mainstream media, Bowser said some people recognize that *Living Single* was truly the originator of the twentysomething-friends-living-together format. "Not so much in the white community, but African-Americans see *Friends* as a white *Living Single*," she said. "There's no denying there are similarities, but that's not to say there isn't room for everything. Clearly, there is. According to the Nielsens and other polls, *Living Single* is no. 1 with African-Americans and *Friends* is not in the Top 10. There's a different sensibility."

Then there's the whole stereotype of Generation X that doesn't include anyone who isn't white, middle class, and suburban. "I would be surprised if the networks were visionary enough to see a black audience as a Generation X audience," *Partners* executive producer Jeff Greenstein said. "I confess I would think the same way. The Generation X slacker experience [is something] I've never heard applied to a black guy or black girl. I'm sure that phenomenon exists, but it seems to be perceived as a white phenomenon. I was surprised when people compared *Friends* and *Living Single* because the comic sensibility is very different on these two shows. I think the story of real black kids in their late twenties and what's on their minds is a story that hasn't been told on TV yet."

Rose Catherine Pinkney, who was television vice-president for Uptown Entertainment during the first season of *New York Undercover,* said *Living Single* is clearly a Gen X show. "It was *Friends* before *Friends,* but with better jobs and love lives," she said, adding that realism in depicting the world is necessary in all programs. "We're not talking about so much regular character as about when people walk into a hallway of an apartment building in New York, you'd think they'd see one black man," she said. "In my generation we look for that content. I can almost tell you the day *Cheers* had the first black person ordering a drink in the bar. The camera just flashed by and my phone started ringing. People were talking about it, and it was not even a featured extra. So it's not to say we're expecting a black character, it's that we want the show to look like the world."

Bowser also brought up the *Cheers* example.

"For many years, there was a great deal of criticism of *Cheers,* and that was problematic for a lot of African-Americans," she said. "The fact is, not a lot of African-Americans hang out in those kinds of bars in Boston, so they were true to their reality. There aren't a lot of opportunities, but if people create what they think should be on TV instead of complaining, it will exist. We'll keep pushing and pushing."

Pinkney said people have called *New York Undercover* a "groundbreaking series," which she doesn't necessarily think is a good thing. "It's a buddy cop show that we've seen 10,000 times before," Pinkney said. "They happen to be two young people of color. It's a shame that's enough to make a show groundbreaking."

Pinkney also points out that the reality of TV is that it's a business first and an art second. "It's called show *business*," she said. "There are so many things I'd take personally, but when you follow the money lines it all becomes clear. This is why it's called commercial television. TV isn't always up for what's right. There is no altruism in the TV business even though that might be right and good and moral—but does it make more money?"

Building
a
Hit

Midway through its first season, the ratings and notoriety of *Friends* began to pick up. The cast was on the covers of *Entertainment Weekly* and *TV Guide* during the same week in January 1995. By May, they also landed on the covers of *People, Rolling Stone,* and the *New York Times* Sunday Arts & Leisure section. Still, in February 1995 when *Friends* moved to the 9:30 P.M. post-*Seinfeld* slot, *Washington Post* TV critic Tom Shales refused to admit that the show might be capable of standing on its own. "*Friends* is one of the least-deserving hits on television," Shales wrote. "It may not become more deserving, but it's almost sure to become more of a hit; as of tonight it moves into the time slot between *Seinfeld* and *ER* on NBC. Al Gore reading the party platform could get a rating in a plum position like that. . . . The show is an hors d'oeuvre that could never pass as an entrée. It's finger food."

Not long after he wrote that piece, *Friends* surged in the ratings. Throughout the May 1995 sweeps period, the show beat *Seinfeld,* ranking no. 2 in the weekly ratings behind *ER*. During the summer 1995 rerun season, *Friends* was no. 1 for six consecutive weeks, which isn't how time slot hit shows usually perform. Jeff Greenstein, one of the show's first-season supervising producers, attributed the show's success to the time slot in the beginning but also to the attractive cast and good writing. "Not including me, there were a lot of terrific writers on the show," he said. "We tried to tell stories about us and people we knew. To us, the ultimate compliment is 'Oh my God, that's so my life,' 'I am that character,' or 'My girlfriend is totally Rachel.' That's what we tried to bring to the show, characters people could relate to. That's why it found an audience to begin with."

As its popularity grew, more critics climbed aboard the *Friends* express with glowing profiles of the show's stars and reviews of the series. At the same time, *Friends* had its detractors, including *Time* magazine's Richard Zoglin, who complained in a March 1995 issue that the characters on *Friends* spent too much time in the coffee bar. "Where *Seinfeld* is smart and appealingly free-form, *Friends* is inane and gimmicky," Zoglin wrote. "In *Friends,* the crowd is always around to share their latest personal woes or to offer a

118

shoulder to cry on. But who would want advice from these dysfunctional morons with their obsessive pop-culture references?"

That last line explains why Zoglin hates the show more than anything else in his critique: He doesn't like the pop culture stuff. Perhaps he feels left out? Maybe he's just too old to understand some of it. Whatever the reason for his objection, it's clear that Zoglin just doesn't get it. The use of pop culture references is the biggest difference between *Friends* and its predecessors such as *Seinfeld*. This device is clearly a trademark of Generation X. For example: "Oh! I think this is the episode of *Three's Company* where there's some sort of misunderstanding," Chandler said in one episode.

In another, Rachel asks, "Guess what?" to which Chandler replied, "The fifth dentist caved and now they're all recommending Trident?"

Baby Boomers are less likely to pepper their conversation with these sorts of pop culture and media references. That's a trademark of Generation X. But Boomers and Xers can both understand this dialogue because members of both age groups have watched enough episodes of *Three's Company* to know that the same thing happens every time. And it's probably during those episodes that they saw the commercials proclaiming that four out of five dentists recommend Trident gum.

"We use a lot of pop culture," said story editor Jeff Astrof. "Some of it's pretty esoteric. We did some Ikea references, and people on the Internet had no idea what it was. We do a lot of TV references. We're a TV generation, so we were all brought up on the same shows."

Although Baby Boomers may have been the first generation to make TV a large part of pop culture, it's the Xers who have taken it to a new art form. Just look at the depiction of Gen X life (over the top and narrow though it was) in the 1994 film *Reality Bites* in which every conversation was filled with pop culture references. Certainly there were pop culture references on *thirtysomething* and other Boomer favorites but none to the extent of *Friends* and other Gen X shows. *Entertainment Weekly,* a journal of popular culture, reported in spring 1995 that 56 percent of its readers were in the 18 to 34 age group. The Boomers may have started the mass media fixation, but Xers are hooked. "It's a set of references and shorthand used by the characters that people can connect with," Jeff Greenstein said. "People in their twenties love seeing characters that have the same cultural reference points they do."

Media
References
Galore

TV talking about TV was a trend that emerged during the 1994–95 television season. It wasn't entirely new; *St. Elsewhere* and several other 1980s shows had made references to other TV shows. Whereas the writers of *St. Elsewhere* made jokes that only a few TV insiders would get, Gen X TV programs include references that are easily identifiable to teleliterate viewers. *Friends* started the trend, and other programs quickly followed suit. Again, these were shows that appealed to the Gen X audience. It's unlikely that Jessica Fletcher on *Murder, She Wrote* would talk about *90210*, but that didn't stop other TV shows, especially *Hope & Gloria*, which had the NBC 8:30 P.M. Thursday time slot the second half of the season. When *Hope & Gloria* debuted, it didn't have as much of the *Friends* TV talk, but as the weeks went by, it became clear that NBC might have mandated that the series become more *Friend*ly.

On the April 20, 1995, episode, Hope mistakenly thought Adam West (TV's *Batman*) could be her real father. Julie Newmar (one of the three actresses to play Catwoman in the campy late 1960s series) also appeared as herself. "So then, the Boy Wonder, would he be your brother or your uncle?" Gloria asked. In that same episode, the hairdresser on the *Dennis Dupree Show* pulled out Adam Wests's autobiography, *Back to the Batcave.* "Well what can I say, I'm a child of television," he said. Later in the episode, Gloria arrived at a grand realization: "You know, when you scratch the surface, we're all a lot closer to *Melrose Place* than we'd care to admit."

The next week, April 28, 1995, Hope thought she might have slept with her half-brother. "This is just like a story on *Models Inc.*," Gloria said. "Oh no, you're going to commit suicide! The girl on *Models Inc.* jumped out a window."

"Did she die?" Hope asked.

"I don't know, I was making a sandwich," Gloria replied.

On the *Seinfeld* episode that followed *Hope & Gloria* that night, George brought up the subject of TV when talking to his mother: "I think we really need to be in front of a television set. You take the TV out, and this relationship is just torture."

Just one week later, May 4, 1995, a *Hope & Gloria* episode featured series star Alan Thicke as both his *Hope & Gloria* character, Dennis Dupree, and as himself, when the fictional *Dennis Dupree Show* hosted a *Growing Pains* reunion. At one point, Hope told another character, "If you're going to call someone, call your niece, those are the demographics we need." This dialogue plays on the fact that viewers know advertisers want the young, Gen X demographic. But by mentioning it, the producers proved that they wanted the show to appeal to this same audience too. When it's suggested that Dennis (who blames look-alike Alan Thicke for ruining his career with the disastrous *Thicke of the Night* late-night talk show) should confront Thicke on the air, Hope explained that the idea came from the station manager, who "says it's very *Talk Soup*-able."

Before *Growing Pains* was chosen, someone else suggested a *Brady Bunch* reunion. "I think several hundred people beat you to that one," announced the station manager.

"Another *Brady Bunch* reunion without Cindy?" Gloria said. "What's the point?"

Again, this all plays into Xer knowledge of pop culture. Xers know there have been countless *Brady Bunch* reunions: sequels, talk show appearances by the stars, and retrospectives. Xers also know that there was a fake Cindy in *A Very Brady Christmas*, although actress Susan Olsen has participated in most of the retrospectives. Using Jan here would have been funnier, because Eve Plumb has been especially snotty in public in recent years when people mention *The Brady Bunch*.

An episode of *The X-Files* referred to a genre competitor during the 1994–95 season when Mulder went to visit the Lone Gunmen, a group of computer hackers and Internet geeks. One of them, who looked like Garth from *Wayne's World*, invited Mulder to join them for weekend festivities. "We're gonna surf the Net and point out the technical inaccuracies in *Earth 2*," he said. In a 1996 episode about a TV microchip that led viewers to commit murder, Mulder refers to NBC's promotional slogan for its blockbuster Thursday night lineup when he said, "All I know is television does not make previously sane men go out and kill five people, thinking they are all the same guy. Not even 'Must See TV' could do that to you."

Melrose Place became an important plot point in episodes of both *Ellen* and *Seinfeld* during the same season. Ellen fell for a guy because he was an intellectual, so different from her regular friends. When she introduced him to *Melrose Place,* he got addicted, left his intellectual life behind, and Ellen lost interest. On the February 9, 1995, episode of *Seinfeld,* Jerry fell for a female cop who didn't believe him when he said he didn't watch *Melrose,* so she hooked him up to a lie detector.

"Did Kimberly steal Jo's baby?"

"Did Billy sleep with Alison's best friend?"

"Did Jane's fiancée kidnap Sydney and take her to Las Vegas, and if so, did she enjoy it?"

Seinfeld replied "I don't know" to all of these, but the last question was just too much for him to stand.

"Did Jane sleep with Michael again?"

"Yes, yes, the stupid idiot, he left her for Kimberly, he slept with her sister, he tricked her into giving him half the business, and then she goes and sleeps with him again!" Jerry shouted as he wigged out. "I mean, she's crazy, how could you do something like that? That Jane, oh she just makes me so mad."

Later as the *Seinfeld* gang watched *Melrose Place* (with the *Melrose* theme song quietly playing in the background), Jerry let loose with another outburst: "Oh Michael, I hate him. He's just so smug."

Melrose Place coproducer Kimberly Costello said the staff on her show loved the tributes from *Seinfeld* and *Ellen.* "I found it really, really interesting that two half-hour sitcoms would spend half of one episode talking about another show," Costello said. "It's a buzz word for people to say, 'We hang out to watch *Melrose Place.*' And you noticed that in both [*Seinfeld* and *Ellen*] they watched in groups. That's the way people watch, in groups, or they're on the phone after or they talk about it the next morning at the office."

To bring things full circle, the 1995 season finales for both *All-American Girl* and *Roseanne* refered to *Friends.* The final episode of *All-American Girl* was actually a back-door pilot, a retooled episode that got rid of most of the original cast and introduced a *Friends*-like set of roommates for series star Margaret Cho. At one point during the episode, Margaret's grandmother was reading *TV Guide* and came across a listing for *Friends.*

"Six gorgeous young people sitting around drinking coffee all day, and they're not sleeping with each other," she said. "Yeah, right!"

On *Roseanne*, TV referring to TV was made into an art with levels of reality colliding as the cast of *Roseanne* pretended to be the cast of *Gilligan's Island*. At the end of the episode, the surviving *Gilligan's Island* cast turned the tables, playing the characters from *Roseanne*. Not only did the episode play with reality on these levels but also on the personal level of the show's lead actress and her reputation.

"Hey, nice drivin', Ahab," Ginger (Roseanne Conner) said to the Skipper (Dan Conner, as played by John Goodman). "That was sure one fun Carnival Cruise, huh? As soon as we get rescued, I'm gonna strangle that bitch, Kathie Lee." Of course, Kathie Lee Gifford is the spokeswoman/singer for Carnival Cruise Lines. Later, Ginger (Roseanne) sulked, saying, "Lost and forgotten, I should have known better than to sign with William Morris."

When Gilligan (Jackie, as played by Laurie Metcalf) ran by with crabs stuck all over his (her) body, Ginger said, "Here comes another Emmy," a knowing reference to Metcalf's multiple wins. Roseanne's life came into play again after Gilligan predicted that things couldn't get any worse.

"Oh, it could get way worse," Ginger said. "I just heard on the radio that Fox is doing my life story."

"What's so bad about that?" Gilligan asked.

"Four words: Denny Dillon is Ginger," Ginger replied, a reference to the horrible Roseanne bio movie that aired on the Fox network and starred Denny Dillon.

"Hey tall, dark, and flesh-eating," Roseanne said to a native on the island. "You're about the sexiest little cannibal I've ever seen. I could do wonders for your career. Trust me, I've done it before and for people less civilized than you."

Clearly, this was a reference to Roseanne's second ex-husband, Tom Arnold. During the episode's end credits, actors from the original *Gilligan's Island* appeared portraying the *Roseanne* characters who had just played their parts. At one point, David (the real David, as played by Johnny Galecki) walked through the scene and said, "We definitely watch too much TV."

Sherwood Schwartz, creator of *Gilligan's Island* and *The Brady Bunch*, appeared as himself, and Roseanne (played by Tina Louise) fired him as the real Roseanne has been known to do to her show's writers. "Get me the guy who wrote *The Brady Bunch*," the fake Roseanne ordered.

"I'm afraid that's me, too," Schwartz replied.

"Great, you're hired again, welcome aboard," the fake Roseanne said.

And the *Friends* reference? David, still himself, climbed out of the wrecked S. S. Minnow on the *Gilligan's Island* set and said, "What am I doing here? I don't even like this show. I wanted to be on *Friends*." *Roseanne's* invoking names of other TV shows is one of the more complex examples because it mixes fact, fiction, and tabloid gossip to such an extent. Although it can be confusing to the uninitiated, TV show writers continue these inside jokes because they know that TV is the most pervasive medium. Producers know they can get away with joking about TV because they know it's what people are watching. TV has become the universal contemporary literature. Although every viewer may not understand these jokes, enough of them will so that TV show writers and producers need not worry about alienating their audiences. At one time, these jokes would all have been regarded as inside jokes, but because of TV and the Internet, everyone is now an insider—and wants to be treated that way. Xers don't want to watch TV, they want to commune with it. By offering these nuggets, viewers who "get it" feel as if they belong, as if they're a part of the process.

Various aspects of the media have become a major preoccupation among TV shows not only in their references but also in their settings. *TV Guide* even caught onto this and included it in the "Jeers" section of the May 13, 1995, issue. Among the programs during the 1994–95 season with characters involved in the media or performing arts were *Martin, Home Improvement, Murphy Brown, Cybill, The Critic, Mad About You, The Larry Sanders Show, Full House, Hope & Gloria, Platypus Man, Frasier, The George Wendt Show, NewsRadio, Bringing Up Jack, Dave's World, Lois & Clark: The New Adventures of Superman,* and *Living Single*. At the beginning of the 1995–96 season, the list expanded to include *The Preston Episodes, Strange Luck, Almost Perfect, Caroline in the City, New York News, The Naked Truth, The Bonnie Hunt Show,* and *Live Shot*.

The reason this is happening is because most of the people who are writing for these shows are in their twenties or thirties and being a part of the media

is all they've ever dreamed of; it's all they've known. No sitcoms are set on farms because it's not something TV show creators aspire to. They aspire to create TV shows, but when they get the chance to create a show, the only thing they know to make their show about is another aspect of the media because that's been their main preoccupation.

From Constructed Programs to Reality Shows

If *Friends* is the most realistic sitcom about Gen X life, what does that make the MTV docudrama series, *The Real World?* Different Xers have different answers. Graduate student Gregory Weight said he gets a kick out of *The Real World* because it makes him feel better about himself. "I like it for some of the same reasons I watch *The Simpsons*—to feel superior. With *The Simpsons*, I feel superior when I get jokes or notice things that probably only 5 percent of the audience will get. I feel superior with *The Real World* because I know I would handle things better than these idiots do. The show plays to our biggest weakness: Gossip among close friends. I like it just to be a voyeur, basically."

Although Weight thinks he understand things in *The Simpsons* that escape others and feels superior to the *Real World* folks, the fact is, most regular viewers of these two shows probably feel the same way. Just as Xers watch *Melrose Place* to feel smarter about themselves, they watch *The Real World* for the same reason. And why not? Xers are constantly being told how stupid they are, that 50 percent of them can't find the United States on a world map. Is it any wonder that some Xers turn to TV to feel more intelligent? With *The Real World,* the satisfaction level rises a notch because instead of watching characters, viewers get to eavesdrop on the lives of real people. That voyeuristic appeal of *The Real World* is the reason cited by Xers most often for watching the show. People watch soap operas for similar reasons, which is exactly what MTV had in mind when they commissioned *The Real World.* The appeal of such a TV show was first made clear during the broadcast of *The Real World* antecedent, the 1973 PBS series *An American Family.* At a December 1994 seminar on *The Real World* at the Museum of Television & Radio in

New York, Lisa Berger, vice-president of talent development for MTV, appeared with *Real World* producers and cast members. Berger said the network had been seeking to increase its original programming and wanted to do a soap. Their timing was right: *The Real World* debuted in the summer of 1992 just before the tidal wave of youth ensemble dramas. The *Real World* brought MTV tons of publicity and some of the best ratings it ever received.

"I've watched *The Real World* mainly because I can relate to the people," said Jennifer Stratakis, a 25-year-old alumni specialist at Carnegie Mellon University. "It's also interesting to see real conflict and to analyze how people relate/react to each other. I guess that's it—I like to study the way these people communicate."

> ## Show Stats
>
> ### *The Real World*
>
> Created by: Mary-Ellis Bunim and Jonathan Murray for MTV
> Season 1: New York
> Premiered: May 21, 1992
>
> Primary cast:
> Eric Nies
> Julie
> Heather
> Becky
> Kevin
> Norman
> Andre
>
> Plot:
>
> Eric worked as a model (who went on after *The Real World* to host MTV's *The Grind*. He also landed a bit part in *The Brady Bunch Movie*); Julie was a dancer from Birmingham, Alabama; Heather was a rapper; Becky was bohemian; Kevin was a writer who often got angry; Norman was a bisexual artist who dated talk show host Charles Perez; and Andre was in a band called Reigndance.

"I like watching their everyday lives play out," said Joyce Woodjetts, a 25-year-old marketing program manager in Mountain View, California. "I liked the first one the best because it was the most genuine; no one was putting on a show for the camera. In the other seasons, everyone knew they had something to gain by being on the show."

Chris McCarthy, a 30-year-old actress who lives in Los Angeles, is not a big fan: "*Real World* just plain *sucks*," she said. "Who cares about those whiny brats? With the notable exception of the late Pedro, he stood out, alone, as reasonably intelligent."

"Oh, please don't let everybody think that this is what all twentysomething people are like!" said Kevin Wilkinson, 25, a computer systems analyst in Norristown, Pennsylvania.

Obviously, *The Real World* is not representative of everyone in the Gen X age group. Rather, the people on the show exist as types: the Republican, the gay activist, the rapper, the Asian medical school student, the innocent suburban white girl, the liberal Jewish cartoonist. At this writing, there have been five incarnations of *The Real World*. The first year was set in New York City and pre-

miered in the summer of 1992. The second edition was set in Los Angeles and was originally broadcast in 1993. In year three, which debuted in summer 1994, a new group headed to San Francisco. Year four, summer 1995, was the first international installment of *The Real World* with a London setting. A fifth installment, set in Miami, aired in 1996.

Perhaps the strangest thing about watching *The Real World* is that it turns reality on its head. Here are a group of real people who have been plugged into the culture of television so that viewers watch them on a weekly basis and treat them the same way they treat characters on all TV shows. They talk about them as if they're characters, even referring to them as characters at times. By the end of a season's worth of *Real World* episodes, viewers know who they like and who they dislike, but unlike most show's during which they're reacting to characters from a writer's imagination, with *The Real World* they're reacting to real people. At the Museum of Television & Radio seminar, Kevin Powell, from the first *Real World* cast, spoke about this confusion.

"I'm a writer, and we are only known by our bylines, and to be walking through New York City and have people running behind me, 'Kevin, Kevin, Kevin,' it was like, 'Whoa!' That was stressful. People saying, I liked your character, I hate your character—all these extreme things going on. But I was like, it's me, it's my real name. . . . A lot of the letters we got, people were talking about things that were real about us. For example, 'Kevin, why are you so angry?' I wasn't acting, that's how I really felt at the time."

Putting the show together is much like scripting a sitcom or drama except that the storyline is created after the action is filmed. "We're letting them tell their own sto-

Season 2: Los Angeles
Premiered: June 24, 1993

Primary cast:
Dominic
Jon
Tami
Aaron
David
Beth S.
Irene
Glen (replacement no. 1)
Beth A. (replacement no. 2)

Plot:
Of all the *Real Worlds* to date, this one featured the greatest number of kids with musical aspirations. Dominic managed a band; Jon and Tami were singers; and Glen was in a band. Aaron was a student at UCLA; Beth S. was an aspiring actress. Beth A. announced that she was a lesbian after being brought in by the show's producers to replace Irene, a cop who left the show after getting married. In the most controversial group decision, David was thrown out of the house after the cameras captured his horseplay with Tami that came to be regarded as a rape attempt. Glen was picked by the remaining housemates to be David's replacement.

Season 3: San Francisco
Premiered: June 23, 1994

Primary cast:
Puck
Pedro
Cory
Rachel
Judd
Mohammed
Pam
Jo (replacement)

Plot:

Puck was a San Francisco bike messenger who quickly grossed everyone out with his scabs, lack of hygiene, and tendency to pick his nose and then use the same finger to scoop out peanut butter from the community jar. Eventually, he was kicked out after butting heads with Pedro, an AIDS activist who tested HIV-positive and died the day after the show's last original broadcast. Cory was a naïve college student from Orange County. Rachel was a conservative who still managed to bond with Pedro because of their similar Hispanic heritage. Judd was a cartoonist who landed a job during the show's run with the *San Francisco Examiner;* Pam was a medical school student; Mo wasn't around the house much, concentrating instead on his budding music career. Jo, selected by the roomies to replace Puck, was a Brit with baggage who quickly bonded with Rachel, who swiftly ditched Cory.

Season 4: London
Premiered: June 28, 1995

Primary cast:
Jay
Kat
Mike
Neil
Sharon
Lars
Jacinda

Plot:

This international version of *The Real World* began by setting up Neil, a pompous Brit, to be the next Puck. It didn't work. Although Neil's smugness was almost as annoying as Puck's, he never upset anyone to the point of getting kicked out. This *Real World* also featured the youngest cast to date. Kat was a student at New York University; Jay was a playwright who had recently graduated from high school in Portland, Oregon; and Mike was the per-

ries," Jonathan Murray, a creator of *Real World*, said in a September 1995 interview. "We're just really acting as their editors. Sometimes that's an easy process. If we have a situation in which the roommates get together and decide to kick Puck out of the house, we end up during the evening with a perfect three-act play. Other times, we have to wait for enough to happen in a particular area to tell a story."

One complaint about *The Real World* from fans is that they don't get to see enough of some characters and see too much of others. "It's always going to be that some people don't do as much as you hope or do it off-camera, and there's no way to control that," Murray said. "Some people's lives fit TV better than others do. Mo's complaint [in *Real World III*] was that he was never seen, but the other roommates say he'd go off on his journeys and not tell anyone he was going, or he was having a philosophical discussion not grounded in anything happening in the loft and didn't fit into any kind of a story. It was disappointing for him and for us. Then other people like Rachel just seemed perfect for television."

Clearly, being on *The Real World* changes the lives of the young adults in the cast. In August 1995 after sending an e-mail to Rachel of *Real World III* for an interview to be included in this book, I received a phone call from her brother, who said he was acting as her attorney/agent. He wanted to know how long an interview would take and if my book would compete with MTV's *Real World* fan book. He was also the only person to ask whether I paid my interview subjects (fat chance). He said I'd probably hear from Rachel soon. I never did.

Real World cast members are unlikely to get sympathy from viewers who know they weren't forced to be on the show. "I watch *The Real World* because it's nice to know

there are people more screwed up than I am," said Brandi Murray, 20, a college student in Logan, Utah.

"It seems contrived, oddly enough," said Jennifer A. Basil, 32, a biologist living in Woods Hole, Massachusetts, "mostly because these folks were handpicked to interact in interesting ways together. I don't like the majority of them, and they all seem fairly immature. Each one seems like such a stereotype."

"*The Real World* makes me want to shoot myself," declared *Friends* staff writer Adam Chase. "This is whatever incarnation of *The Real World* we're talking about. It's as if they're holding those six disparate people up, like, 'Here's a sampling of people that age,' and I think I was really much less dorky than those people."

"I'm not sure that's true," Ungerleider replied. "It's just so contrived; it's so *not* the real world. If it were called *The Contrived World,* it would be kind of ironically funny."

Murray defended the show's title. "I've always interpreted *The Real World* as the time in life when you're out on your own and you're responsible for your own actions," he said. "You've left your parents' nest, and you've got to make decisions for yourself. This is a television show, and we say that in the opening. We're admitting it's a TV show, this *is* a set-up situation."

The fifth installment of the series (summer 1996) was set in Miami. In a new twist, the housemates were given money to start a business, provoking more criticism about the reality of *The Real World.* There's no denying that the makeup of each *Real World* would be unlikely to occur in real life. In the real world, would a gay activist choose to live with a Republican? Would a medical student want to have six other roommates? Would anyone want to live with Puck? Probably not. At the MT&R seminar, *Real World* executive producer Jonathan Murray said that bringing these different people together is the whole point of the show.

"If you bring seven people together who all like each other, and that's the

fect stereotype of an American frat boy. Sharon was a singer from England who talked constantly; Lars was a German DJ; and Jacinda was an Australian model.

Season 5: Miami
Premiered: July 10, 1996

Primary cast:
Joe
Cynthia
Mike
Flora
Dan
Melissa
Sarah

Plot:
This time the housemates not only lived together they were supposed to run their own business. Joe came to the series with one business under his belt already; Cynthia was a waitress who put herself through college; Mike had a background in accounting and restaurant management; Flora immigrated from the Soviet Union when she was three and worked as a bartender while attending art school; Dan talked a lot and was editor of his college newspaper; Melissa was from a traditional Cuban family living in Miami; and Sarah was an editor at a comic book company.

kind of people we generally surround ourselves with, nothing's going to happen. It would be very boring. I don't think you can be so arrogant as to say let's take the cat and dog and throw them in and watch them claw each other to death. What a lot of people forget is these guys have to wake up and look at each other every morning; they have to live together. So I think what we learned over the course of this is that you have to have people who, yeah, on the surface have those stereotypes hung around their necks, but there's more depth to them. After a while, they're going to stop playing those games."

Although the beginnings may be calculated attempts to ignite conflicts that produce exciting TV, what actually plays out on *The Real World* appears to be pretty realistic. No one could have predicted that Puck would stick his fingers in the peanut butter jar in *Real World III* or that David would be kicked out of the house in *Real World II*.

"We thought Puck might be a little more accommodating, a little more willing to compromise," Murray said. "We expected a little bit of trouble, he's a strong personality, but most people generally will bow to the will of the group."

Puck didn't, and the roommates threw him out. Puck was still trailed by MTV cameras and eventually landed on MTV as a VJ for a short time. He also found himself parodied on an episode of *Beverly Hills, 90210*. This was, no doubt, motivated by the discussion of *90210* during *Real World III*. On *90210*, David and Clare had a class assignment to follow someone for 24 hours and create a *Real Life* documentary. Their chosen subject, a bicyclist named Tuck who wore a leather aviator's helmet, turned them down. "My roommates are too P.O'd at me these days," Tuck explained. "We didn't sign a contract or anything. Find some other lab rat or blow it out your shorts. . . . What can I say? The Tuckster has his own program and you dorks are not on it."

Later, Brandon Walsh ended up playing the role of Tuck in a fictionalized account. Although the *90210* episode was a fairly obvious and unoriginal attempt at parody, the Tuck/Puck dialogue sounded pretty genuine. During the same season, *All-American Girl* did a *Real World* takeoff as well, but it was more a parody of the format than of any of the characters. During the summer of 1994, Comedy Central ran a series of short subjects called *The Real Bowl,* which focused on the lives of seven fish living together in one bowl. Every *Real World* house has had a fish tank as part of the set. Another refer-

ence to *The Real World* was made at the beginning of the 1995–96 season, again on *90210*. After Ma and Pa Walsh moved to Hong Kong, Brandon and Valerie had the family house to themselves, so Steve moved in for a true group home experience. When Dylan visited the first time, he commented, "Well, at least there's not a fish tank."

Questions of authenticity continue to plague *The Real World*. During the London-based fourth season, cast members told *Entertainment Weekly* about the show's tricky editing. In a scene from the first episode, Mike's dad told him that Big Ben is a clock. "I said, 'Yeah, Dad, I know Big Ben's a clock.' And the [editors] took off the 'Yeah, Dad, I know' and made it 'Big Ben's a clock'," Mike told *Entertainment Weekly*. "All of a sudden, *Newsweek* writes an article about how stupid Mike is when there's no way anybody in the world doesn't know Big Ben's a clock." Actually, Big Ben is the bell inside the clock tower.

Jonathan Murray, executive producer/creator of *The Real World*, defended the editing of that scene. "If you look at the raw tape of that overall conversation, I think what we edited was fair," he said. "Mike was overall pretty naïve about what was in England, and his father had a general knowledge, but nothing specific. What we showed reflected what happened over a half-hour discussion."

In the same *Entertainment Weekly* article, the roommates accused one another of acting, hamming it up for the cameras, or filtering out elements of their lives they didn't want made public. "Once Mike asked me something when the cameras weren't there, and five minutes later he repeated the same question because now the cameras were there," Lars told *Entertainment Weekly*. "Mike isn't usually like that."

Sharmila Mali, 22, has thought about how participating in *The Real World* benefits not only the housemates but also those they come in contact with. "I'm interested to see how their careers work while living with MTV," she said. "Usually it turns out well; if you have MTV cameras following you everywhere, that's great exposure for both parties."

"*The Real World* seems quite true to life," said Brian D. Hadfield, 22, a student at the University of Michigan. "The constant bickering among friends—friends play a very important role in my life—is something I can relate to. I think this is also the reason I don't tune in regularly. I get this in my own life enough."

MTV may live by Gen X, but they also have to deal with Xers' distrustful and cynical natures. Despite some disdain from its target audience, MTV ordered up *Road Rules* (also from Bunim/Murray Productions) for summer 1995. Described by many critics as "*The Real World* in a Winnebago," this series took *Real World* voyeurism, added extreme sports, and set it all in a smaller space. Murray said the idea behind this series came out of the second *Real World* when Jon, Dom, and Tami took a road trip across America to reach Los Angeles. The producers also wanted a series focused on life in small towns all over the country instead of on life in a big city. "We wanted to send these big city kids through small towns so they'd get a dose of that Americana that's out there," he said. "We think a lot of exciting stories can come from road trips. It's *Mission: Impossible* meets *The Real World* meets *MTV Sports*."

Bunim and Murray even saw their successful *Real World* concept ripped-off by the Disney Channel when it introduced *Hollywood Lives* in August 1995. This *Real World* for a slightly younger audience didn't feature kids living together; instead it was a more traditional documentary series with camera crews following a diverse array of mostly teens who all wanted to make it in show business.

Music

MTV really helped mold Gen X's interest in popular music. Now this music has become a hallmark in all Gen X TV programming, not just shows on MTV. How important is music in Gen X TV? Important enough that the producers of *Friends, My So-Called Life,* and *Party of Five* all chose to use the Gen X angst anthem, R. E. M.'s "Everybody Hurts," in their pilot episodes. It's also important enough to warrant soundtrack spin-offs. *The Heights, My So-Called Life, Party of Five, Melrose Place, New York Undercover, Saved by the Bell, The X-Files,* and *Friends* have all spawned soundtracks, and *90210* has had two albums. The *Friends* album went platinum, leading to plans for a sequel soundtrack.

The *Friends* theme song, "I'll Be There For You," was performed by the Rembrandts (music by Michael Skloff, lyrics by Allee Willis, David Crane, Marta Kauffman, and the Rembrandts' Phil Solem and Danny Wilde) specifically for the series. When DJs began taping it off their TVs and playing it over the radio, the Rembrandts hurriedly recorded a newer version that

lasted longer than the show's short intro, adding more verses and creating a Top 40 hit in the process.

Ironically, in July 1994 just before *Friends* premiered, ABC Entertainment president Ted Harbert declared a moratorium on TV show theme songs in an effort to reduce the opportunity for channel surfing. Instead of a 40-second theme with credits, he suggested that the credits should play over the show's first scene. Obviously, this was a bad idea from the start. TV show theme songs have played an important part in the insinuation of programs into culture. Theme songs also make good business sense because they create awareness of a TV show. Just as a hit song from a movie can power ticket sales (see the box office results from *The Bodyguard* or *Dangerous Minds* for proof), a hit TV show theme song can help draw viewers to the tube. Is it just coincidence that once the Rembrandts released their extended version of the *Friends* theme that the show shot to no. 1? By July 1995, Harbert changed his mind, realizing the importance of TV tunes.

By March 1996, the *Party of Five* theme song, "Closer to Free" by the BoDeans, became a Top 20 radio hit that spawned a single. Music also plays a big role on *New York Undercover.* Each episode's entire introductory scene (before the credits and theme song) plays like a music video—no dialogue, just music as the scene plays out MTV-style. The NBC show *Homicide: Life on the Street,* although not filled with glamorous Gen X actors, has used modern rock from the likes of Nine Inch Nails, Belly, Candlebox, Morphine, Live, Matthew Sweet, and Barenaked Ladies. "I think you have to speak in a language that's going to reach the people you're aiming your show at," said *Real World* executive producer Jonathan Murray. "A lot of Gen Xers grew up knowing words to songs better than words to a poem in school. We're trying to speak to them in their language, which is often music."

The Flops

The inclusion of music, or any other part of what seems to be the Gen X TV formula, doesn't guarantee a hit. Other sitcoms that attempted to depict Gen X life in the 1994–95 season included *Wild Oats* on Fox and *Blue Skies* on ABC. Both flopped. *Wild Oats* premiered to terrible reviews that complemented the sheer baseness of the program. "This wobbly comedy is, itself, confused and confusing, a jumble of setups and shtick that evidences neither wit nor wile," wrote Miles Beller in the *Hollywood Reporter*. "*Oats* is a rickety transport traveling a trivial distance for comedy and laughs." Tom Shales called *Wild Oats* the sleaziest show on the Fox Sunday night lineup. "*Wild Oats* is not really a situation comedy; it's a fornication comedy," Shales wrote in the *Washington Post* in September 1994.

In the pilot, roommates Jack (Tim Conlon), the jerk, and Brian (Paul Stephen Rudd), the sensitive guy, went out to a bar. "Everybody here looks so desperate," Brian said.

"Oh, I don't like to think of them as desperate," Jack replied. "I prefer to think of them as horny losers chummin' for nasty." Later, Brian assured Jack that he's "heard the gentle thump of the headboard against the wall." Sex-obsessed and lacking in real laughs, *Wild Oats* sank quickly to the bottom of the Nielsen ratings, landing in 111th place among households for the season.

"In retrospect, we put it after a family show," Fox vice-president of research Charles Kennedy said. "Even though *Married . . . with Children* is a very dysfunctional family, it's still a family show. It has a lot of teens and kids watching it. So you go from a broad-based show to a narrow-based show; if you're not in that particular situation, you may not be watching it. So a lot of it was the time period. We had high hopes for that; we thought, we've got the right one. I think the reason *Friends* won out was because it had longer to develop into a really good show."

Fox executive vice-president of comedy and drama development Robert Greenblatt was less forgiving of *Wild Oats*. "It was a bad show," he said. "The idea was, I think, narrow. The idea was two guys in love with the same woman, and I think it just wasn't written that well and wasn't cast that well. All the things *Friends* has going for it, brilliant writing, really good casting, it didn't have. . . . I just think it wasn't executed very well."

Mercifully, Fox Entertainment president John Matoian canceled *Wild Oats* just four days after joining the com-

---

Show Stats

Wild Oats
Premiered: September 4, 1994, on Fox

Primary cast:
Tim Conlon as Jack Slayton
Paul S. Rudd as Brian Grant
Paula Marshall as Shelly Thomas
Jana Marie Hupp as Liz Bradford

Plot:
Roommates Jack (the jerk) and Brian (the sensitive guy) both fell in love with the same woman, Shelly, Jack's ex-girlfriend. As this short-lived series began, Brian started dating Shelly, which only made Jack more lustful and interested in winning her back. Liz was Shelly's roommate, who often accompanied the gang to the Hanger, a Chicago club/bar.

pany in fall 1994. By the summer 1995 annual Television Critics Association press tour, he admitted the show was "sophomoric" and not in line with what the network would strive for in the future. All these slams against *Wild Oats* for its obsession with sex begs the question, what about *Friends*, which each week offers plenty of innuendo and sex talk? In the episode during which Ross and Rachel consummate their relationship, Rachel was heard to yell, "Oh, come on, would you just grab my ass!" That same episode also had a joke involving a juice box and premature ejaculation. The difference between *Friends* and *Wild Oats* is that on *Friends* sex may always be on the minds of the characters, but on *Wild Oats* it was the *only* thing on their minds. The cast of *Wild Oats* even looked dirty, but *Friends* can make a sex joke in one scene and have a touching moment between realistic characters in the next.

Blue Skies wasn't raunchy like *Wild Oats*, but it did feature Gen X partners (played by Matt Roth and Corey Parker) in an L. L. Bean-type catalog business called Blue Skies. Things got wacky when they hired an attractive female accountant (Julia Campbell) for the company and the partners squabbled over which one got to date her. The show aired between *Coach* and *Monday Night Football*, but the competition from *Melrose Place, Blossom*, and the CBS comedy block proved too intense, and *Blue Skies* was yanked from the schedule and retooled as *A Whole New Ballgame*, starring Corbin Bernsen as a chauvinistic sportscaster in Milwaukee. Julia Campbell, Stephen Tobolowsky, and Richard Kind from the *Blue Skies* cast returned, but Xers Matt Roth and Corey Parker were nowhere to be seen. Not that it mattered, *A Whole New Ballgame* was thrown out before the end of the season.

Quality Gen X TV

Because *Wild Oats* and the like helped reinforce the perception of Gen X TV as shallow programs filled with sex-

Show Stats

Blue Skies
Premiered: September 12, 1994, on ABC

Primary cast:
Matt Roth as Russell Evans
Corey Parker as Joel Goodman
Julia Campbell as Ellie Baskin
Stephen Tobolowsky as Oak

Plot:
   Two young guys, Russell and Joel, started a catalog mail-order company (like L. L. Bean) in Boston but soon discovered that their accountant, Kenny (Richard Kind), was stealing the profits. They hired smart and sexy Ellie to fix things up. Because she was smart and sexy, Russell and Joel quickly forgot about their business and became more interested in being fixed up with Ellie.

crazed young adults, many people probably think quality television and Generation X are mutually exclusive, but that's not the case. Although most of Gen X was too young to appreciate the first wave of shows in the quality TV genre (*Hill Street Blues, St. Elsewhere*) in the 1980s, they have jumped on the quality TV train of many shows since, including *China Beach, Twin Peaks, L. A. Law,* and, more recently, *My So-Called Life, Party of Five, ER,* and *NYPD Blue*. Quality TV shows have come to be viewed as prime time dramas (and to a lesser degree, some comedies) with large ensemble casts that tell realistic stories often in a surprising, moving manner. Quality TV shows also tend to be ground breaking—the cinematic weirdness of *Twin Peaks*, the hand-held camera movements and realistic cop talk on *NYPD Blue*—and forward thinking in representing racial, gender, and sexual equality. These programs also borrow the nighttime soap's continuing storyline format and sometimes even the romantic entanglements and cliff-hangers. "What we are doing here, really, is a soap opera," said *ER* star Anthony Edwards in *TV Guide's* April 13, 1996, issue.

The most prominent group of viewers who enthusiastically encourage quality TV is Viewers for Quality Television(VQT), an advocacy group that lobbies the networks on behalf of intelligent programs. So far, VQT has offered support to a number of Gen X programs, even *Beverly Hills, 90210,* which received "tentative support" (the category that is now "qualified support") in spring 1992. "That surprised me," said VQT founder and president Dorothy Swanson. "I didn't agree with it. I was somewhat appalled as a matter of fact."

The first Gen X show that can really be mentioned in a genre study of both Gen X TV and quality TV is the short-lived Fox series *Class of '96*. This show never won any level of VQT support, possibly because it was on the air such a short time. But some VQT members were taken with the program. Janet Harding, a longtime VQT member, wrote in the April 1993 issue of the VQT newsletter that she was impressed with this ensemble drama: "The stories and characters develop in a natural, believable way. Anyone who went to college will recognize the atmosphere that pervades college life. Issues may change with time, but some things never change. Dorm life, dealing with professors, pressure to make good grades, temptations, newly found freedom, and responsibility are heavy loads for almost-adults."

As Robert Greenblatt explained, this show had everything going against

it from a poor time slot to coming at the tail end of the first wave of Gen X dramas. *Class of '96* was not a unanimous critic's darling, so it is frequently ignored in discussions of Gen X and quality TV.

VQT included several programs with high Gen X appeal on its list of "endorsed" series in July 1995. Among the VQT-supported shows that ranked in the Top 20 Nielsen ratings (ages 18 to 34) for the 1994–95 season were *ER*, *Grace Under Fire*, *Roseanne*, *Mad About You*, *Frasier*, and *NYPD Blue*. Other Gen X appeal shows endorsed by VQT were *The X-Files* and *My So-Called Life*. Shows with high Gen X viewership that received "qualified support" from VQT in July 1995 included *Friends*, *Seinfeld*, *Party of Five*, *Star Trek: Deep Space Nine*, and *Star Trek: Voyager*. By January 1996, VQT moved *Friends* and *Party of Five* up to the endorsed list, and *Seinfeld*, which saw a resurgence in critical acclaim in fall 1995, returned to the group's top list too. After hearing the list of programs in the 1994–95 Nielsen Top 10 for ages 18 to 34, VQT founder and president Dorothy Swanson, who is in her fifties, said that Gen X seems pretty similar to most TV viewers. She said many of the programs that have attempted to lure Gen X to the tube are lackluster at best. "Until *Friends*, too many of the Generation X shows were stupid, and people weren't watching," Swanson said, citing the programs on the Warner Brothers network. "Youthful doesn't have to be stupid; I think that's insulting to that generation."

Swanson pointed out that VQT's membership (which numbers about 2,500) is predominantly much older than Generation X, yet VQT members appreciate many shows featuring Xers, but only if they represent quality. "I think the success and critical acclaim of *Friends* has little to do with the fact that the characters are in their twenties," Swanson said. "The success is based on a show with likable people who care about each other, and that affection also transfers to viewers who are watching. If [the characters on the show] care about each other that much, then I care about them."

VQT **Viewers for Quality Television** was founded in 1984 after a successful campaign to save *Cagney & Lacey*. The group got another big boost in 1986 during its successful campaign to save *Designing Women*. So what is quality television? VQT used the following definition in its November/December 1995 newsletter: "A quality program enlightens, enriches, challenges, involves, and confronts the viewer. It surpasses entertainment. It dares to take risks. It is honest and illuminating, appeals to the intellect, and touches the emotions. It is interesting and compelling. It requires concentration and attention. It provokes thought. Characterization is explored. A quality comedy touches the funnybone *and* the heart. It is unique and honest and intelligent."

For more information on VQT or details on how to join, write to VQT, P.O. Box 195, Fairfax Station, VA 22039. Send e-mail to VQT at info@VQT.com or visit the Web site (http://www.vqt.org/).

Still, Swanson said that the networks' overwhelming desire for programs that reach the younger demographic could come at a cost to quality TV. "Let's face it, I think a lot of the older population views young people as being shallow," Swanson said. "Therefore, the producers and writers who write it will portray them that way. If the fact [is] that *Under Suspicion* was canceled because it skewed too old, then I would say [appealing solely to Gen X viewers] will have a [negative] impact on quality television. Remember when we had a newsmagazine show every night? If you get too much of something, it is going to become mediocre."

Swanson admitted, however, that although she admired *My So-Called Life*, she didn't always enjoy watching it because she said, "I got tired of the way they talked. . . . It definitely had a narrow appeal. There were people who just didn't care, thank you very much, to watch teens in angst and that wasn't entertainment to them. . . . I find teenagers annoying anyway, and I think a lot of people do. You're going to take a risk of alienating a percentage of your audience immediately. They won't even give it a try."

This is where the generation gap develops. Although Swanson certainly doesn't speak for all VQT members, as the head of the group she frequently sets VQT's agenda in terms of which programs will receive the most support and coverage in the VQT newsletter. VQT's predominantly older membership also plays a part in setting the group's agenda, and although it's understandable that some members of the organization may not have the patience for the "teens in angst" on *My So-Called Life*, the show did exemplify VQT's own definition of quality TV.

Although VQT certainly provides a worthwhile service on behalf of viewers concerned about quality television, it's clear that the organization is not always in sync with quality programs appreciated by members of Generation X. Several active VQT members wrote to VQT in support of *My So-Called Life*, Swanson said, but not many. *My So-Called Life* was named best drama series by the Television Critics Association in July 1995, but it failed to receive a single 1995 VQT "Q" award. Swanson herself could have given the show the annual Founders Award (often given to shows overlooked in other categories with past winners including *Homefront*, *Life Goes On*, *South Central*, and *Alien Nation*) but opted instead to give that prize to *Homicide: Life on the Street*.

It will be interesting to see in the future if this generation gap widens. Will VQT be seen as an organization that represents the interests of a majority of viewers who want quality television or the ideals of a graying membership?

Whatever the future of VQT, it's clear that quality TV is here to stay. "The number of choices has raised the bar over the years so that the average show is more intelligent and entertaining than it was 20 to 30 years ago," said David Bianculli, *New York Daily News* TV critic. "TV is better now than it's ever been." Viewers may get enough of a kick out of throwback shows to make *Nash Bridges* and *Walker, Texas Ranger* hits, but the realism found in shows such as *ER* and *Homicide* is becoming mainstream, which means quality TV is becoming mainstream. No longer will viewers tolerate TV schedules littered with the garbage that was omnipresent in the 1970s. Although not all quality TV shows will survive, it's doubtful that viewers will ever see a return to the days where every show looked like *The A-Team*.

A Year in the Life

Although *My So-Called Life* was about high school students who barely made it into Generation X (as per the Strauss and Howe formula [1961–81]), it did appeal to some twentysomethings. The show ranked 38th with teens 12 to 18, 88th with Xers 18 to 34 and 107th in households. Still, older Xers had the perspective to appreciate the emotional struggles of Angela Chase, whereas younger Xers watched a mirror of their lives. Sometimes painfully accurate in its portrayal of teen angst, *My So-Called Life* was the anti-*90210*. The characters on *90210* were class presidents and homecoming queens, while the students featured on *My So-Called Life* were all outsiders who didn't seem to fit in. Whether it was the nerdy and sensitive Brian Krakow or the wild and irresponsible Rayanne, these kids were far more realistic. Characters from both shows dealt with many of the same issues, but on *MSCL* it was always more believable. Rayanne's relationship with her absentee mom and her envy of Angela's nuclear family made sense. The melodramatic comings and goings of Kelly and David's parents on *90210* were overwrought. Whereas

90210 was born out of the optimistic late 1980s, *MSCL* was clearly a part of the nihilistic 1990s. "*My So-Called Life* was one of the first shows we've seen that pitches the formula to that young, MTV-bred, Fox-crazy audience and tries to deliver a true quality drama that's not part of a [definable] genre," said Matt Roush of *USA Today.* "So you're not dealing with a traditional franchise. What you're basically doing is a family drama thing, which is the most endangered species of all the drama shows."

The irony of *My So-Called Life* is that although it's the touchstone quality show for Generation X, it was created, produced, and written by the people responsible for *thirtysomething,* the ultimate Baby Boomer program. Yet *My So Called Life* still managed to capture not only the universal pain of adolescence but also the specific details of growing up X. *My So-Called Life* creator Winnie Holzman said she never intended her show to speak to only one age group. "That definitely was not my aim. I wanted it to be something that I felt spoke up to the highest in people and did not condescend. But I didn't think of it in terms of teenagers or a teenage audience; that's not my approach. I was thinking in terms of having characters that would be interesting. I was attempting to be honest . . . and I did not want the teen characters to be cliché, but at the same time it was important to me that the parents not be cliché, and in many ways, it was harder."

The show caught attention for its realistic portrayal of teen life, but *My So-Called Life* was championed by people of many ages, including Xers. "Many people in their twenties were saying it brings them right back to that time," Holzman said. "A lot of people in their twenties felt—I don't want to make too many sweeping statements—very far from their teen years, even though they were closer than I was to mine. The show was bringing back emotions they'd never dealt with completely. The show was bringing up emotions regarding their teen

Show Stats

My So-Called Life
Premiered: August 25, 1994, on ABC
Created by: Winnie Holzman

Primary cast:
Bess Armstrong as Patty Chase
Wilson Cruz as Rickie Vasquez
Claire Danes as Angela Chase
Devon Gummersall as Brian Krakow
A. J. Langer as Rayanne Graff
Jared Leto as Jordan Catalano
Devon Odessa as Sharon Cherski
Lisa Wilhoit as Danielle Chase
Tom Irwin as Graham Chase

Plot:
   This realistic and compelling contemporary family drama focused on the life of teenager Angela Chase and her high school friends. Angela was a brooding, introspective, angst-ridden teen who dumped her life-long best friend, Sharon, for her new best friend, wild child Rayanne. In the swap she also got Rayanne's buddy, Rickie, a sensitive teen coming to terms with his homosexuality. Jordan was the dim-witted hunk Angela lusted after, and Brian was her nerdy, but devoted, neighbor. Angela's parents, Graham and Patty had their own problems to deal with while her sister Danielle just watched, taking it all in.

years or begun in teen years that were very profound for them. . . . 'How do you know my life' was a phrase I read many times in a fan letter. That has to do with just tapping into something that's universal."

Xers who watched the show responded to that honesty and realism. Having great alternative music on the soundtrack probably didn't hurt either. "I care about the characters to a rather absurd extent (usually at the end of an episode, I'm an emotional wreck)," wrote Brown graduate student Andy Perry, 26, in an e-mail.

"It is the first show that actually takes life seriously," said Jodie Zwart, 20, a college student in Sioux Center, Iowa. "These people know what it is about and go after it."

Holzman, who was 38 when *My So-Called Life* began, said her secret for writing teen dialogue was to never think of them as teenagers but as characters.

"Teens don't think of themselves as quite young; they feel quite old, like, you've really arrived," Holzman said. "Sometimes you feel exhausted and old like your childhood is over and now you're an adult. You feel like you have it all together right now. In other words, in order to capture teens, I thought of them as feeling that way, as very complex people with very complicated lives."

Holzman said she was actually relieved that *My So-Called Life* appealed to younger viewers. She said the producers were secretly worried that teenagers would watch and say, "Oh no, that isn't us." Holzman said she received one of the most memorable compliments about the show early on when a teenage actress came in to audition and asked the casting director, "Is Winnie a teenager?" Holzman pointed out that today's teens are struggling with many of the same questions although some issues have been replaced by others. "I don't think the true things people are caught up with ever really change," Holzman said. "I'm not pretending that AIDS is not a huge shadow falling over a generation, but every generation has had its huge shadow and that's what we forget sometimes. They just have different names: Is it World War II? or Is it AIDS? The fact is people have similar struggles when you dig deeper. Who am I? What does it mean to be a friend? What does it mean to find yourself? These are the basic struggles, and they don't change with the generations. That to me is the meaning of my show. We may divide ourselves into generations, but it's important to remember that it is just a label."

It was those universal themes that appealed to critics, many of whom quickly hailed *My So-Called Life* when it premiered in August 1994. "*My So-Called Life* is the best new show of the season," wrote Paul Lomartire in the *Palm Beach Post*. "There is a mood to this drama that many will mistakenly paint as too dark. Nonsense. It isn't dark, it's real. . . . This is appointment television for everyone who loves excellent drama." Dusty Saunders wrote in the *Rocky Mountain News* that "*My So-Called Life* is not predictable, easy television. Rather, it's a thoughtful, sometimes disturbing reminder that life is not easy—for teens or adults."

In a most unusual and unprecedented move, ABC allowed MTV to air re-runs of *My So-Called Life* in April and May 1995 before ABC even announced whether the show would return for a second season. *USA Today* TV critic Matt Roush said *My So-Called Life* going on MTV made more sense for MTV than for the show. "It's more of a feather in the cap for MTV to get it and run it," Roush said in an interview. "What else can they run in that hour? Better that than they actually create a new show for us to watch."

There's no exact count from ABC on the number of pieces of mail and e-mail they received in support of the series, but it was at least enough to warrant the printing of a special postcard sent to viewers who wrote in support of the show. The amount of praise and the number of columns by TV critics urging ABC to save the show became so great that Mike Duffy of Knight-Ridder Newspapers wrote a column in which he urged critics to cool it. "The best new show of the season has a splendid season finale Thursday night," he wrote. "Trouble is, *My So-Called Life* is also the one show TV critics just can't stop writing about. And we're perilously close to the whine borderline." No matter, their pleas went unheeded. Poor ratings in a bad time slot (a quality drama at 8:00 P.M.? On Thursday against NBC's comedy block?) led ABC to cancel the show after just 19 episodes. Some blamed series star Claire Danes, whose mother and agent supposedly went to the network before the fall schedule announcement and informed the ABC brass that Claire didn't want to return for a second season. Certainly, that wouldn't

have encouraged the network to renew a show that was already on the bor-
derline. "There's not a way for me to ever know, but certainly that was a con-
tributing factor among other factors," Winnie Holzman said.

Steve Joyner, who led the on-line crusade to save *My So-Called Life*, also
points a finger at Claire Danes, her mother, and her agent. "The bottom line
is the show was very close to coming back," he said. "Although it's impossible to know for sure if it would have been canceled, why would [Danes'
camp] be making these efforts to contact [ABC's Ted] Harbert to make sure
that if the network had any idea of bringing back the show that she had no
desire to return?" TV critic David Bianculli said a lack of interest from Danes
may not have been the issue. "She didn't have any choice; she signed that
contract," he said. "The history of TV shows that are significantly different
from everything around them is that they usually click in their second season or when no one's looking. Deep into the first season it happened with
Friends. Mad About You and *Seinfeld* took a few years too." Whatever the
reason for the short-sighted decision by ABC, Bianculli believes ABC shot itself in the foot. "I think ABC was so stupid to let that go," Bianculli said. "I
think their problem was they didn't realize they had a really rare show there
that could appeal to teenagers, to Generation X, to me, to old farts all in the
same room and with each member of the audience wondering why the hell
the other was watching. That was just a really, really well-written show.
Danes will be such a big actress. I don't understand how TV programmers
who have somebody under contract can let her go. If for nothing else they
could say, 'I've got this talent.' You might as well come in second with something really good."

Bianculli also speculated that if *My So-Called Life* had returned for a second season its ratings might have improved as a result of the MTV exposure.
"That girl was so filled with angst that anybody who ever listened to Nirvana
would watch her," he said. But even the audience for Kurt Cobain and company may not have been enough to get the numbers *My So-Called Life* needed
on ABC. "It really aimed high in its production, writing, and emotional content, so much more than even *Party of Five*," said Matt Roush. "There's no
question *My So-Called Life* is a deeper show, but I found *Party of Five* to be a
much more enjoyable TV show to watch."

Joining the *Party*

Although it premiered the same year as *My So-Called Life*, *Party of Five* never received the same sort of hero's welcome. There were several reasons for this. First, it was on Fox, a network not known for providing quality programs. Second, the *Party of Five* premise of five siblings whose parents died in an automobile accident reeked of high-concept plotting. Third, it wasn't as good a show as *My So-Called Life*, but it was still far superior to much of the programming on TV.

Fox development vice-president Robert Greenblatt said the network wanted to do a family show, but not the type that had been done before. Instead, they wanted to look at a family that was more contemporary with kids trying to survive without the benefit of the classic two-parent household. Although the story of kids living with a divorced parent was an option, the network chose to go with a scenario in which the parents were removed from the equation completely.

"We thought it would be interesting to do it in a very realistic and dramatic way as opposed to *Melrose Place*," Greenblatt said. "We wanted to look at these issues and have fun with the characters and have them live lives that aren't completely overcome by the grief of the loss of parents."

Party of Five executive producers Amy Lippman and Christopher Keyser had just finished a three-year stint writing for *Sisters* when they were approached by Fox to write "a show about a family living without parents," Lippman said. "On the basis of that one sentence we thought of lots of things, stories we could tell with that premise, the viability of a series with a premise like that. Initially, we were not convinced about the idea. What we brought back to them was different from the show they envisioned. Their intention was to create a series about kids with no responsibility, no curfews, partying, no parents to say, 'Enough's enough.' They may have initially conceived the show as more of a lark."

Lippman, 31, said the premise of the show, kids surviving in the shadow of their parents' deaths, was a tough sell to both critics and the viewing public. "Once people got past the franchise of the show, something attached

Minus the baby, the cool cast of *Party of Five* chill out in Bailey's jeep. (*Clockwise from top left*) Scott Wolf, Lacey Chabert, Matthew Fox, and Neve Campbell star in this youth ensemble drama. Fox Broadcasting.

Show Stats

Party of Five

Premiered: September 12, 1994, on Fox
Created by: Christopher Keyser and Amy Lippman

Primary cast:
Matthew Fox as Charlie Salinger
Scott Wolf as Bailey Salinger
Neve Campbell as Julia Salinger
Lacey Chabert as Claudia Salinger
Brandon Porter and Taylor Porter as Owen Salinger
   (1994–95)
Stephen Cavarno and Andrew Cavarno as Owen
   Salinger (1995–96)
Paula Devicq as Kirsten Bennett
Scott Grimes as Will
Mitchell Anderson as Ross
Michael Goorjian as Justin Thompson
Jennifer Blanc as Kate Bishop (1994)
Megan Ward as Jill Holbrook (1994–95)
Jennifer Love Hewitt as Sarah (1995–)

Plot:
   This is a one-hour family drama minus pesky parents, who were killed in an automobile accident. As the series began, the kids, who ranged in age from 11 months to 24 years, had to learn to survive on

to us early on, people stopped looking at it as 'This is so unrealistic, you're appealing to the orphan demographic.' Then we found we were actually touching a nerve in people. The definition of family these days is not two kids, mom and dad, and a dog in the suburbs. Today's family is much more complex, diffused, and undefined. Kids are figuring out the value they have to each other without any parental presence enforcing them. They have to find their way to it themselves, and I think that really seemed to hit home for a lot of people."

   Although most of the Salinger kids are at the younger end of the Generation X age spectrum, the oldest sibling, Charlie, was 24 when the series began. Greenblatt, 35, said a conscious decision was made to go against expectations and portray him as the least responsible kid in the family. "Up to the point of his parents' deaths he was kind of the irresponsible kid," Greenblatt said. "He followed his whim, didn't go to college, and decided to sleep with girls and just kind of have fun with life, which is one approach to the Generation X life-style. I think Gen X gets a bad name because it's a blanket description that I think is describing slackers, but I would say it is a group of characters in this age group working to do things differently. It's not like they're turning against doing anything and just floating around and have no aims and no goals; they've just seen the generation above them screw around and screw it up, and they're starting to struggle with how do we do things differently. It's not that they have no values; they have different values. It's not that they have no goals or no aspirations; they just want to do it in a different way."

   Although many TV critics were too busy trying to drum up support for *My So-Called Life* to notice *Party of Five* during its first season, some journalists did find the show praiseworthy. "*Party of Five* takes a serious tone," wrote Tom Jicha in the Fort Lauderdale *Sun-Sentinel*. "With this party, you can cry if you want to." Robert P. Laurence of the *San Diego Union-Tribune* called the

show "a true sleeper: a sensitive, unpretentious, often humorous drama that immediately leaps beyond its unlikely premise and wraps itself in irresistible charm and utter believability."

Party of Five also struck a chord in a small but loyal group of viewers in its first season. "I care about what happens to the characters," said Joanne Cosker, 25, an executive assistant. "I like that their house is a mess all the time. That's real. Sometimes they get TV-ized—more than likely your everyday kid won't get involved with someone like Jill and take off to L. A. for four days. But a real kid would fail his classes. The way they don't know what each other is doing is very realistic. It's kind of like warm and fuzzy, and it makes me cry. I like that in a TV show and not many TV shows do that."

their own while keeping a pact to dine at their parents' restaurant once a week as a party of five. Charlie, the oldest, found himself as a legal guardian, but he wasn't prepared for the responsibility. Eventually, he got the hang of it but then screwed up his relationship with his live-in girlfriend, Kirsten. Bailey, 16, began as the most sensible family member but soon went loopy over Kate and then broke up with her when she wouldn't have sex. He ended up with sex-loving Jill, but she was a drug addict who died of an overdose in the May 1995 season finale. Julia, 15, has had her share of heartaches too, including the breakup with her boyfriend Justin after she suffered a miscarriage. Claudia, 11, is a talented but precocious musician. Owen just drools a lot.

Vince Hamner, a 31-year-old graduate student at Virginia Tech, also said realism is what draws him to *Party of Five.* "The episodes and characters are believable," he said. "[The show has] realistic story lines. Each show deals with current issues, most of them pertinent to my age group."

Sandy Candioglos, a 26-year-old engineer in Portland, Oregon, had a similar reaction to the series. "It's one of the first shows I've ever watched that comes close to dealing with real-life situations realistically," she said. "It's a tearjerker, and it's easy on the eyes, as well. None of the characters are over-the-top; they're all very normal upper-middle-class kids who are trying to deal with each other and with losing their parents."

Party of Five was one of the four shows listed in *TV Guide's* 1995 Save Our Shows viewer's poll. It garnered the top spot with 34 percent of the vote (*Earth 2* received 32 percent; *My So-Called Life,* 26 percent; *Under Suspicion,* 8 percent). *TV Guide,* however, is owned by Rupert Murdoch, who also owns Fox. It's interesting to note that during its first season *Party of Five* never received the same sort of overwhelming on-line support that the three other shows did. More important to the show's survival that first year was a first-season script that won the Humanitas Prize for communicating human values, beating out all the other dramas on TV.

"Party of Five is about life, and it's harder for people to find the show," Greenblatt said in March 1995. "We believe it's a very well-done show, and in time will deliver the audience, we hope. The same thing happened with *90210.* It went on the air and nobody cared for about 20 episodes and then, finally, we got people into the show."

In January 1996, *Party of Five* was named best TV drama at the Golden Globe awards, beating out such favorites as *E.R.* The ratings continued to improve steadily, leading Fox to renew the series for a third season before its second season was over. *Party of Five* is probably the first example of a Gen X show that's a hybrid of two earlier shows. By combining the relationship melodrama and good-looking cast of *90210* with the more believable writing, acting, and moody atmosphere of quality shows such as *thirtysomething*, *Party of Five* was eventually able to have it both ways. It could be popular and remain quality. It could appeal to both the cool people and the alienated outsiders. With a little time, a lot of promotion, and a unique balance, *Party of Five* remained true to the vision of its creators and still attracted an audience that satisfied Fox executives and advertisers.

The Season of the *Friends* Ripoffs

Quality TV and Gen X TV can coexist within the same programs, but by the fall of 1995, the quality component was forsaken in an attempt to ride the coattails of *Friends* (and its predecessor, *Living Single*). No fewer than 10 Gen X sitcoms jumped on the bandwagon. CBS, in a desperate attempt to woo younger viewers, spent its biggest promotional bucks on Darren Star's *Melrose Place* clone, *Central Park West.* The Tiffany network also unveiled the *Friend*-ly sitcoms *Can't Hurry Love* (Nancy McKeon and friends) and *Dweebs* (nerdy computer programmers who had no friends).

ABC offered *The Drew Carey Show* (fat midwestern guy and friends); NBC went with *Caroline in the City* (cartoonist and friends) and *The Single Guy* (single guy and his married friends); and WB introduced *First Time Out* (Latino comic and friends) and *Simon* (Forrest Gump-like TV programmer and friends). The Fox attempt to get back into the Gen X TV genre it pioneered

included *The Crew* (flight attendants who are friends), *Partners* (two best friends and one's fiancée), and *Too Something* (two slacker guys and friends in a show later retitled *New York Daze*). *The Last Frontier* (friends in Alaska), a Fox sitcom that aired in summer 1996, even admitted to its pedigree in an episode that featured "I'll Be There For You," the *Friends* theme song.

That's just the stuff that made it to the air. Some of the Gen X TV development projects that weren't picked up included ABC's *The Ward* (an ensemble comedy about the lives and loves of college students from the creators of *Moonlighting*), *Jam Bay* (13 young improvisational actors live and work at a California beach hotel from the creators of *The Real World*), and *Pier 66* (*Melrose Place* meets *Baywatch* in Fort Lauderdale from Aaron Spelling and *Melrose Place* producer Kimberly Costello). CBS passed on *Nowhere Fast* (*The Odd Couple* in their 20s), *Clarissa* (based on Nickelodeon's *Clarissa Explains It All*), *Staten Island, 10309* (an East Coast version of *90210*), and *Crosstown Traffic* (*New York Undercover* in Los Angeles). NBC ignored *Crazy Love* (singles who hang out at a San Francisco diner from *Lois & Clark* creator Deborah Joy LeVine). Fox abandoned *Glory Days* (high school friends now in their mid-20s muddle through from Witt-Thomas Productions), *Hell* (young waiters at a trendy New York restaurant), *Divas* (the chronicles of female R&B singers), and *Planet Rules* (a caucasian *Divas*).

Of the *Friends* clones that made it to the air, none managed to duplicate the *Friends* phenomenon. *The Single Guy* survived as a result of a cushy time slot and a tone that combined *Friends* and *Seinfeld*. *Caroline in the City* survived on time slot alone until finding its way creatively by midseason. Most of the *Friends*-like shows flopped because of their nature—they were clones. They weren't created for any reason other than to cash in on what producers and programmers saw as the trend of the moment. History has shown that whenever this is the motivating factor behind TV shows, they scarcely are ever successes either creatively or in the ratings. That's not to say all these shows failed because they tried to be *Friends*. Some suffered from poor time slots and lack of promotion, but for the most part, shows such as *Can't Hurry Love* and *First Time Out* just couldn't overcome the fact that they were poorly executed imitations. Of all the Gen X shows introduced in fall 1995, the best of the bunch was the Fox sitcom *Partners* from *Friends* first-season supervising producers Jeff Greenstein and Jeff Strauss (known in TV circles as "the

Too good to last, the smart and funny *Partners* featured Tate Donovan, Maria Pitillo, and Jon Cryer. Fox Broadcasting.

Jeffs"). *Partners* was the tale of best friends Bob (Jon Cryer) and Owen (Tate Donovan), who worked together in a San Francisco architecture firm. Owen's fiancée, Alicia (Maria Pitillo), was a partner of another kind.

"This was an idea Jeff and I had in our back pocket for a while," Greenstein said. "To a great extent, it's about our relationship. You're really good friends with somebody, you depend on each other for your livelihood, and it's kind of like a marriage. Both of us are married now, and we wanted to show the challenges of maintaining these relationships. When you get engaged, the woman doesn't realize her husband-to-be has another husband. He's caught in the middle, trying to balance the two strongest relationships in his life."

Greenstein was quick to add that the show was about the changes marriage creates in friendships, but he didn't want the show to become "the lovely young couple and their annoying friend" or "friends and the woman who tears them apart."

Although some critics agreed that *Partners* warranted applause, many simply labeled it a *Friends* clone, an accusation it never overcame. "To a certain extent, it has some of the sound and feel of *Friends*," said Jeff Strauss. "I would hope there are stylistic similarities because that would mean we write consistently." *Partners*, however moved at a slower pace (fewer characters, fewer storylines) and focused on an older group of characters who had matured beyond the *Friends* years. Unlike the other *Friends* clones, *Partners* had a more distinct voice. It was about something other than just being friends. Sure, *Partners* dealt with many of the same themes, but it did so in a different way. Although Chandler of *Friends* and Bob of *Partners* appeared to be cut from the same cloth (wise guys desperate for relationships), Bob was far less sarcastic and not as fast on the draw with a quip. Although *Partners* did become a little too slapstick during the 1995–96 season (probably on orders from Fox to make the show fit better alongside its horrible neighbor, *Ned and Stacey*), at least the show became more than the sum of its parts. Even people on the Internet thought it was another *Friends* clone. "We saw a promo for *Partners* that looked like *Friends* only with more flannel and goatees," wrote Terra Goodnight, 27, a computer programmer in Washington, D.C. "Is this a sign that my fellow Gen Xers watch enough TV to have them target shows at us, or are they just sadly misunderstanding their viewing market and stabbing in the dark? I hope it's the latter, and we're not watching *that* much!" *Partners* turned out to be too smart and sophisticated for its own good. This intelligent sitcom with potential didn't fit the Fox mold and was canceled after one season.

Missing the Target . . . by a Mile

Because CBS was desperate to reach a younger audience, it gave the green light to the soapy *Central Park West*. Of all the programs on the fall 1995 schedule, *Central Park West* got the biggest publicity push, including a two-page spread in the *New York Times* the Sunday before its debut. It was all for naught. Fox wisely counterprogrammed, putting together two episodes of *90210* for a two-hour season premiere September 13. The second hour went head-to-head with *Central Park West*, and the new show was left in the dust. *Grace Under Fire* and *The Naked Truth* on ABC won the hour; Fox came in second. The second hour of *90210* averaged a 12.4/20 (rating/share; each rating point equaled 959,000 households in 1995) and the two-hour block ranked 23rd for the week; *Central Park West* only managed a 7.5/12, tied for 61st for the week. CBS, struggling to get its best new hope for salvation seen by more people, quickly scheduled a rebroadcast for Friday, September 22, but that did even worse: 5.4/10 and 84th for the week.

The next week, Fox counterprogrammed again, playing the 100th episode of *Melrose Place* opposite *Central Park West*. *Melrose* drew a 10.3/16 share (47th for the week) and *Central Park West* only a 6.0/9 share (tied at 85th for the week). In its third week, *Central Park West* was even beaten by ratings weakling *Party of Five*. The week after that, *Central Park West* was beaten by a Fox repeat of *Beethoven*, a kids' movie about a slobbering St. Bernard.

Central Park West, a "surefire hit" that inexplicably drew decent reviews, flopped for several reasons: a poor premiere it couldn't recover from; a lack of young viewers on CBS, who missed the promos and simply didn't know it existed; cardboard characters without much humor; and an oversaturation of continuing dramas. Whereas *90210*, *Melrose Place*, and *Sisters* were the only

one-hour programs called soaps, established series such as *ER, NYPD Blue, Chicago Hope, The X-Files, Picket Fences, Party of Five*, and *Homicide* also featured continuing storylines. *90210* and *Melrose Place* started slowly, but Fox gave them time to grow, which CBS couldn't afford to do with *Central Park West*. With all the other continuing dramas on the air, *Central Park West* faced greater competition not just in its time slot but for attention. Xers were already committed to other programs and didn't have the time to devote to a trashy knockoff such as *Central Park West*.

The network gave up going after Xers exclusively, and instead tried to lure back the traditional CBS audience who had proved to be faithful viewers of *Dallas* and *Knots Landing. Central Park West* was retooled, jettisoning star Mariel Hemingway and other cast members in favor of older actors such as Gerald McRaney and Raquel Welch. The final four episodes featuring Hemingway's character never aired in the United States (they did air overseas). The remaining *Central Park West* episodes aired twice a week (so they could get rid of it as quickly as possible?) in summer 1996 under the title *CPW* (to make viewers think it was a different show?).

By December 1995, with *Central Park West* failing and its new sitcoms in disarray, CBS realized its strategy of seeking younger viewers at the expense of its traditional older audience was a failure. "Too much, too soon," CBS Entertainment president Les Moonves admitted in January 1996 to the assembled members of the Television Critics Association in Pasadena, California. "Yes, we do want to get younger. But the way to get younger is to expand what is already our traditional core audience—not to try to do a kamikaze type of show that brings us way down immediately."

CBS jettisoned its underperforming youth shows in favor of old stalwarts such as *Diagnosis Murder*. CBS also got a boost from the surprise success of its Saturday night lineup featuring *Dr. Quinn: Medicine Woman, Touched by an Angel*, and *Walker, Texas Ranger*. At the same time that CBS was on the rebound, ABC was falling fast. The no. 1 network for the 1994–95 season, ABC fell to second midway through 1995–96 and came in third behind NBC and CBS during the February 1996 sweeps period. With no new hit shows and its past hits fading, ABC began to assume the loser status held by CBS only months earlier. One of the ABC shows that got away was *3rd Rock from the Sun*, which became a Tuesday night hit for NBC as soon as it premiered in early 1996. ABC developed *3rd Rock* but rejected both the original pilot (filmed in January 1995) and reshoots as well. ABC's loss became NBC's gain. *3rd Rock* features the same "outsider looking in" observational humor that was a hallmark of *ALF* in the 1980s. *3rd Rock* also features several Gen X TV appeal ingredients: a crew of aliens pretending to be a family, a sarcastic teen, and sexual innuendo aplenty. A stellar performance from John Lithgow as alien high commander Dick Solomon and a ready for prime time Jane Curtin rocketed this *Rock* into the Nielsen Top 20. It also helped that the show was completely different (broad, slapstick comedy instead of relationship/character comedy) from all the *Friends* clones of fall 1995.

Boston Common also benefited from differentiation, although in a much milder form, when it joined the NBC Thursday night lineup in March 1996 (sending *The Single Guy* on a short hiatus). Although *Boston Common* has a young, Gen X cast and is set at a fictional Boston college, the comic situations come from the fish-out-of-water situations faced by the lead character, Boyd Pritchett (Anthony Clark), a hick from southwest Virginia.

Despite the failure of *Central Park West* on CBS, WB found a keeper in the soap opera format with *Savannah* when it premiered in January 1996. This drama featured southern belles from hell, including bad girl Peyton (Jamie Luner), naïve Reese (Shannon Sturges), and intelligent Lane (Robyn Lively). The show was developed by Dianne Messina Stanley and James Stanley (for Aaron Spelling productions, of course) and relied on every trick they learned from their years working on *Knots Landing, Homefront,* and *Hotel Malibu. Savannah* is injected with a sense of fun missing from *Melrose Place* in its fourth season. The WB soap also benefits from better-than-average soap writing and the good sense not to take itself too seriously. How could it, when, as *TV Guide* pointed out, each of the three main characters speaks with a different bad Southern accent. Although *Savannah* ranked at the bottom of the Nielsen list every week, it pulled in the best numbers ever for a WB show. The network rewarded *Savannah* with an order for a second season. The failure of *Central Park West* and the success of *Savannah* brings to light the distinct identities of the networks. CBS had a failure because it promoted *Central Park West* as Gen X TV, something completely unfamiliar to its core audience. For WB, *Savannah* appealed to the young viewers already watch-

ing the network; in addition, its original Sunday 9:00 P.M. time slot offered counterprogramming to the movie-of-the-week on the Big Three and the tacky sitcoms on Fox.

At the same time that *Savannah* began its successful run, a *Friends* backlash (fanned by the same media who touted the show only one year earlier) started to grow. Maybe it was the fact that viewers couldn't visit the newsstand without seeing a *Friend*-ly face staring back at them from a magazine cover; maybe it was the Diet Coke commercials that featured the cast playing their *Friends* characters; maybe it was the gobs of promotion for the hour-long episode after 1995's Super Bowl XXX, featuring Julia Roberts, Chris Isaak, Brooke Shields, and Jean-Claude Van Damme. Whatever the reason, it quickly became hip to hate *Friends*. This had no effect on the show's ratings. It still ranked among the top three most-watched TV shows every week, but its luster began to dim. Even Internet geeks got into the bashing, creating a newsgroup devoted to hating the show (alt.tv.friends.puke.puke.puke).

NBC tried to launch a Spelling-backed show midway through the 1995–96 season with *Malibu Shores*, a *90210* for the next generation, featuring Tori Spelling's little brother, Randy. This *West Side Story* ripoff pitted the rich Malibu kids against the not-so-rich valley folk, but it didn't stir up much public interest. Although the show improved the NBC 8:00 P.M. Saturday performance in all the young female demographics, *Malibu Shores* flopped in the overall household demos.

Fox thought it could take a bite out of the Nielsen ratings with a vampire show, so once again the Spelling forces were mustered to bring audiences *Kindred: The Embraced*. Unfortunately for Spelling and Fox, few TV viewers embraced *Kindred*. Set in San Francisco, this gothic-themed soap focused on five clans of vampires lead by Julian Luna (Mark Frankel). Although the vampires were an intriguing lot, the human protagonist was not. C. Thomas Howell played a human cop in a performance so lackluster it was easy to confuse him with the undead. Even after the first hour of the 90-minute pilot, discriminating viewers were rooting for his character's demise. It didn't happen. The blame shouldn't all go to Howell; much of the dialogue was turgid, too. The show went on to distinguish itself by getting lower ratings than the previous occupant of the Wednesday 9:00 P.M. time slot, *Party of Five*.

Another Fox entry, *Profit,* fared no better in the ratings, but creatively, it was a smashing success. This drama of office politics from Stephen J. Cannell Productions was one of the most innovative shows Fox ever put on the air. But because quality and Fox tend to be mutually exclusive, viewers didn't tune in. Adrian Pasdar (a Charlie Sheen soundalike) starred as Jim Profit, a 28-year-old Machiavellian businessman with plans to manipulate his way to the top of Gracen & Gracen, a fictional Fortune 100 conglomerate. Profit was clearly the bad guy, committing several murders and ruining other characters' lives, but he was so smooth that audiences cheered him on anyway. Profit had an unusual past that explained his backstabbing, murderous behavior. He was abused as a child and forced to sleep in a cardboard box with a hole cut in its side so that he could watch TV, his sole companion. This was one of the boldest anti-TV statements about the effects of television on our nation's youth ever to come from a network TV series. And that was a large part of the show's appeal. The fact that *Profit* was different should have distinguished it and made it appealing to Gen X audiences, but the show turned out to be too different in its premise but very much the same in its execution as Profit conducted his dirty deeds week after week. Despite its intriguing premise, even this conniver's bad behavior became boring.

Cyber-space—The Final Frontier

During a *Friends* writers' meeting in March 1995, story editor Alexa Junge mentioned the latest piece of minutiae to be discussed on a newsgroup devoted to the hit show (alt.tv.friends). In an episode that aired the week before this meeting ("The One with the Poker Game"), Ross's pet monkey, Marcel, was seen putting a CD of the song "The Lion Sleeps Tonight" into a CD player. Marcel then appeared to dance to the music—or was it trick photography?

"The monkey dancing, that's the big thing [being discussed on the newsgroup]," Junge told other members of the writing staff, not all of whom were on-line. "People are saying, 'Was he really dancing or was it. . . ?' They're actually playing it back. There's stuff like, 'Somebody rerun it and check the clock'."

"Oh my God!" another *Friends* writer replied. "People are sick. That's amazing."

Although many of the people who post to TV show newsgroups are well-adjusted young professionals, there is a segment that falls into the "get a life" category. At the same time, there are those who are not on-line who look down upon the entire on-line world as simply an arena filled with nerds and geeks. As always, reality lies somewhere in between. After all, how different is posting one's own textual analysis of a TV show from a graduate school English class during which a whole semester is spent discussing a single novel? There are both TV watchers and English scholars who take things too far, but the majority are pretty normal people with a specific interest.

"I think people need more things to do," said *Friends* executive producer Marta Kauffman. "They need friends; they need to go out more. I mean, it's sort of neat. I like to read about it; I like to hear about it. The [*Friends*] Inter-

5

Cyber Glossary

Cyberspace: Not a place; it doesn't have walls. Some have called it the fourth dimension. It's where computer users travel on a computer on-line service or the Internet.

Download: The transfer of photo or text files to a personal computer via modem.

FAQ: Frequently Asked Questions. A file of questions and answers compiled for Usenet newsgroups and mailing lists to help inform new users so they don't keep asking the same questions. FAQs are usually posted to each newsgroup on a regular basis.

FTP: File Transfer Protocol. A way of moving files from one computer to another.

Internet: The worldwide, noncommerical network of interlinked computers. Frequently called the Net.

Mailing lists: Instead of going to a newsgroup for discussion, the discussion comes to the user via e-mail, usually as a listserv list.

Newsgroups: Usenet message areas grouped by subject that are accessible from the Internet. On-line services feature similar areas of their own called bulletin boards or forums.

On-line service: A commercial service that gives a computer user access to different features, including news, chat areas, discussion groups, and usually the Internet.

Postings: Messages (posts) added to a bulletin board or newsgroup.

World Wide Web: The collection of multimedia (can include sound, pictures, and even video) pages on the Internet. Because of its unique linking system called hypertext, WWW users can navigate from site to site by simply clicking on highlighted words or objects.

net drinking game I think is sort of terrifying, but I thought it was pretty funny."

Kauffman, who is not on-line, said reading the *Friends* newsgroup can be fun because it gives her a chance to hear the gossip that is spread. Kauffman's favorite on-line tale was an example of mistaken identity. Someone came into the show late and was asking about Ross, Carol, and Susan. Another person wrote back that Ross's ex-wife is living with her lesbian lover, she's pregnant with his child, and the three of them have decided to raise the baby. Then the person posting added that the character of the ex-wife was based on executive producer Marta Kauffman. "And I thought that was so funny. I called my friend in New York and said, 'Sorry, they think it's me'."

Friends story editor Jeff Astrof said he was not fond of the people on the Net, but at the same time he enjoyed reading positive comments about his work. "It kind of pisses me off," said Astrof. "I use it solely for ego to see which of my jokes people like. I think a lot of those people really need to see the sunlight; they really need to get out. We get on 10 minutes everyday, and we make fun of people, but it gives [us] a passive link to the community, which I wouldn't say is our broad audience. It is neat to see that certain things do work and [which] things people like. When people obsess over what Spanish words we used or whether the monkey was actually dancing that doesn't help us at all."

Perhaps the most amazing thing about the so-called *information super-highway* (a term some Netters hate as much as some Xers hate the label *Generation X*) is the speed with which it bulldozed its way into the mainstream. Before 1993, the terms *Internet, newsgroups, mailing lists, the World Wide Web, FTP*, and *gopher* were not part of the general lexicon. To Xers, the Internet is becoming a way of life.

"Isn't it scary how on-line we're all getting?" wrote Jennifer Hale, 25, in an e-mail message. "It always surprises me now when I'm talking to someone and I say, 'Oh, I'll e-mail you that address,' and they say, 'I don't have e-mail,' and a little part of me glances at them momentarily with a 'What are you, nuts?' expression. Let me tell you, my AOL bill is getting kind of scary, and my computer was costly, but I'm hooked."

The relationship between TV and the Net continues to develop. The Internet is used as a gathering place for people to post their thoughts about TV shows, network personnel, and network decisions. Viewers also use the Net to lobby against the cancellation of their favorite programs. Sometimes TV show producers and writers read these postings and network researchers use the Net for feedback. Netters compile vast lists of episode titles, guest stars, and other specific details about their favorite programs. They create "drinking games," write their own fan fiction, and debate the sexual orientation of various actors. Furthermore, the networks have all established a presence on the Net through on-line services and by creating their own World Wide Web sites.

Going On-Line
As viewers look toward the next century, a new medium is springing up all around them, even though it barely existed at the start of the decade. Sure, the Internet has been around since the 1960s when it was created by the government for military use. And college students have had access to e-mail accounts for more than a decade, but the real boom in on-line came in late 1993 with the maturing of the on-line services. What was once seen as a weird hobby (spending hours on the computer talking to strangers?) suddenly became not only mainstream but even fashionable as the big three commercial services (America Online, CompuServe, and Prodigy) battled for consumers' attention.

Although the on-line world is not limited to Generation X, people in this age group are among its most active users. It should be noted that the on-line world is considered to be very white and very male. Although there are no official figures to debunk this stereotype, Matrix Information & Directory Services, a market research firm, published a survey (titled "The Internet Gender Gap") in which the gender balance was slightly less than 2:1 at the end of 1994. In a late 1995 survey by the Emerging Technologies Research Group (titled "The American Internet User Survey") 35 percent of Internet users were women. In the same study 31 percent of Internet users were younger than 30 and 57 percent used the Internet for locating information on entertainment and music.

In October 1995, O'Reilly & Associates, a California-based publisher of books about computers and the Internet, reported (in a study called "Defining the Internet Opportunity") that almost 10 million Americans were on the Internet or an on-line service. They expected that number to rise to almost 16 million in 1996. In the same report, O'Reilly found that Internet users are 67 percent male, 33 percent female, and that 55 percent of Internet users are between ages 18 to 34.

TV fits in a discussion of the Net in two ways: viewer-generated TV talk and corporate promotion. Viewers can post their thoughts on a specific show in that show's newsgroup (many programs now have a newsgroup created by a fan, not the show's network or production company) or in a folder devoted to the series on an on-line service or on the network's Web site. Some people also create World Wide Web sites devoted to TV shows, actors, directors, and genres. Most of the networks (broadcast and cable) have both WWW sites and forums on the major on-line services. Viewers can go to these sites to obtain press releases, actor bios, photos, and lists of upcoming episodes.

In April 1995, the most popular photo to download from the ABC site on AOL was of Teri Hatcher, costar of *Lois & Clark: The New Adventures of Superman,* another indicator that young males are spending the most time on-line. More than 18,000 people had downloaded the photo. The least popular were pictures from *Matlock.*

Judging by the rally for low-rated shows on the Net, cybernauts are also more likely to have an interest in cult TV shows. Canceled sci-fi and cult programs, such as *Twin Peaks,* still have a devoted following on-line. Fans of the low-rated *My So-Called Life* posted enough messages to warrant the creation of 25 folders (each holding 500 messages) at ABC's AOL site, whereas the top-rated *Grace Under Fire* had only 141 postings in one folder during an April 1995 visit.

The networks also offer bulletin board areas on their commercial on-line service sites where viewers gather to discuss their favorite programs and sometimes spew professions of love for Connie Chung. Such a declaration appeared on the CBS Prodigy site a few weeks before she was fired from the *CBS Evening News* in summer 1995. More frequently, people posting will beg the network to keep a show on the air. "As a 43-year-old, upper-middle-class male with disposable income (just showing that you reach the right demographics), as well as a lifelong critic (both favorably and unfavorably) of TV, I've got to tell you that without a doubt, *Chicago Hope* is the best thing on television today," wrote one cybernaut in the CBS Prodigy site. "*Pleeeease* do whatever it takes to keep it on. We'll do our part by faithfully watching."

Network executives like the on-line world because it affords them yet another way to promote

Andy J. Williams, 27, is manager of the computer resource center at Dartmouth University. He says many of the same people who watch Gen X TV shows are likely to participate in Net discussions of these programs. "We're supposed to be the TV generation, and we're also the Internet generation," Williams said. "So there's a link in the age of the whole thing, but at the same time the Internet is about interaction, and TV's about passive watching."

Charles Kennedy, vice-president of Fox research, points out that in the history of television only a few TV shows have provoked a devoted following. For programs such as *Star Trek,* people created fan clubs and attended conventions. Now viewers can find discussions of any TV show. "There'd have to be structure and a network that they could plug into to show off their minutiae and intellect and command over this small area of life," said Kennedy. "But now the on-line [world] allows you to do that. It's a way to show off. Those people often know more about *X-Files* than any of the producers do. There are people who compile huge lists of credits and information and bios and listings and everything, and it's nice; they build the system for us. They help promote for us. It is kind of scary sometimes. Whatever floats your boat, I guess."

their programs. "We've been on-line on Prodigy since the 1994 Winter Olympics," said Jim Byrne, director of marketing communications for CBS, in an article I wrote for the *Times-Dispatch* in April 1995. "That was the first time we went on and opened a bulletin board. During 16 days we received more than 12,500 messages. That told us we had something that really was a way to extend our relationship with our viewers."

In the same April 1995 *Time-Dispatch* article, Mike Dubester, vice-president of the Capital Cities/ABC Multimedia Group, said the creation of temporary specialty areas (the Academy Awards and Super Bowl sections) are important. "We will utilize our production resources to create as much as possible," Dubester said. "It merits programming, not regurgitated TV programming, but programming just for this medium."

All four networks also send the stars of their programs on-line for question-and-answer sessions with viewers. Anthony Edwards, from NBC's *ER,* visited America Online in March 1995. "Being able to type naked covered in edible oil is a freedom that only cyberspace can give me!" Edwards wrote. "Ow! I feel good!" Part marketing tool, part fourth-dimensional water cooler, cyberspace is the place to be for chatting about TV.

Although many of those who are involved in this on-line universe are perfectly normal people, this new medium provides yet another opportunity for addiction. "I was in a chat [room], and this person gravitated toward me because my [on-line] name is Foxnet," Kennedy said. "She's somebody who's into animals and fur or whatever, I still haven't quite figured that out, and she has her own little world revolving around this. I just swirled up into it for a moment and then swirled out of it." Kennedy said he thinks the Internet has become popular in part because it fills a void in people's lives. It provides a community. "It gets back to that sense of community that's missing in America, so this provides it," Kennedy said. "If you have a particular interest, whatever it may be, you'll find people on-line who can share it with you."

On-line conversation also varies a great deal, depending on the TV show being discussed. Whereas *My So-Called Life* fans talked about substantive issues and *Earth 2* fans created their own fiction based on the characters in the series, posters to the *90210* newsgroup were more likely to speculate on whether any of the show's male stars is gay.

TV-crusading Cybernauts

Ian J. Ball, 25, is a graduate student studying chemistry at UCLA and a 1993 graduate of Harvard, but in his spare time he's taken it upon himself to catalog all the TV-related newsgroups, mailing lists, FTP, and Web sites for the rec.arts.tv newsgroup. "Generally, if I see that a major need isn't being met in a newsgroup I subscribe to, I will attempt to meet it," Ball wrote in an e-mail interview. "I also want the Net to be as user-friendly as possible. One of the best ways of doing that is to catalog useful Net features and databases."

In a follow-up phone interview, Ball described himself as "a TV head" and said the rec.arts.tv group is the first thing he looks at when he goes on-line. "I'm a firm believer in giving back information as well as taking it out," Ball said. "A lot of people bring information there, so if I can bring information to other people, I'll do that. [There's an] incredible reservoir of knowledge out there; there are people who are incredible libraries of knowledge. I'm pretty good, but there are people who can easily out-do me. This is true not just of TV and movies but also of current events and politics and just about anything else."

This attitude toward sharing information goes back to the origins of the on-line community, but as more and more people sign on, observance of netiquette is becoming scarce. "On the downside, the thing that has surprised me the most is the ferocity with which some people attack not just other Netters, but more alarmingly, shows and actors," Ball wrote. "Comments such as, 'Not only can [so-and-so] not act, but he (she) is ugly,' or, 'That show stinks. Everyone who watches it should be shot.' If I were an actor, I would never read the Net because some people are just so mean and thoughtless sometimes."

Ball also cited the high incidence of rumors that run rampant on the Net. Although many of these rumors may start elsewhere, once they hit the Internet, nothing can stop the spread of information. Perhaps the most infamous rumor (debated for months on alt.showbiz.gossip) had actor Keanu Reeves marrying openly gay media mogul David Geffen. It got to the point that Reeves had to tell interviewers he'd never even met Geffen. As much as celebrities may dislike being talked about on-line, they certainly have no problem putting in promotional appearances on America Online, Compu-Serve, or Prodigy.

Another person responsible for bringing TV culture to the Internet is Jol E. Padgett, a 27-year-old software engineer who created the Internet Television Ratings (ITR). Padgett said he created the ITR in December 1994 because people who had posted the Nielsen ratings on the Net received cease and desist e-mail from Nielsen employees.

"The second reason I started the ITR is because people on the TV newsgroups were always complaining that the Nielsens didn't reflect what they watched," Padgett said.

Clearly, the ITR was not intended to be a comprehensive reflection of national viewing as are the Nielsens. Instead, it represented the views of a specific group of people—computer users who care about TV. Padgett's ITR system only lasted until September 1995 when he had to give it up because of problems with his Internet provider and the conflicts it caused with his job. But in the short time it existed, the ITR showed another link between TV and the Net. Padgett conducted the ITR by having people on the Net keep diaries of their own viewing habits. Each day they e-mailed what they watched the previous night to Padgett, whose computer cranked out the results, which were then sent to the participants. During the 1994–95 season, the number of people filling out the survey averaged 600 to 900 daily. Padgett said he heard from a few people in the TV industry, including a producer from *Cybill*.

Nielsen Compared to ITR

(TV Ratings, week of May 22–28, 1995)

Nielsen's household ratings

1. *Home Improvement* (9:30 P.M. Tuesday)
2. *Home Improvement* (9:00 P.M. Tuesday)
3. *NYPD Blue*
4. *Friends*
5. *Seinfeld*
6. *ER*
7. *Full House*
8. *Frasier*
9. *Wings*
10. TV movie: *The Face on the Milk Carton*

Padgett's Internet TV ratings

1. *Friends*
2. *Frasier*
3. *Star Trek: Voyager*
4. *Wings*
5. *Seinfeld*
6. *Melrose Place*
7. *Mad About You*
8. *Beverly Hills, 90210*
9. *ER*
10. *Murphy Brown*

"One of the vice-presidents for Warner Bros. used the data in a meeting with the American Research Association, and the president of Nielsen was there and he was interested in it as well," Padgett said. "And there's someone with a user account at Nielsen on the [ITR] mailing list."

Padgett said the younger, youth-oriented shows (Gen X TV) or science-fiction shows did better in the ITR. Indeed, Padgett's list was much more similar to the Nielsen 18 to 24 or 18 to 34 demo than to the household ratings, which again supports the theory that Generation X has a large presence on the Net. For example, on May 28, 1995, *Murder, She Wrote*, a show with a notoriously older audience, ranked no. 22 on the Nielsen list but tied for no. 84 on the ITR. It's also worth noting that of the Top 10 programs on the ITR list, eight were also found on the survey I conducted partially on the Internet (see chap. 1).

Further proof of the Gen X influence in the ITR can be found in the rankings of several specials that aired that week. *Brady Bunch Home Movies* on CBS ranked no. 57 in the Nielsens, but no. 23 in the ITR. It was a much closer margin for the *Laverne & Shirley* reunion special, which came in no. 27 in the Nielsens and no. 25 in the ITR. Given the no. 3 rank of *Star Trek: Voyager* on Padgett's list the week of May 22, 1995 (compared to a Nielsen no. 66 ranking), and a follow-through correlation with other shows that tend to skew to the sci-fi audience (*Earth 2* was no. 28 in ITR, but no. 81 in the Nielsens; *X-Files* was no. 17 in ITR, but no. 44 in the Nielsens), it's clear that people who reported their viewing habits to ITR are a definite niche audience. But it's not necessarily an all-boys club, which the Internet has often been accused of being. In fact, *Walker, Texas Ranger*, a show with a high male viewership, ranked no. 72 on the ITR, but no. 36 in the Nielsens.

Even though the show hasn't been in production since 1994, fans of *Star Trek: The Next Generation* still talk about it on the Net thanks to the continuing *Star Trek* franchise that includes *Star Trek: Deep Space Nine, Star Trek: Voyager,* and the *Next Generation* movies. The series featured (*back row*): Whoopi Goldberg, Gates McFadden, Michael Dorn, Marina Sirtis, Wil Wheaton; (*front row*): LeVar Burton, Patrick Stewart, Jonathan Frakes, and Brent Spiner. Paramount Pictures.

One speculation about the Internet that can't be disproved is its exclusion of minorities and the poor. Many articles have stated that the Internet is not an inclusive community because of the cost to get on-line. The fact that there are no newsgroups devoted to *Martin, Living Single*, or *New York Undercover*, makes it clear that only a small number of minorities are on-line. Until a major on-line service takes the narrowcasting approach Fox took in the late 1980s with programs geared to minority viewers, the on-line world is likely to remain segregated.

There's no lack of discussion about anything related to *Star Trek*, a TV show that has spawned so many different newsgroups, Web sites, and mailing lists that a book (*NetTrek*) was published about the *Star Trek* presence on the Internet. These *Star Trek* newsgroups have, perhaps, the most fervent fans, which makes sense because *Trek* fans are well known for their devotion. By lurking in the *Star Trek* newsgroups, viewers can also find one of the pitfalls of the Net—spoilers. These are messages posted and usually labeled *spoilers* that contain upcoming storyline information for TV shows. They may give away information about who lives and dies or maybe a fact as unimportant as a character's promotion in rank. Although much of the information is reprinted word for word from tabloids such as the *National Enquirer*, leaks from the set also make it to the Net. In 1994, the script for the film *Star Trek Generations* was posted six months before the movie made it into theaters. A summary for the plot of the fall 1995 premiere of *Star Trek: Deep Space Nine* appeared long before the episode it described was broadcast. Granted there have always been leaks and illegal distributions of scripts from any number of TV shows, but one has to wonder if *Dallas* were on the air today, would "Who Shot J. R.?" really have been kept a secret? Probably. The answer to "Who Shot Mr. Burns?" on *The Simpsons* remained a secret in 1995 despite rampant on-line speculation and theorizing.

On-line Attempts at *Life* Saving

On-line buzz can help create awareness that turns into network ratings, but it doesn't always work that way. Steve Joyner was 27 when he started Operation Life Support, an on-line campaign to save the critically acclaimed television series *My So-Called Life*. And he doesn't even like television. Joyner had been on-line before the show's launch, but when he found himself drawn into *My So-Called Life*, he checked the ABC area on America Online to see what people were saying about the show. "I noticed something I wasn't aware of; the show was not doing well," Joyner said. "I saw a lot of people making this fact known, suggesting you write ABC, and they'd post an address, saying you should write. So there was all this enthusiasm, but it was sort of sporadic and sort of individual, noncentralized."

Thanksgiving weekend 1994, Joyner, an author, was tired of working on a book project, so he put together a proposal, "A So-Called Call to Arms" and coined the name Operation Life Support (OLS), inspired by military actions such as Operation Desert Storm. "Basically, I was just saying, let's create and sustain awareness of the show by putting out a newsletter, *Sustaining Life*, and also raise money maybe to take out a full-page ad in *Daily Variety*," Joyner said. The cost of that ad would be $2,250 and Joyner volunteered to put up $600 in start-up costs. With the help of other fans, Joyner's on-line campaign was in full swing. Despite people's fears of being ripped-off on the Internet, Joyner secured $1,000 in pledges within the first week. After the *New York Post* broke the story of Joyner's campaign in early December, the media madness descended. "From there everything just started getting out of control," Joyner said. "Other members of the press picked it up, and at that point, I didn't have to post on-line anymore. It was certainly nothing I expected."

By the day of *My So-Called Life's* final original episode broadcast, January 26, 1995, OLS had raised more than $6,000, enough to buy ads in both *Daily Variety* and the *Hollywood Reporter*. OLS was featured in articles in *USA Today*, the *Wall Street Journal, TV Guide, People,* the Associated Press, United Press International, CNN's *Showbiz Today*, E! Entertainment Television, and *Entertainment Tonight*. Once the show was off the air, Joyner thought that would be the end of his campaign. But on-line fans urged Joyner to continue because without episodes airing someone had to keep the spotlight on the program. Joyner said he half-heartedly went along with their request.

MTV began airing reruns of *My So-Called Life* before ABC had even decided whether or not the show would return for a second season. "I think the fact that it was picked up by MTV would not have happened unless we existed," Joyner said. "But I don't know how anyone could prove or disprove that." The *Sustaining Life* newsletter that was originally planned never came to be because Joyner had no time to prepare it and respond to e-mail, which arrived at the rate of almost 1,000 messages per day at the height of the campaign. The campaign remained on-line with Save *My So-Called Life* T-shirts offered as a premium for people who donated $20. Video tapes of the show were another premium for people who donated $90. A book about the OLS campaign was planned for publication in 1996. In the end, Joyner said the OLS campaign took in $70,000 in revenue, which was used to pay for the premiums, on-line time, a 1-800 number (that was announced only on MTV and generated 20,000 calls), and an ad that ran in *USA Today* in May 1995, urging ABC to renew the series. All this effort and time was spent, but *My So-Called Life* was still canceled.

"I know we had an impact," Joyner said, "certainly in this country in giving people something to rally for. In terms of a charity, there are so many plain vanilla solicitations for Cancer, AIDS. People get so much mail. But our largest individual contribution was $500. At first I thought [spending that kind of money] for a TV show was depressing, but I realized that this doesn't come around a lot, the opportunity to rally behind something. This show saved lives with Wilson Cruz's [gay] character. A number of schools have been getting tapes for use in classroom discussion. It's become a public service, and as [the show] spreads to different cultures in different parts of the world, every week someone else has just discovered the fact that we are here."

Although it's specific goal was never achieved, OLS did set the groundwork for future on-line campaigns. Joyner showed how the Net can be used to rally support and to attract media coverage. The question now becomes, because on-line campaigns are so much easier to conduct, will they really make a difference in the future? Now that anyone, anywhere can start a campaign via the Net (and they have), will the networks and news media continue to pay attention? OLS made headlines because it was seen as a new, unique way to get the network's attention, but now that it's not new, will newspaper writers care when future campaigns start? Chances are they will if the on-line campaign is for a show that critics unanimously support and if the people involved in the campaign put as much effort into it as Steve Joyner did. Many on-line campaigns will go unnoticed, but a select few will make it through to garner the attention of the nation's news media.

Whether or not OLS itself will be used as a blueprint for save-a-show campaigns in the future will depend on whether anyone else is willing to expend the time, resources, and energy that Joyner spent. "I think Bess Armstrong said this, and I've been parroting it: 'If ever there has been a campaign that should save a show, it's this one. And if it doesn't work, I don't know if it's worth trying again'," Joyner said. "Going back you hear about campaigns for *Star Trek* and *Cagney & Lacey*, but I think we set a precedent. The money, I think, was unprecedented. It remains to be seen what sort of precedent OLS becomes, a good one, bad one, or both."

Viewers for Quality Television founder and president Dorothy Swanson said that the on-line world is becoming a part of VQT as well. "I wish there were more of us on-line because as Steve Joyner knows, there's no better way for instant communication. It's time has come. . . . I've tried to push it, and I'll try to push it again, but the Internet is for—I was about to say young people—but I don't know. It's for people with the means to buy a computer and a modem and for those willing to learn a new technology. It's not for everybody."

Although Steve Joyner's campaign to save *My So-Called Life* got the most press, similar Net-based campaigns to save *Earth 2, VR.5, seaQuest DSV, Models Inc., Twin Peaks,* and *Party of Five* have appeared as well. Charles Kennedy, vice-president of Fox research, said the effectiveness of an on-line campaign may not be as great as some people think. "People who take the time to write a letter and address it, put it in an envelope and lick the stamp and put it in a box have taken more time and care in presenting their arguments and ideas," Kennedy said. "It also shows a greater level of effort to save the show."

Almost every show now generates a Save Our Show e-mail campaign on-line that would not normally happen through snail mail because it's too much effort, Kennedy said. This means the networks will adjust their expectations; 500 e-mail letters may mean nothing, Kennedy said, whereas 100 written letters may mean something more. The Viewers for Quality Television organization realizes this as well. The June 1995 issue of the group's newsletter stated, "VQT wants to go on record as believing that U.S. Mail letters rather than e-mail sent to the networks is more effective as it shows that a viewer took the time to write a letter, address an envelope and mail it."

Kennedy said campaigning to save a show on-line does help in one important area—getting the word out that a program is in danger. "Now you can go on-line and spread the word to your friends and create word-of-mouth and, we hope, that will encourage people to watch and when they start watching, that drives up ratings," Kennedy said. "Then we have a reason to save the show. If it changes people's behavior, then it will have an impact. If it's just merely a series of letters saying 'save it,' it's not going to do as much."

Updates and Drinking Games

Ian Ferrell, a 25-year-old program manager for the Microsoft Corporation, has been on the Net for five years. When *Melrose Place* began, Ferrell was living in a group house (like the one depicted in Douglas Coupland's book *Microserfs*) where he and his housemates would gather once a week to watch the show.

"We were all living together, but we didn't see each other very much, so we decided one night a week to make dinner together and do the family thing," Ferrell said. "All of us grew up far away from here, so [your housemates] are the only family you've got in the area. So we'd watch what we considered to be the worst possible TV show. We started with *Cop Rock* until, thankfully, the network minions took it off. The next thing we knew *Melrose Place* was coming out, so we started watching it. Then we started getting promoted [at work] or getting stuck in other jobs, and people were making the evening date less and less until I was left watching with the dog."

That was when Ferrell decided to help out his housemates by typing up a weekly "Melrose Place Update." They sent it to their friends; those friends sent it to their friends; and soon Ferrell's just-for-fun updates were spreading throughout the Internet. "It went from 4 to 5 people to 150 people at Microsoft to overnight hundreds of subscription requests pouring in from all over the place," Ferrell said. "At any given time there's something floating around the Net that's been forwarded from the dawn of time. It's like viruses floating around. It's very much this organic entity, so you can use organic metaphors."

The update contained a summary of the most recent episode, analysis and commentary, statistics, quotes, and a listing of songs played. "Sydney is sent off to Hidden Hills Sanatorium," Ferrell wrote in the September 19, 1994, update. "Great name for a salad dressing, stupid name for a sanatorium." At its peak, the update reached almost 3,000 subscribers a week. But by late fall 1994, Ferrell was promoted at work and ran out of time to write the spirited weekly synopsis. "They were 12 pages long and tended to go into gory detail," he said. "It took five to six hours to write in the evening. When I was doing it, *Melrose Place* was kind of cool; they weren't aware they were such a cliché and really campy and now they're playing it up and it's kind of depressing."

Ferrell is no fan of the Usenet newsgroups. "It's an extraordinary waste of time," he said. "Newsgroup quality has really declined. In some ways, it's infantile. I don't read the *Melrose Place* group anymore because typically its flame wars about Matt's homosexuality or spoilers."

Ferrell said one of the mailing lists he subscribes to is called Transient Images.

"Predominantly, it's an amalgam of all the gossip and chatter, leaning toward *X-Files* and talk about upcoming episodes and things about the cast and crew," he said. "Mindless trivia you can say in front of people to impress the crap out of them."

The Internet is also responsible for the escalation in the number of TV show drinking games. There was a popular drinking game in the 1970s for *The Bob Newhart Show* (drink whenever someone says "Hi, Bob"), and more recently, *The Grinch Who Stole Christmas* (drink whenever someone says "Who") has become a college favorite. But the number of drinking games and their complexity has certainly risen with the increase in Internet population. Just as there are newsgroups for most prime time TV shows, there are also drinking games being created daily. Many shows have more than one drinking game as more and more people try their hand at creating them. Jon Singer, a 26-year-old graduate student studying molecular biology at the University of California at Los Angeles, took charge of the *Melrose Place* drinking game Memorial Day weekend 1995. "Someone else posted it on a German Web

Take two drinks if you can name everyone in this *Melrose Place* fourth-season cast photo. *Front row* left to right: Kristen Davis, Andrew Shue, Heather Locklear, Courtney Thorne-Smith, Daphne Zuniga, Josie Bissett, Patrick Muldoon, Grant Show, Laura Leighton; *back row*: Doug Savant, Thomas Calabro, Marcia Cross, and Jack Wagner. Fox Broadcasting.

site," Singer said. "The original author is unknown, so I think it's been revised by several people. I just saw it was out of date with regard to the plot so I started working on it."

Singer said he thinks most people don't actually download the drinking game and use it; they're more likely just to read it and get a kick out of how much they recognize in it. That's what makes these games so much fun. They're all about familiarity and recognizing the formula to these shows, which again gives viewers a few moments of feeling superior because they get it. In the case of early *Melrose Place*, it's clear that the smug superiority viewers felt toward the show was much deserved. Although most of the characters have better jobs and better bods than viewers or their friends, viewers can take comfort in the fact that they are much smarter. For example, chances are real people would never move back into an apartment building that had been blown up only weeks before. Real people would not continue to live in the same apartment complex as their arch enemies. Once the show's writers saw they were unknowingly appealing to the audience in this way, they went out of their way to create opportunities for viewers to feel smarter than the show as in a sample from the *Melrose Place* drinking game: Amanda shows up at someone's door to chew them out—1 drink (extra gulp if it's about the rent. Two extra gulps if it's about the rent and the person is in the middle of a tragedy or personal crisis.) In the context of the show, this is dead-on. Amanda always pops up on someone's doorstep to tear into them, and she often chooses the worst possible time. Singer said the move of *Melrose* by Fox from Wednesday to Monday in 1994 diluted the fun of actually drinking along with the drinking game. "It's kind of early in the week to be drinking that much," Singer said. "It was better when it was on Wednesday and you were starting into the weekend."

Melrose Place Drinking Game No. 8

These are excerpts from the *Melrose Place* Drinking Game, posted to alt.tv.melrose-place by Jon Singer ("I recommend Zima for game play with a true Generation X feel.")

Billy
- Shot of Billy in jeans at the office—1 drink
- Billy wears a horrible tie (party vote)—2 drinks
- Billy looks dumbfounded—1 drink
- Billy says, "Ah wuv eu,———"—1 drink
- Billy without a shirt—1 drink
- Billy playing soccer—1 drink

Alison
- If Alison drinks, by all means drink with her
- Alison drunk (it's an ugly sight, ain't it?)—1 drink
- Alison and Amanda fight—1 drink (if it's over Billy—2 drinks)

Brooke
- Brooke makes her perky/concerned/helpful face—1 drink
- Brooke calls Billy "Campbell"—1 drink
- Brooke's father throws his weight around—1 drink

Jake

- Jake roughin' someone up, or gettin' roughed up —1 drink per punch
- Jake flees the scene—1 drink
- Jake is seen with no shirt on (extra gulp if he's carrying tools)

Amanda

- Amanda strides by the pool in a mini—1 drink
- Amanda looks bemused when someone criticizes her—1 drink

Sydney

- Sydney insults Jane—1 drink
- Sydney comes to Jane to plead for help, swearing that she's changed—1 drink (extra gulp if Jane slams the door in Sydney's face)
- Syd shows up in a dress that makes her look sweet and innocent—1 drink (extra gulp if the dress has a nice and sweet lace collar)
- Someone calls Sydney a whore—1 drink

Jane

- Jane in disbelief (for gettin' stepped on)—1 drink
- Jane tucks her hair behind her ear—1 drink
- Someone tells Jane she's gullible or too trusting —1 drink

Michael

- Michael uses medical lingo—2 drinks
- Michael threatens someone—1 drink (2 if you laugh while he's doing it)
- Michael seen without a shirt—1 drink
- Michael tells a lie—1 drink (if he's smirking, drink 2)

Kimberly

- Kimberly's "evil bitch look"—1 drink
- Kimberly's *scar!!!*—5 drinks (if you can stomach it)
- Kimberly without her wig—2 drinks
- Kimberly threatens someone—1 drink
- Kimberly uses medical lingo—1 drink
- Kimberly lies—1 drink

Matt

- Matt—1 drink for every line
- Matt and a man lustfully staring at each other —1 drink
- Matt is used in a gay context—1 drink
- Matt mentions his job as a social worker —1 drink
- Matt flips his bangs out of his face—1 drink
- Matt seen with no shirt (does he have a chest?) —2 drinks

Jo

- Jo with hand on womb—1 drink per hand
- Jo whines—1 drink (rubs her stomach while whining—2 drinks)
- Jo tells Jake she needs time to think (or vice versa)—1 drink

Cool Commercials

It's not just a love of TV shows that can be found on the Net. There's also an obsession with some commercials (see alt.tv.commercials), particularly those for Mentos, the candies advertised in goofy TV spots that feature Xers using the candy as an empowering device to sneak into a rock concert, get a car moved, and escape from a crazy woman at the mall. In September 1995,

Newsweek described the Mentos spots as "the world's most annoying commercials," but they'd already been a Gen X rage for more than one year.

Heath Doerr, 24, created the Mentos Frequently Asked Questions (FAQ) in September 1994 during his senior year at Purdue University where he majored in economics and psychology. The FAQ includes details about Mentos from information on the foreign-made commercials to the ingredients in the candy and the size of each piece. The FAQ begins with Doerr's summary of these corny TV commercials. Here's his take on what he calls "the Backstage Crew (or 'Those Crazy Kids II')," also known as commercial no. 7: "Once again the establishment has prevented some teens from achieving their goal. At the backstage door to a rock concert, our friends are star struck and must find a way backstage to meet their idols, demonstrate their freshness, and enjoy each other's minty clean breath. Musical paraphernalia is being unloaded, and with the aid of a bandanna, one teen slips through the line undetected. At the last moment, a security guard spots him, but instead of pouncing on him and beating him to a bloody mess with his nightstick, he lets him go, showing an expression that could only mean one thing, 'Those crazy kids!' Bravo!"

Of all the bad TV commercials out there, why Mentos? In an e-mail, Doerr explained his love for these particular bad commercials. "In the vast strip mall of images that commercials flash past our eyes in the fleeting minutes between car chases, Mentos was different. It told a story and an iconoclastic socially misguided one at that. The appeal is that it just seems wrong, or at least not normal, which is what most of us want to be. Normal is boring, and Mentos (and, hence, the viewers) are no longer dull. We are exciting, popular, and have fresh breath. Nuff Said."

In a phone interview, Doerr explained that his interest in Mentos had a simple origin. He was frequenting humor newsgroups and noticed that Mentos kept coming up, so it seemed natural for him to write something about the candy. Doerr said he sat down one night and remembered all the commercials in about 10 minutes. He revved up his computer and wrote up his summaries of each commercial, labeled his post a Mentos FAQ and posted it (to alt.tv.commercials and rec.arts.tv). "A lot of people have the misconception I was somehow mystified by Mentos," Doerr said. "But I was just in a humorous mood. I thought I'd write this thing and that would be the end of it. The only reason I called it an FAQ was to give it a context, but people really took it seriously and sent in all this information. After I took what they sent me and added it in, the thing started to become a real FAQ. It was a happy accident."

Doerr said much of the credit for the FAQ goes to the contributors, saying that all he did was get the ball rolling and collect the information that dozens of people contributed via e-mail. By the time he began graduate school at Wake Forest University in summer 1995, he had given the FAQ to someone else to manage, and it's now kept at a Web site (http://www3.gse.ucla.edu/~cjones/mentos-faq.html). "It started out as a joke and became something serious," Doerr said. "That's the beauty of the Internet. We created something out of nothing."

Among the many Mentos debates were whether or not the commercials were foreign-produced, with the jingle translated into English, which would explain why the commercials don't always make sense. "'The Freshmaker' is very German," he said. "Germans have a tendency to put two words together to make a new word, like 'toaster' becomes 'breadwarmer.' It's those subtle differences that don't scream foreign, but make the commercials seem not exactly right."

The November 1994 issue of *Sassy* magazine also included a Mentos deconstruction in its article titled "Working Our Nerves: Those Stupid Frigging Mentos Commercials." "It's not the bad acting, lack of technical flash, or wide-eyed sincerity of these commercials that's got me riled," wrote Mike, the surname-free author of the *Sassy* piece. "It's that they aim so low and depict such mundane scenarios." For all Mike's complaints, he admits to bounding "toward the TV set like a Pavlovian dog upon hearing their breezy, cheesy jingle, just to punish myself." Mike also dissected the ending of each commercial, which always features the teen hero "defiantly thrusting an upright roll of Mentos at the persecutor like one big middle finger." Doerr said that theory had been bandied about on the Net even before the *Sassy* article was published.

Doerr said Mentos are also frequently mentioned on the hit cable series *Mystery Science Theater 3000*. "There's sort of a different style of humor [on that show] and you either love it or hate it," he said. "It's sort of that sarcastic humor, and I think the Mentos commercials are inherently sarcastic.

They're such a cliché, it amazes me that they were even made. It's like, how stupid do they think I am? Then you watch longer, and it's funny to get into it." Once again, irony, sarcasm, and an opportunity to feel superior are the basic tenets behind a media icon with Gen X appeal. The only difference this time is that the appeal has led to the creation of a document by devotees to further cement their feelings of ownership.

Mentos have also been gaining a spot in popular culture lore as a result of mentions in TV shows, including *Friends.* In that show's first episode, Chandler and Joey are consoling Ross, whose wife has left him for another woman.

"Between us, we haven't had a relationship that's lasted longer than a Mento," Chandler says.

The 1995 film *Clueless* included a scene in which one of the characters sang along to a Mentos commercial. No joke was made, but just the sight of the commercial got a laugh from movie theater audiences. In early 1996, the modern rock band Foo Fighters released a music video for their song "Big Me" that was a parody of the Mentos commercials. The video featured lead singer Dave Grohl and other band members reenacting the Mentos commercials all the while attributing their success to "Footos: The Fresh Fighter." The video quickly became a heavy rotation hit on MTV.

Tricia Gold, 29, is the Mentos brand manager for Van Melle USA, the Kentucky-based company that imports Mentos from its parent company in Breda, Holland. Gold said Mentos have been sold in the United States for the past 20 years, but only in the past few years, with the introduction of the TV commercials in July 1992, have sales been strengthening. An *Advertising Age* article reported that sales of Mentos jumped from $20 million in 1991 to $40 million in 1994.

Gold described the commercials as part of a "global campaign" with three ads filmed in the United States and seven created overseas. She said the Mentos ads weren't designed specifically for Generation X although people in that age group are part of the Mentos target market. "We weren't trying to exploit anybody," Gold said. "I can think of other commercials that have done that and backfired. [Generation X] doesn't want advertising to bow down to them."

Despite their success in attracting not only buyers but a cult following too, the advertising community has turned its collective nose up at Mentos ads.

"*USA Today* picked us as the second worst campaign [in January 1994], but we're not out to win advertising awards," Gold said. "What's important to us is that people remember [the ads]."

Gold said she's aware of the Mentos interest on the Internet, but she said Van Melle has no plans to respond to it. "We like it, but we have no desire to add our input," Gold said. "With the Internet, you can't change anything that's said, even if something's not right, but if we start interfering with what's going on, we'd sort of stifle the flow of communication, and we have no desire to do that."

Van Melle's reluctance to defend its product on-line, to explain its commercials, or to give out much information about where they came from only enhances the mystique. It keeps the Netheads who worship Mentos guessing, and it ensures that these candies will continue to be viewed as cool because they're seen as weird rather than as corporate creations (even though that's just what they are). Letting people say what they like about Mentos on-line is the proper approach, according to advertising insiders. "Highjacking time or attention [on-line] is perceived as theft unless immediately qualified as truly imaginative and useful," wrote a group of digital marketers (including Nicholas Givotovsky) in the February 6, 1995, *Mediaweek.* "Net citizens will respond coldly to synthetic or contrived 'impressions,' which lack currency, depth, applicability, relevance, and credibility."

The writers went on to use the Mentos case as an example of how people on the Net acted as the source of discussion for this product and how that approach differs from advertising initiated by a corporation, that is, a corporate creation. "Before the Internet and its attendant culture of hyper-hip critique and parody, these ads would have gone unremarked. While the hapless qualities of the Mentos campaign made the brand some friends, what will be the reception to such advertising on the Net itself? False or hollow impressions on-line will be a big bust, for users and advertisers alike."

Cybersoaps

A company that hopes to avoid such pitfalls is Prophecy Entertainment, a division of the Los Angeles–based ad agency Fattal & Collins, which has created *The Spot,* perhaps the most obvious melding of TV and the Internet at a

World Wide Web site (http://www.thespot.com). This "episodic Web site" was the first soap opera in cyberspace when it premiered in June 1995. The brainchild of Prophecy employee Scott Zakarin, 32, *The Spot* features a cast of fictional characters living in a beach house with a long history. Part *Real World*, part *Melrose Place*, *The Spot* offers cybersurfers the opportunity to drop by for daily updates in the form of diary entries by the five fictional housemates.

Russell Collins, 46, director and executive producer of Prophecy Entertainment, said *The Spot* was developed as a way to get people to come routinely to a specific place. Selling any products would have to come later. Eric Hirshberg, 27, senior vice–president/associate creative director for Fattal & Collins, points to the beginnings of television as a blueprint for how the Internet should be colonized.

"TV became TV because thousands of people were watching it," he said. "The problem with the Internet is that people are starting to deliver advertising before the programming. MCI is putting up everything [on their Web site] about MCI without giving any compelling entertainment value, and people are tuning in just because of the novelty of the technology. Until *The Spot*, there was never a traditional model of entertainment available on the Internet. The idea of doing an episodic soap opera is not a new idea, but doing it on the Internet is a new idea. Now people will want to go there and want to go back. It will become a place people go to for entertainment and a place people can be reached by advertisers."

What makes entertainment on the Internet so different is that interactivity is available today, whereas interactive TV is much further in the future than people once imagined. Collins said interactive TV is at least five to seven years away, which is why he thinks it's important to make the Internet experience more TV-like but richer than any current television experience. Collins said *The Spot* received about 300 e-mails a day in July 1995 and that each one is responded to by one of the characters from the Web site. In March 1996, the number of people visiting the site averaged 40,000 daily.

"I think anyone who creates anything on the Internet had better be ready to collaborate with his audience," Hirshberg said. "The paradigm of TV producers as artists in an ivory tower who come down with a show will change. People won't tolerate not being included. The Internet is about inclusion. *The Spot* is about including people in their own story."

Clearly, this perspective has an appeal to Gen Xers who can't be included in the production of real TV shows, so they turn to newsgroups for inclusion. "Obviously *The Spot* is geared toward that age group," Collins said. "They're pioneering [the Internet], they're reinventing it, they're populating it. It is really their medium. . . . It will be like television for them; that is our belief and that is what is so compelling. In our opinion, it will replace television as the dominant mass medium."

Hirshberg pointed out that members of Generation X grew up with remote controls, VCRs, and computers and the opportunity to create their own entertainment experiences using that technology. "They relate to *The Spot* because this is the first form of entertainment where they feel in control of the creation," Hirshberg said. Through the interactivity of e-mail between people in the real world and characters from *The Spot*, the plot lines and characters are affected by the audience, Collins said. "Your e-mail advice to Tara would affect her," Hirshberg said. "She would consider it, and her pondering on your input could be a part of the storyline. It's a dialogue between the creators and the audience."

Collins said the daily diary entries at *The Spot* are created internally by young employees ("They work together here, which is like living together," Collins said), some of whom share the faces of *Spot* characters.

Terra Goodnight, 27, works in a Washington, D.C., Internet design firm as a programmer and consultant, and she thought *The Spot* was a step in the right direction. "The site is really interesting in that it captures that missing element—interactivity," she wrote in an e-mail message. "The 'characters' ask the viewers what they should do in their lives (one guy wanted to know how to break up with his annoying girlfriend) and it gets incorporated into the action. Yeah, it's still stupid, voyeuristic, and content-free, but I'll take it over *Melrose Place* any day if only because I really want to know what it is all about and why it is there."

Because the Internet is such a dispersed medium with no beginning and no end and because it's constantly changing, it's impossible to completely catalog everything that's out there. "The experience of being on the Internet is more like kayaking than it is like selecting a TV program," Collins said. The Net is all about linkage, he said, and each Web site may refer to another related Web site. For example, viewers' first stop might be the Sony Pictures site, which may have a link taking them to a film school, which may give them the opportunity to connect to criticism of Charlie Chaplin films written by a monk in a monastery.

"It's fluid and ongoing and never takes you back to a central location," Collins said. "There's no home base. When you get done with one show, you can't see what's on next, and that's the challenge of the Internet. It's totally counterculture and subversive."

As with Gen X's infatuation with *The Simpsons* and the humor of David Letterman, subversion and defiance of authority are well-regarded traits. Advertisers, however, are necessary to pay for the programming on this new medium. "This is a very sophisticated audience," Collins said in July 1995. "One speculation is [about] when advertising is going to start [on *The Spot*]. If we mention anything that could even remotely be considered a product, we get e-mail. We acknowledge, yes, somebody has to pay for production of *The Spot*, and there will be advertising. People are ironic and cynical about it, but nobody really imagines we can produce *The Spot* without support from advertisers."

By the end of 1995, advertising began on *The Spot* with such sponsors as Hugo Boss, Honda, K-Swiss sneakers, and others paying a $16,500 per month fee. Hirshberg pointed out that as much as people joke about commercials, they watch them on TV, so why not on the Internet? "When the remote control was new, people had to elect to watch commercials," Hirshberg said. "That paradigm will become intensified on the Net. Advertising has to be as engaging as the program itself."

Although advertisers may be slow to accept this new place to advertise, if the Net becomes known as a new entertainment medium as Collins and Hirshberg expect, the demand for more episodic Web sites like *The Spot* will continue to grow. Collins said he's anticipating this and is already at work on five additional shows that he expects to premiere during 1996. That sounds a lot like a TV network programmer trying to build a night of viewing, and indeed, Collins founded the American Cybercast Network (ACN) in May 1996 with its debut show *Eon-4* (http://www.eon4.com/) from veteran sci-fi scribe Rockne O'Bannon. "Because the Internet is such a free-flowing experience, that creates the demand for organization," Collins said. "It's an opportunity to organize people's experiences, so when you're on the Internet, you go to a site, and you're provided with a whole block of experiences. The key to the ACN concept is that we already have an audience coming for entertainment; we have to hold onto them for a while and provide them with more entertainment." American Online tried to make itself more TV-like when it unveiled a new version of its software in summer 1996. The "Main Menu" that listed some of the different areas was replaced by a list of "Channels."

As the technology for visiting Web sites continues to become more elaborate, the experience will continue to become more "real." Collins expected to introduce audio links to *The Spot* so visitors could hear conversations of the characters. Although people may tire of *The Spot,* Collins expects it to be around for at least a few years, just like a TV show. By then, TV and the Internet may work together. Scott Zakarin said they'd had offers to turn *The Spot* into a TV show. In February 1996, NBC hired Zakarin and *Spot* cocreator Troy Blotnick to create new interactive programs for its Web site. NBC will also have an option to turn the duo's Web creations into TV shows.

The Spot won acclaim early, receiving the first annual Webby award, given to the most popular World Wide Web site. Kristin Herrold, 25, who portrays recovering alcoholic model Michelle Foster on *The Spot,* was included in *People* magazine's "Fresh Faces '95" for her groundbreaking on-line role. *The Spot* also spawned a parody, *The Squat* (http://theory.physics.missouri.edu/~georges/Josh/squat/), where a collection of hillbilly characters fill their diaries with spelling errors. America Online entered cyber entertainment in September 1995 with *Lost in America*, a site where a group of five travelers posted their daily accounts of driving around America (Think of it as MTV's *Road Rules* on-line with the opportunity to interact with the stars and vote on their next destination). In March 1996, AOL introduced *The Hub*, which was produced by New Line Television and featured 25 "programs" on eight "channels." Other Cybersoaps include *Lake Shore Drive* (http://www.chiweb.com/chicago/lsd/), *Madeleine's Mind* (http://www.madmind.com), *Ferndale* (http://www.ferndale.com/), and *The East Village* (http://www.theeastvillage.com).

Clearly *The Spot* and other cybersoaps are onto something. By combining the conventions of TV with the new technology of the Internet, this new hybrid form of entertainment is able to attract a small portion of Gen Xers who would otherwise spend their time in front of the TV. As technology improves and Net access continues to grow, the Net will continue to draw viewers away from the tube in the living room to the tube on their desks. So far, TV has only begun to fight this encroachment by acknowledging that the Internet exists, but soon enough it will have to change, just as radio changed with the advent of television, and just as newspapers changed with the creation of radio. The Internet will not cause the end of broadcast television as viewers know it, but it will force TV to evolve.

Net TV

It's not just a case of TV being talked about on the Internet. TV has also begun to showcase the Net. The dense and confusing 1993 ABC miniseries, *Wild Palms*, was the first to use the idea of a futuristic world filled with virtual reality. The 1995 Fox series, *VR.5*, was the most transparent attempt so far to cash in on the newfound technology and the cult phenomenon of the show that aired after it on Friday nights, *The X-Files*.

VR.5 starred Lori Singer as Sydney Bloom, a Los Angeles telephone worker who spent her nights in virtual reality (VR), trying to untangle the secrets of her family's past (her father worked on early VR equipment and was seemingly killed for it). When Sydney strapped on her VR gear, she'd enter another realm, and she always returned shaking from her discoveries.

"I think people layer their shows more carefully now in hopes that people will hook up to it," said *USA Today* TV critic Matt Roush. "I know *VR.5* wanted that so bad. They want to be obsessed upon." Indeed, *VR.5* took the *X-Files* mantra of "The Truth Is Out There" and concocted its own slogan, "Virtual Reality Is Real." "As a critic I found *VR.5* to be a very interesting show not to respond to because it's the kind of show we should be responding to," Roush said.

Many other critics gave the show positive reviews, citing it's attempt to be different and to stand out from the crowd. David Bianculli was among the TV critics who applauded *VR.5*. "This series definitely had an art and a place to go, it just wasn't allowed to get there," Bianculli said. "This comes from someone who watches a lot of MTV and likes it. It had the visual artistry and the constant character development that I liked." Despite its tireless attempts to lure *X-Files* fans to the tube an hour earlier, *VR.5* got zapped.

In September 1995, CBS introduced the world to *Dweebs,* a sitcom about a Bill Gates-like visionary (Peter Scolari) who oversaw a computer company staff of techno geeks (including Cory Feldman). On the newsgroup alt.society.generation-x, contributors mistook it for a takeoff on Douglas Coupland's novel *Microserfs.* One person even observed, "CBS is going to beat Fox for a TV show about the Microserf types." Saddled with a poor time slot (opposite the ABC TGIF powerhouse and Fox's offbeat *Strange Luck*), *Dweebs* never had a chance.

Mentions of the Internet have started popping up in shows all across the TV spectrum from *Picket Fences* to *Beverly Hills, 90210,* which featured several episodes with Internet-related activities. In fall 1994, an episode showed David and Clare going on-line to post an announcement about a party, but they accidentally sent it to the wrong newsgroup—one devoted to lesbian issues. Consequently, one of the women who read the posting showed up at the party and developed a crush on Kelly after being trapped with her in a fire. It was fall 1994 when the Peach Pit After Dark was introduced as the night club where the *90210* gang hangs out. It featured the After Dark screensaver logo of a flying toaster on the door of the club and as the stage backdrop. In the September 1995 season premiere, Brandon corresponded with his parents (now living in Hong Kong) via e-mail on America Online. That same night, the AOL sign-off screen featured a small note: "Best regards to Brandon Walsh, Beverly Hills, CA, 90210."

As a result of its large following of Netheads, writers for *The Simpsons* have had fun taking potshots at the show's fans. In a September 1995 episode, a comic book store owner tapped into his computer and logged onto the newsgroup "alt.nerd.obsessive." In a fall 1995 *Law & Order* episode, a criminal was tracked down via a computer bulletin board; *New York Undercover* featured an episode about pedophiles who troll the Net; and Hope accidentally sent a love note via e-mail to a global mailing list on *Hope & Gloria.*

Big Brother Wants You (To Tell Him How to Improve His TV Show)

6

Thousands of newsgroups, mail-ing lists, and World Wide Web pages are available for viewers to see as long as they have computers, modems, and access to the Internet. Many of these areas are created by the same people who use them—the fans. Andy J. Williams, 27, is manager of the computer resource center at Dartmouth University. He's been on-line for nine years, but was never into TV show newsgroups (except alt.tv.twin-peaks) until the debut of *Friends*.

Because he works at a university and has direct Internet access, he was able to create a *Friends* mailing list in late October 1994. Newsgroups and mailing lists are usually created by people at institutions. World Wide Web sites are more likely to be created by individuals at colleges or on their home computers. Once the *Friends* mailing list was off the ground, people started asking Williams to create a newsgroup, which he did in January 1995. With the rise in the show's popularity, the number of daily posts to the newsgroup also rose. There are typically about 75 new postings each day, but as in most TV show newsgroups, the number of posts balloons the day after a new episode airs. Although many of the posts ask, "Which is your favorite *Friend???*" or

"Who's the sexiest Friend?" or "I saw Matthew Perry in a *Growing Pains* rerun" or "Are Matthew Perry and Luke Perry related?" there is also some substantive discussion of individual episodes and the show's continuing storyline. More and more newsgroups, however, are being deluged with mindlessness. "There are all these messages posted about us, especially the girls," *Friends* star Lisa Kudrow told *Entertainment Weekly's* Ken Tucker in June 1995. "Some of it's kind of weird; like, there's this whole section on the Net about a 'Jennifer-Courteney sandwich.'"

On the Net **The Internet offers an unbelievable**

wealth of information about TV shows from episode guides to cast bios. Listed below are areas from which viewers can obtain such information. Newsgroups offer an outlet to express opinions about specific shows. FTP sites contain episode guides and FAQs for newsgroups, and World Wide Web sites offer a little bit of everything. Much of the information presented in this volume must be credited to Ian J. Ball who collects, archives, and publishes a list of TV-related Internet sites in the rec.arts.tv FAQ, which can be accessed through his Web site (http://members.aol.com/IJBall/WWW/TV.html)

For discussion of all things Gen X (including TV), one can read the newsgroup alt.society.generation-x. Internet sites (especially fan-created sites on the Web) go up and come down all the time, so something listed in this section may or may not exist by the time viewers check it out.

Newsgroups

Absolutely Fabulous	alt.tv.ab-fab
The Addams Family	alt.fan.addams.family
American Gothic	alt.tv.amer-gothic
Animaniacs	alt.tv.animaniacs

Williams said that sort of topic is less likely to crop up on a mailing list. Instead, mailing list fans are more likely to use the show as a common bond for the formation of a community of cybernauts, friends who only know one another in cyberspace. "I'm amazed at how ready people are to form communities [in cyberspace]," Williams said. "Maybe that's just built into the human animal."

Williams is also one of the many people on the Net who communicates via e-mail with producers and writers of their favorite TV shows. Williams was the conduit for Jeff Greenstein, a supervising producer during the first season of *Friends*. "He delurked to me," Williams said. "The mailing list was not a couple days old, and I got mail from this random person. He sent a picture of the show's logo. Two days later, he told me Phoebe's last name. Then he told me who he was, and we struck up a deal that I would act as his mouthpiece to the list."

Greenstein, 31, is actually a veteran of Net life, having gone on-line six years ago before the hype began. "It was very early in the show . . . and the list probably didn't have more than 25 people asking questions," Greenstein recalled. "I wrote and said, 'I can answer a lot of these questions. Why not give them the benefit of somebody's insight who works on the show?' I always feel kind of isolated as a writer from the audience, so it's a great way for me to keep in touch with people who are actually fans of the show. That kind of feedback was really valuable; that's why I kind of stuck around. I ended up having quite a lot of interactions with people on the list and answering questions people posted."

Williams said he was glad someone on the show was willing to interact with people on the Net and that the arrangement he and Greenstein worked out benefited everyone. People on-line got their questions answered; Greenstein had someone to screen his messages. Greenstein said going on-line with *Friends* fans wasn't terribly time-consuming, and he appreciated the enthusiasm from fans on the Net. Like millions of other Americans, the on-line world has become a part of Greenstein's life. When he prepared for the fall 1995 launch of his Universal-produced sitcom, *Partners* (with writing partner Jeff Strauss), Greenstein said he talked to the people at Universal's Cyberwalk, a WWW site set up by Universal Studios, about how to promote the show on the Internet. These corporate sites, although helpful in providing viewers with information, are generally regarded with skepticism by veteran cybernauts. Corporate sites may have the money and technology to look good, but because they are controlled by huge media conglomerates, there's

Babylon 5	rec.arts.sf.tv.babylon5
Barney and Friends	alt.tv.barney
Baywatch	alt.tv.baywatch
Beauty and the Beast	alt.tv.beauty+beast
Beavis and Butthead	alt.tv.beavis-n-butthead
Beverly Hills, 90210	alt.tv.bh90210
The Brady Bunch	alt.tv.brady-bunch
British TV programs	rec.arts.tv.uk.misc
Canadian TV	alt.tv.networks.cbc
Chicago Hope	alt.tv.chicago-hope
China Beach	alt.tv.china-beach
Christy	alt.tv.christy
Comedy Central	alt.tv.comedy-central
commercials on TV	alt.tv.commercials
The Critic	alt.tv.the-critic
Dark Shadows	alt.tv.dark_shadows
Dinosaurs	alt.tv.dinosaurs
Discovery Channel	alt.tv.discovery
Dr. Who	rec.arts.drwho
Duckman	alt.tv.duckman
Due South	alt.tv.due-south
Earth 2	alt.tv.earth-2
Eek the Cat	alt.tv.eek-the-cat
ER	alt.tv.er
Forever Knight	alt.tv.forever-knight
Frasier	alt.tv.frasier
Friends	alt.tv.friends
game shows	alt.tv.game-shows
HBO	alt.tv.hbo
Herman's Head	alt.tv.hermans-head
Highlander	alt.tv.highlander
Home Improvement	alt.tv.home-imprvment
Homicide	alt.tv.homicide
infomercials	alt.tv.infomercials
The Kids in the Hall	alt.tv.kids-in-hall
The Kindred	alt.tv.kindred
Knight Rider	alt.tv.knight-rider
Kung Fu	alt.tv.kungfu

L. A. Law	alt.tv.la-law
Late Night with	
Conan O'Brien	alt.fan.conan-obrien
The Late Show with	
David Letterman	alt.fan.letterman
Law & Order	alt.tv.law-and-order
Liquid TV	alt.tv.liquid-tv
Lois & Clark: The New	
Adventures of Superman	alt.tv.lois-n-clark
Mad About You	alt.tv.mad-about-you
Mad TV	alt.tv.mad-tv
Magnum P. I.	alt.tv.magnum-pi
The Man from Uncle	alt.tv.man-from-uncle
Married . . . with Children	alt.tv.mwc
M*A*S*H	alt.tv.mash
Max Headroom	alt.tv.max-headroom
Melrose Place	alt.tv.melrose-place
Models Inc.	alt.tv.models-inc
MTV	alt.tv.mtv
The Muppets	alt.tv.muppets
Monty Python	alt.fan.monty-python
Much Music	alt.fan.muchmusic
Murder One	alt.tv.murder-one
My So-Called Life	alt.tv.my-s-c-life
Mystery Science	
Theater 3000	rec.arts.tv.mst3k.misc
The Nanny	alt.tv.the-nanny
NewsRadio	alt.tv.newsradio
news shows	alt.tv.news-shows
New York News	alt.tv.ny-news
Nickelodeon	alt.tv.nickelodeon
Northern Exposure	alt.tv.northern-exp
Nowhere Man	alt.tv.nowhere-man
NYPD Blue	alt.tv.nypd-blue
Party of Five	alt.tv.party-of-five
Picket Fences	alt.tv.picket-fences
Pinky & the Brain	alt.tv.animaniacs.pinky-brain
The Prisoner	alt.tv.prisoner

not a lot of trust in them. Although all the TV networks have their own sites, the populist culture of the Internet dictates that "Joe's *Star Trek* Home Page" is more authentic and believable because it comes from an average Joe. People on the Net like to control information about their favorite TV shows themselves because it's the one place where they can be in control. In the real world, people can't go out and simply publish a magazine devoted to *Murder One* that has the potential to be read by millions. On the Net, people can do just that.

Conversing with the Audience

Although plenty of fans of sitcoms and dramas are on the Net, perhaps the most active contingent of TV talk on the Net is related to science fiction. This makes sense because the whole online universe is like a sci-fi story. Whereas *Star Trek* newsgroups are among the most populated, *Babylon 5* executive producer/creator J. Michael Straczynski is well known for trafficking the Net. In a July 1994 article for the *Richmond Times-Dispatch,* Straczynski said sci-fi TV viewers tend to be interested in the Net because they're most apt to own high-tech video equipment and are comfortable enough with technology. Straczynski, who said he reads 500 pieces of e-mail a day, has been on-line since 1984. Whenever there's news about his show, he's always quick to get to the Net to share it with fans. "Yes, I can confirm that we've been renewed for Year Three," Straczynski wrote in a May 1995 posting. "It's a full order for 22 episodes, and we begin shooting July 31st or thereabouts. Thanks in particular to all of *Babylon 5's* Netted' friends, who have held the line alongside us for the preceding two years and with whom we hope to continue sharing the foxhole for the next three."

As the gap between fans and TV show producers shrinks, the feeling is growing among fans that producers are reading the newsgroups and swiping ideas for their programs. "*They used my idea!!*" wrote one fan in the *Melrose Place* newsgroup in May 1995 after Matt got together with a married man. "You see, this *proves* they read this stupid newsgroup! About four months ago, we had a gay/lesbian debate, and I said if Spelling had *real* balls, he would bring up a *bisexual* plot, and *he did!* Outrageous!!"

In another instance, people had been referring to Kimberly in newsgroup discussions as Kimmie. A few weeks later someone called her by that name on the show, and many people posted to the newsgroup, saying this was proof that producers were lurking. Kimberly Costello, *Melrose Place* producer, said some of the show's producers read the newsgroup, but they don't swipe ideas. The use of "Kimmie" wasn't a wink at newsgroup participants either. "By the time they're seeing episode one, we'll have shot episode 10," Costello said. "So any of their ideas don't matter because we're so far ahead."

At the end of the 1994–95 season when Kimberly was seeing an evil-looking guy (named

public access cable	alt.tv.public-access
Quantum Leap	rec.arts.sf.tv.quantum-leap
The Real World	alt.tv.real-world
Red Dwarf	alt.tv.red-dwarf
Ren and Stimpy	alt.tv.ren-n-stimpy
Road Rules	alt.tv.road-rules
The Rockford Files	alt.tv.rockford-files
Roseanne	alt.tv.roseanne
SCTV	alt.tv.sctv
Saturday Night Live	alt.tv.snl
Saved By the Bell	alt.tv.saved-bell
seaQuest DSV/2032	alt.tv.seaquest
Seinfeld	alt.tv.seinfeld
Sesame Street	alt.tv.sesame-street
Silk Stalkings	alt.tv.silk-stalkings
The Simpsons	alt.tv.simpsons
Sliders	alt.tv.sliders
soap operas	rec.arts.tv.soaps.misc
soap operas, ABC	rec.arts.tv.soaps.abc
soap operas, CBS	rec.arts.tv.soaps.cbs
Space: Above and Beyond	alt.tv.space-a-n-b
Star Trek, current	rec.arts.startrek.current
Star Trek, fandom	rec.arts.startrek.fandom
Star Trek, info.	rec.arts.startrek.info
Star Trek, other	rec.arts.startrek.misc
Star Trek, reviews	rec.arts.startrek.reviews
Star Trek: Deep Space Nine	alt.tv.star-trek.ds9
Star Trek: Voyager	alt.tv.star-trek.voyager
talk shows, daytime	alt.tv.talkshows.daytime
talk shows, late night	alt.tv.talkshows.late
teen idols	alt.fan.teen.idols
teen starlets	alt.fan.teen.starlets
The Tick	alt.tv.the-tick
3rd Rock from the Sun	alt.tv.3rd-rock
Tiny Toon Adventures	rec.arts.tv.tiny-toon
The Tonight Show with Jay Leno	alt.fan.jay-leno
TV discussion, general	rec.arts.tv

TV Nation	alt.tv.tv-nation
Twin Peaks	alt.tv.twin-peaks
V	alt.tv.v
VR.5	alt.tv.vr5
Weird Science	alt.tv.weird-science
Wings	alt.tv.wings
Wiseguy	alt.tv.wiseguy
The X-Files	alt.tv.x-files

**FTP Sites
for Episode
Guides and FAQs**

SRC.DOC.IC.AC.UK:/public/media/tv/collections/tardis/
The most complete FTP site for episode guides. Send
queries to: tv-archive@cheers.demon.co.uk

FTP.UU.NET:/usenet/rec.arts.tv
Formerly the home of the rec.arts.tv FAQ, this site is no
longer maintained, but episode guides still exist.

ftp://users.aol.com/IJBall3/FTP/rec.arts.tv-FAQ/
Current site of the rec.arts.tv FAQ.

RTFM.MIT.EDU:/pub/usenet-by-hierarchy; or
RTFM.MIT.EDU:/pub/usenet/news.answers/tv/
Many FAQs for alt.tv and rec.arts newsgroups can be
found here.

SFLOVERS.RUTGERS.EDU:/pub/sf-lovers
Episode guides and FAQs for science-fiction TV shows.

FTP.FUNET.FI:/pub/culture/tv+film
A European site for episode guides.

Henry) as her reflection in mirrors, many news-group readers (and professional TV critics) called it a *Twin Peaks* ripoff because that show also featured a malevolent character who appeared in mirrors as a reflection. Costello said that was never the intention. "That never came up in the [writers' meeting] room once," Costello said. "It didn't even occur to us. I don't remember hearing *Twin Peaks* come up in our meetings. It's not an homage; it was just part of Kimberly's psychosis." The idea that none of the *Melrose Place* staff knew they were imitating *Twin Peaks* is laughable to veteran TV watchers, but stranger things have happened. Although most TV show producers are sincere when they say they don't get story ideas from the Net (because of legal issues), some producers admit to getting feedback from the on-line universe.

"The only time it had any effect was when we remixed the title theme [during the first season]," said *Friends* executive producer Marta Kauffman. "Everybody noticed and didn't like it as much, and what it made me do was go back and listen to the remix and wonder why. And then when we figured out why, we changed it."

Partners executive producer Jeff Greenstein said advice from the Internet can sometimes be helpful, but it can't be considered the majority opinion. "It's a very specific cross section of primarily white males who make a lot of money," Greenstein said. "It's like when you read a particular film critic. You know Pauline Kael has a point of view, so you put it through your Kael filter." Greenstein is among an increasing number of TV show producers who will go to the Net to get information. He mentioned that in a first season episode of *Friends* there was supposed to be a mention of an episode of *The Twilight Zone* starring Burgess Meredith but another writer thought Meredith had appeared in more than one episode. Greenstein went to the Net and found his answer.

When the UPN series *Nowhere Man* premiered in September 1995, the network insisted on using previews of upcoming scenes every time the show went to commercial. People on the quickly created newsgroup (alt.tv.nowhere-man) complained. The show's creator/executive producer Larry Hertzog was on-line responding to fan's questions and concerns that the bumpers were giving away too much information about upcoming scenes. After only three weeks on the air, he posted this message: "For all of you folks who have complained (rightfully) about the 'giveaway' bumpers between acts—you'll be pleased to know that UPN has been following the chatter here on the Net and has, today, approved dropping them. So you see, if enough of us get together—even the Powers that Be sometimes have to crumble. Don't get too cocky, though; it's only a battle, and the war ain't over."

Winnie Holzman, executive producer of *My So-Called Life,* said she discovered through the Net that fans of her show had questions about Jordan Catalano's reading ability. "I remember people [on the Internet] were confused," Holzman said. "They said, 'If Jordan can't read, how could he write that note?' Well, he could read, just at a low level. Some people said, 'Is he dyslexic?'

World Wide Web Sites

http://www.ultimatetv.com
A site that bills itself as the "Ultimate TV list for the Web."

http://www.afionline.org/CineMedia/
An excellent site with links to Web sites for TV shows, networks, TV organizations, and so forth.

http://www.cinescape.com
The Web site of Cinescape magazine, includes daily updates on TV and film projects, mostly in the sci-fi genre.

http://www.yahoo.com/Entertainment/Television/
An excellent search tool that can help locate Web sites. This address takes viewers right to Yahoo's entertainment section.

http://src.doc.ic.ac.uk/public/media/tv/collections/tardis/
A Web interface to the Tardis FTP site.

http://www.clicktv.com/
http://www.tvquest.com/
On-line guides to what's on TV tonight.

http://www.specialweb.com/tv/
A site with links to pages devoted to actors/actresses, networks, shows, magazines, and more.

http://www.webhangers.com/~tvthemes/
A fan-created Web site containing downloadable TV theme songs from 1980s-era programs. Includes network jingles, commercial music, local news music and themes from prime time comedy and drama series.

http://www.tvgen.com/
The Web site for *TV Guide* magazine.

http://www.mca.com/tv/
An official Web site for MCA-Universal TV shows.

http://www.mtr.com/
The Museum of Television & Radio

http://www.emmys.org
The Academy of Television Arts & Sciences.

http://members.aol.com/IJBall/WWW//TV.html
Web site for Ian J. Ball's rec.arts.tv FAQ.

http://www.nielsenmedia.com/
Nielsen Media Research.

http://livingisland.com
A Sid & Marty Krofft Home Page.

Network Web Sites

A&E	http://www.aetv.com/
ABC	http://www.abc.com
AMC	http://www.amctv.com/
BBC	http://www.bbc.co.uk
CBC	http://www.cbc.ca
CBS	http://www.cbs.com
CNBC	http://www.cnbc.com/
CNN	http://www.cnn.com/
Comedy Central	http://www.comedycentral.com/
Court TV	http://www.courttv.com/
C-SPAN	http://www.c-span.org/
Discovery	http://www.discovery.com
E!	http://www.eonline.com/
ESPN	http://espnet.sportszone.com

So I gave him a title." In the show's final episode, Holzman added dialogue to clarify that Jordan was a "rudimentary reader with low literacy skills." Holzman also encountered a somewhat different dilemma when dealing with the Internet. Her show was floundering in the ratings when Operation Life Support sprang up on the Net.

"That's such a complicated subject," she said. "When it started, I felt nothing but gratitude. Any time you have any type of fans, it's always very intoxicating. Here were people who clearly felt passionately [enough] about the show to try to keep it going. Of course, that made us feel thrilled that people were doing that for the show. Other aspects were less simple."

Holzman said she felt it was important to keep her distance from the campaign because she was the show's creator, not its crusader.

"We were not involved in the save *My So-Called Life* campaign; we were *My So-Called Life*. We were by definition not comrades with these people; we could not join with them; we could not change what they were doing. We were cognizant of it, but nobody had any experience with this Internet thing, and it was a little confusing sometimes to realize the intensity of what was going on. I felt it was important not to get involved with them; there had to be a separation of church and state. I still feel that it was not quite clear to them."

Steve Joyner, founder of Operation Life Support, disagreed. He said it was always clear; they knew Holzman told the cast to keep their distance from OLS. The first contact Joyner had with any of the cast came when cast member Devon Odessa's mother called him followed by a call from Devon Gummersall's father. To Holzman, the on-line campaign was a mixed bag.

"[The on-line support] quickly became a double-edged sword," Holzman said. "These people who I totally thanked—How could I not thank them? But they were going out on a limb not for us [but] for themselves. Sometimes you don't want people doing too much for you because you're afraid of what it will mean." Holzman became frustrated further when OLS started selling tapes of *My So-Called Life*. "It's illegal," she said. "That is how we make our living, and they were selling bootleg copies. That's my work and our work that's supposed to benefit us as a career, not to be bootlegged and sold over the Internet. It's a rather serious thing to us. I'm not accusing anybody of making a profit, this all came of good intentions, but on some level elements of things were happening that I was uncomfortable with."

Food TV	http://www.foodtv.com/
Fox	http://www.foxnetwork.com/
FX	http://www.fxnetworks.com/
HBO	http://www.homebox.com/
History	http://www.historychannel.com/
Lifetime	http://www.lifetimetv.com/
MTV	http://mtv.com/
NBC	http://www.nbc.com
Nick	http://www.nick-at-nite.com/
Pay-per-view	http://www.ppv.com/
PBS	http://www.pbs.org
QVC	http://www.qvc.com/
Sci-Fi	http://www.scifi.com/
Showtime	http://showtimeonline.com/
TBS, TNT, TCM	http://www.turner.com/
UPN	http://www.upn.com/
The WB	http://www.thewb.com
Weather	http://www.weather.com/

Steve Joyner said he was aware that making copies of the tapes was illegal but so was using the show's logo on OLS T-shirts and using ABC photos in his book about OLS. "We violated every copyright in the book," he said. "But no one's making any money off it [because OLS is nonprofit]. Can we be sued? Yeah. Will we [be sued]? Not likely." Joyner said he resisted selling video tapes of the episodes at first but gave in to pressure from fans of the series. He announced their availability as "a premium for donations," so technically he wasn't selling the tapes. A complete set of the 19 episodes of *My So-Called Life* could be had for a $90 donation.

Although some of the actions of OLS bothered Holzman, it didn't stop her and coexecutive producer Scott Winant from going on-line for an organized chat session with fans at the height of the save *My So-Called Life* campaign. "I wanted to go on-line in some way that had some sort of boundaries," Holzman said. "We loved it. We answered peoples' questions, and we did that on purpose. It was my way of responding to what at the time was a huge amount of on-line chat. Everything was reaching a crescendo, and we wanted to talk to the on-line fans."

Even after that positive experience, Holzman shied away from becoming a regular presence on-line. She saw it simply as a matter of keeping herself from the thoughts, suggestions, and desires of fans. "I did not want the show to be what everyone on-line thought it should be. I didn't want it to make me self-conscious. I didn't want to start doing things they asked for, not because they asked, but I wanted to remain true to what I was doing." Holzman did like the fact that the Internet gave her greater feedback on what people liked about the show, especially given its low ratings. When she wrote for *thirtysomething,* Holzman said she received fan mail, but much less and much longer after an episode she wrote aired. "This was like the next day after it aired. It was a living breathing thing, and as a writer there's nothing better than that. . . . It makes me feel like we were having quite the effect. ABC was constantly implying that nobody was watching the show, so in many ways, for me, I could see with my own eyes the intensity of the reaction. It kept me inspired; that was one of the reasons I was so grateful to Steve Joyner. It had nothing to do with staying on air, it had to do with the passion and intensity of the response and saying this is so worthwhile that I'm going to fight for it at a time it was quite helpful to feel that way. It wasn't, 'Thank God, I hope this man and his group can keep us on the air.' I didn't believe that. It was a corporate decision. I thought possibly they'd have influence, but I did not really believe the decision was in my hands or Steve Joyner's hands."

One aspect of the Internet that frustrates many people from all walks of life is its anonymity. Are people who they say they are? Is a person telling the truth? One *My So-Called Life* fan posted a report to the newsgroup in July 1995 about meeting actress Lisa Waltz (who played Hallie Lowenthal in the show) at a Los Angeles restaurant. According to the post, Waltz said a general storyline for the show's second season had been developed. The scenario outlined in the post included such details as the opening of Hallie and Graham's restaurant, where Rickie would work as a busboy. Graham would leave Patti

for Hallie, causing Angela to run away from home. Eventually, Graham would return to his wife, but not until everyone involved had suffered much angst. The show's executive producer denied that anything had been decided about second-season storylines.

"I decided I wasn't going to do that on a serious level," Holzman said. "I'd talked about it vaguely with [executive producers] Marshall [Herskovitz] and Ed [Zwick], but the truth is that I was insecure and felt the show was probably not going to get picked up, so we didn't want to make a lot of plans that weren't going to happen."

As for the storyline suggested in the newsgroup posting, Holzman said it should not be believed. "I may have said something to Lisa at one point, but that does not sound real," she said. "I never seriously thought about that. It just doesn't sound real unless she was making it as a joke."

Did someone really meet Waltz at a restaurant? Did she say that, or was the whole story of the meeting fabricated? Fans on the Net never got an answer. Another rumor that surfaced on-line was that there would be a *My So-Called Life* TV movie that would wrap up the loose ends. Holzman denied that too, saying she was happy with the way the show ended.

Taking a different approach, *Party of Five* coexecutive producer/director Ken Topolsky said in an e-mail interview that he enjoys communicating with fans on-line. "I reply to every letter and try to participate in every chat," Topolsky said. "I see no minus to interacting with the fans. It's very gratifying to 'know' so many of them personally. Too often we feel as if we produce our shows in a vacuum. This more personal touch keeps us honest." Topolsky even posted to the show's mailing list asking fans not to bother the people who live in the house used for exterior establishing shots in the series.

Even Marta Kauffman of *Friends,* who is not on-line, said producers shouldn't totally discount fan input when it's brought to them by network executives, especially if a show isn't working. "Any producer should listen to the network and see if there's a way to make it work," Kauffman said. "If a show is working and the network tries to force changes on you, it's not a good situation. It should be a communication. If they read something on the Internet and want a change based on that, it would depend on what it was and if it was a good idea. The network wants to keep the monkey [on *Friends*]; I don't know if that has to do with the Internet, but we have to get rid of the monkey."

Former *90210* executive producer Charles Rosin said feedback from the Net has become less important the more popular it's become. "I think some of our people surf through to see what is being said, but it's less of a germane barometer than it was 2 to 4 years ago," Rosin said in 1995. "In the first year, people were on the *Beverly Hills* group talking among themselves, and they had no clue that people were looking to see what they had to say. At this point, there's a self-consciousness about it."

Suits on the Net

Just as TV producers are using the Net in varying amounts, so are researchers at the major TV networks. Larry Gianinno, vice-president of program research for ABC, said his network uses on-line services to research the teen audience, which watches that network in large numbers because of the network's Friday TGIF strategy. But even if they set up a special bulletin board to conduct research, one hazard remains—they never really know who they're talking to.

At CBS, David Poltrack said they use on-line services to research in two ways. When *The Late Show with David Letterman* premiered in August 1993, the network sponsored a demographics survey on Prodigy, offering to enter participants in a drawing for a new VCR. He said 15,000 people took the survey. The information was used to develop a panel of 1,000 people who were given free access to the bulletin board. "These people were polled regularly about different things and that helped us get an idea of the initial reactions," Poltrack said. "It was helpful because it was very tightly structured."

Poltrack said CBS would never make any definite moves or assumptions about a program based on the dialogue picked up off the Internet. He said a fairly fanatical fringe element populates these boards and the same people direct the discussions in ways they might not naturally go if people were just sitting around a room together talking about a show. Because these people feel passionately about "their show," they can't be regarded as a reliable sample. Poltrack said lurking on bulletin boards and newsgroups offers clues that can lead to the shaping of further studies.

"You still have to do quantitative studies, telephone tracking studies, and all the other research," Poltrack said. "If the ratings for a show are going down, and you're trying to find out why, you can get indications. People on the Internet felt a show got screwed up when this character left, so in a survey of the general public, let's ask a question and focus it in that way."

The network cybernauts encounter most often in newsgroups is Fox. Charles Kennedy, vice-president of program research at Fox, said his network often uses the Internet to gauge viewer feedback, but again it's used in conjunction with more traditional research methods such as focus groups and phone surveys. "I really like the instantaneousness of the response I can get," Kennedy said in an article I wrote for the *Times-Dispatch* in July 1994. "I'm able to hop on and place a message on a bulletin board, and within five hours I'll have 150 messages. The other thing I like about the Net is the honesty of people. I think they feel much more open and blunt when typing something. In a focus room or on the phone, they feel compelled to be somewhat polite. On the Internet, you don't have to be polite. The drawback is that sometimes you get extreme reactions."

Kennedy has been on-line since late 1993 and has access to the various on-line services and the Internet itself. Although he can pick up a copy of the Nielsen ratings in his office every morning, the Nielsens only say how many people watched a program, not what they thought of it. That's when Kennedy gets on the Net. "In our business, shows often will get a very big number when they premiere because everyone wants to check it out, so a big number may have no relationship to success," Kennedy said in a March 1995 interview at his office on the Fox lot in West Hollywood. "It may mean people were tricked into watching a lousy show they hated and will never come back, or the reverse could be true. When *90210* premiered it was a small number, but the people who showed up loved it and it grew. I never had the opportunity to be on-line back then to know what was going on. We had to go out and test it and that takes time. It takes almost a week to set up a test and get people in there and have them respond and look at the results and analyze what they said and come up with the result. We have a show tomorrow night, *VR.5*, which is going to air, and by midnight . . . I'll have a pretty good idea of what people thought about the show. What the on-line environment won't tell me is how many people shared that feeling."

Kennedy said he will pass along Internet comments to a show's producers although he said many of them are on-line themselves, gathering such information. They can find out the flaws and the things that work right away from reading people's on-line posts. Instead of helping producers discover what the problems are, he can keep track of the messages to quantify how deeply rooted the feelings are and how many people share that view. In fall 1994, Kennedy went on-line after the first *Alien Nation* reunion movie aired and asked viewers what they thought about it: "We'd like to hear what people think of the *Alien Nation* movie that just aired this Tuesday (October 25). Would you like to see this come back as a regular series? As a series of movies?"

When the *Melrose Place* spin-off *Models Inc.* was being developed, Kennedy said he did a phone and Internet survey to see what the show should be called. Some of the titles participants rejected were *Cover Girls*, *Dream Chasers*, *Objects of Desire*, *Glamour Girls*, *Jet Set*, *Exposure*. On the day *Models Inc.* premiered in summer 1994, Kennedy posted a message to the *Melrose Place* newsgroup and for the first time solicited feedback on a program. Elissa Milenky, a 24-year-old newspaper reporter in Roanoke, Virginia, fired off this response to Kennedy after watching the first episode of *Models Inc.* She shared a copy of her message with me: "1. Someone please get Sue Ellen's son—I mean Hillary's son—some acting lessons. 2. Making the photographer an obsessive psycho is a nice touch. 3. How could Teri have had Sue Ellen's—I mean, Hillary's—clothing fibers under her nails when Hillary was wearing leather? 4. I like Carrie; she seems more normal than the others. I'm curious to see if she kidnaps *The Greatest American Hero*'s son."

Many of Milenky's comments, particularly those concerning the character of Hillary's son, were echoed on the *Melrose Place* newsgroup (before the creation of the *Models Inc.* newsgroup). A few months later, that character was sent on a trip to a fashion show in Europe and never returned. "We were given feedback and we met with the producers and we met with Aaron Spelling . . . and we explained the concerns that people have," Kennedy said.

"We had research from focus groups and surveys and, at the same time, we said when we go on-line, we hear the same things. Which one the [producers] believed, we don't know, but because they were hearing it from multiple sources, [Spelling] gave it more credibility."

Kennedy said on-line comments are also passed along to Fox programming executives who have input on creative decisions. He said, sometimes hearing about something on-line helps confirm ideas that executives have already bandied about. Someone sent him e-mail suggesting a *Married . . . with Children* bloopers show after watching the series' 200th episode special, an idea that had been discussed internally in the past. Fox executives were told a suggestion for the same type of show came from a viewer via the Net. "Because we brought it up as a perspective outside the core circle of executives, suddenly the president of the entertainment division, John Matoian, is going, 'Yeah we should look into that.' Turns out they don't keep that material so there's a reason we couldn't do it, but we went ahead and investigated it anyway. So their perspective is often given more weight, and I think what happens is that their comments are used more for confirmation of what is already going on and taking place at Fox."

Echoing Poltrack's earlier comments, Kennedy said the on-line world acts as a leading indicator and helps in decision making rather than being the sole reason for a decision. He added that the speed with which opinions are offered on the Internet is also beneficial. "In this business, decisions are made quickly," Kennedy said. "You have to make it that day often times because scripts are being written in advance and things are being cast and shot in advance and you have to decide. By the time we get feedback to an episode that's on the air, they're shooting the sixth episode down the line and they're already writing the script for the tenth. If I have to test something, it will take one week sometimes, and we've lost all that time. This will help us."

Net Law

Many producers are going on-line and chatting with fans, and the networks love the free publicity their shows get, but legal issues are beginning to muddy the waters. Gary Goldberg, 31, of Bowie, Maryland, created a site devoted to *The Simpsons* (http://www.digimark.net/TheSimpsons/) in winter 1993 that featured copyrighted *Simpsons* pictures, sounds, and video clips. Goldberg said he realized he was violating copyrights, so after founding his own company, DigiMark, he made a preemptive effort to smooth things over by contacting a publicist for Fox and Gracie Films.

"I explained what the nature of the site and what its special relationship to alt.tv.simpsons was and the fan impact, etc.," Goldberg wrote in an e-mail interview. "I also provided [the publicist] with a copy of the FAQ and copies of magazine articles and newspaper reports of our activities (*Philadelphia Inquirer, Phoenix Gazette, Entertainment Weekly*). All of this was to obtain the proper permission to continue what we were doing. I offered to sign over control of the content, and I also offered the full services of DigiMark for free. She seemed very interested and enthusiastic and promised a call back within a few days. When I called her a week later, she was very frosty and said I could expect a cease/desist order from Fox legal. Of course, the fact that the www.springfield.com [official Fox] site appeared two months later would not have been connected to this—sure."

Goldberg said he never received the cease and desist order, but he removed the material anyway for fear of the consequences. His *Simpsons* site still exists but without any of the copyright-violating material. This however was not the case for *Spellingland,* a Web site created by Tom Zoerner, a 26-year-old computer science major at Friedrich-Alexander University in Germany. "I began with the *90210* FAQ only," he said in an e-mail interview. "Later I added some updates that I had saved from the alt.tv.bh90210 newsgroup. Then Rose Ellen Auerbach contacted me; she was searching for an archive site for her *90210* and *Melrose Place* summaries. So I added *MP* to my archive. I think that was when I started calling it *Spellingland.* The original idea was just to have a permanent place for the frequently asked stuff so that it doesn't need to be posted over and over again. Later, I added everything I found. It was fun maintaining a well-visited Website."

Zoerner said this all started in February 1994. The site grew to the point where it received 80,000 visits per week. Zoerner said he even corresponded with *90210* supervising producer Larry Mollin and Charles Kennedy of Fox research and received no negative feedback about his site. That changed June

14, 1995, when his supervisors at the university received a letter from Greer Bosworth, senior counsel for the Spelling Entertainment Group. She wrote that Zoerner was using the university's computers to "load and retrieve unauthorized information about Spelling's productions." Zoerner said her complaint also cited the use of names and logos, which are protected by the laws of trademark and copyright.

"My boss took this first letter quite relaxed, so I decided I could risk a second of Spelling's attacks and just took the complaint literally: I removed all of the logos, replaced the names with shortcuts or some other sort of identification (like *9*210* for *90210*), removed a few more stuff that might infringe someone's copyright (frameclips, sounds, articles) and went on-line again," Zoerner said.

But only a few days after Zoerner's revised site went on-line, his supervisors received another letter. "Mr. [*sic*] Bosworth told us how 'surprised' he was, that I intended to 'resume use of Spelling materials'." Zoerner wrote. "He was basically repeating his demands—totally ignoring the modifications at my site. There were no further explanations what exactly he was referring to, why he wanted me to remove it, or which legal basis his complaints had. . . . So I got a direct order to remove all of my material about Spelling's shows, even despite the fact that I wasn't doing anything illegal."

"Our point is to protect the marks," Bosworth said in a phone interview. "They're registered in the U.S. Trademark office. Anytime we see someone using it without our authorization it behooves us to send a cease and desist letter informing that it is a protected mark." Certainly this is understandable. Zoerner's original site did contain material that violated copyright laws. But what about the second site that contained no copyrighted material, no pictures, no logos, no sound clips, just episode summaries and information about the Spelling TV shows? Wouldn't Spelling Entertainment be happy for the publicity and for a fan-created site devoted to its programs?

"That's your take on that," Bosworth responded. "Our concern again is the misuse of our trademarks, logos, and copyright."

She said another reason for Spelling's concern is that use of logos not only infringes on Spelling but also on Spelling's licensees who sell Spelling merchandise. If Spelling doesn't protect the use of its trademarks, then the value of the marks will be less and the amount of money Spelling can get from a licensee will be less. This may be the case with Zoerner's site. Not long after it was shut down in summer 1995, an official *Melrose Place* Web site debuted (http://www.melroseplace.com/). "OnRamp has exclusive rights to use the characters, character names, and title for *Melrose Place*," Bosworth said in October 1995. "It's a pretty new relationship."

The connection between the closing of Zoerner's site and the creation of the official site could not be verified, but it's a safe bet that 1 + 1 = 2. What if Zoerner had defied the second demand that he shut his site down? Could Spelling have won a lawsuit? Aren't episode summaries and FAQs protected under fair comment and criticism? That's just one of the many questions facing Internet denizens who build shrines to TV shows. It's a question that will undoubtedly be answered in the next few years as more Internet litigation makes its way through the court system.

In the end, the relationship between the Internet and TV can be broken down into four segments:

1. Sheer corporate hype at the Web sites created by the networks and studios. These on-line commercials are somewhat useful for viewers if they include episode guides, downloadable pictures, and interviews with a show's stars.
2. On-line chat by random people giving their opinions about TV shows in newsgroups and chat rooms. This independent community of viewers can produce intelligent thoughtful discussions or pure drivel.
3. Insiders participating in the more thoughtful Net-based discussions by offering explanations and inside information not available elsewhere. These people can also take back suggestions from viewers that have the potential to be incorporated into their programs.
4. On-line entertainment in the form of actual programs such as *The Spot* whose roots can be traced back to television.

Channel Surfing into the Sunset

Speculating on the future of Gen X TV is a no-win task. Things are moving so fast today that even by the time this book is published any predictions may already be proved inaccurate. The multimedia revolution is on, and nothing can stop it. Still, it appears some clear trends won't be changing soon.

Future Sights and Sound

7

The pace of television will never return to what it once was. Leisurely paced dramas are ancient relics. Serialized sitcoms and dramas will continue. The fast-moving feel of *ER* and *NYPD Blue* will become common. Likewise, music will continue to play a big part in television. Forget Ted Harbert's 1994 decree; despite audience erosion, the theme song is not yet a relic. Music not only draws in viewers and helps a program maintain a quick pace it also benefits the entertainment conglomerates that now control all aspects of the media. Warner Bros. doesn't just make a TV show anymore. They make a TV show with the potential to be spun-off into a soundtrack, a World Wide Web site, a CD-ROM game, and, eventually, a motion picture, all created in-house by one of its many subsidiaries. Although this won't happen in all cases, when the opportunity presents itself, the entertainment empires (Disney-ABC, Time-Warner-Turner, CBS-Westinghouse, Fox, Paramount-Viacom, Sony) will take full advantage of their synergy, at least until they're declared monopolies and are forced to cast off some of their segments.

Future
Demographics

TV will probably never see a slip back into the 1980s when there were few twentysomethings anywhere on the tube. Even after Gen X has moved out of its 20s, youth will maintain a presence on TV because of networks such as Fox, WB, UPN, Cartoon Network, Sci-Fi Channel, MTV, and Nick. Even as Xers age and are replaced by future generations, TV will likely continue its fascination with young adult life. Just as the Boomers are feeling younger than their parents, Xers will feel younger than Boomers and continue to stay in tune with some aspects of youth culture. TV's demographic dial is set for youth and that is unlikely to change.

Viewers are already seeing a Gen X backlash from the *Friends* clones that flooded network schedules in 1995. Even older actors are becoming resentful of Gen X dominance. Taylor Negron, who played TV station manager Gwillem Blatt on *Hope & Gloria*, denounced Gen Xers in *Total TV*, a cable TV magazine. "TV will lose touch with what's really happening," he said. "This whole Generation X thing. These people go, 'What about my generation?' I didn't even have a generation when I was 25. I didn't even know I was in a generation'."

For fall 1996, the trend was away from sitcoms focusing on twentysomethings to *X-Files* ripoffs such as *Dark Skies* (NBC), *The Burning Zone* (UPN), and *Millennium* (Fox) or movie spin-offs such as *Dangerous Minds* and *Clueless* on ABC and *Party Girl* on Fox. Fox didn't add any new programs aimed at black viewers, so the WB and UPN decided to focus on this audience. *The Steve Harvey Show* and *The Jamie Foxx Show* received time slots on the WB while UPN picked up *Sparks* starring Robin Givens, *Homeboys in Outer Space*, *Goode Behavior*, starring Sherman Hemsley, and *Malcolm and Eddie*, featuring former *Cosby Show* kid Malcolm-Jamal Warner.

Of the approximately 40 new shows on tap for fall 1996, only a few (Fox's *Party Girl* and *Lush Life*, ABC's *Townies* and *Relativity*) seem geared specifically to Xers. In the immediate future, shows about and catering to Gen X will continue to be created although probably not at the rate they were in 1995. The failure of so many Xer-based sitcoms has undoubtedly left a bad taste in the mouths of network programmers. Viewers will see more of Gen X, but not more of the same Gen X. As Xers continue to age, the depiction of friends as family will eventually decline as Xers form more traditional nuclear families. The failure of Darren Star's *Central Park West* proved there is a saturation point for prime time soaps, so that cycle is probably on its way into hibernation, waiting for the next generation to reinvent it again. "Maybe the lesson [the networks] are going to learn where this generation is concerned is that even though this generation seems very willing to be pandered to, you can't condescend to the product," said *USA Today* TV critic Matt Roush in an interview. "You can't just put out crap and expect them to buy it just because it looks like the other crap they've been buying. You've got to find your own twist to it."

At this writing, *Beverly Hills, 90210* is in its sixth season and Fox is grooming *Party of Five* to take its place. Although people continue to tune in to watch the exploits of Brandon, Kelly, and Steve, even this hit show will not last much longer. The characters are growing tired, the plots are weak, and the characters are in their senior year of college. Charles Rosin, *90210* executive producer during its first five seasons, admitted that the show's time has come and gone. Rosin said during his show's first season there was a feeling in America that things were beginning to change. The Republican domination of the 1980s soon gave way to the Clinton 1990s. "There really was a notion that something was changing," he said. "We were a show of a different era that was not as bleak as what exists now. We had changes in Eastern Europe, the promise of peace, that we could make inroads and strides. That idealism was all around." There's nothing ironic, cynical, or angry about *90210,* which makes it seem particularly out-of-touch with the audience that once adored it. Now that a pessimistic, paranoid, apathetic stagnancy has taken over the country and the culture, *90210* seems particularly quaint.

A new era is beginning, and television will be forced to change along with society. Today's teens have infinitely more choices than most Xers had. Today's young people grew up in a world in which MTV and Fox always existed. Cable TV is a part of most households. While today's teens can't come home and watch *The Brady Bunch* on a local station everyday at 4:00 P.M. as Xers did, they can just click over to cable and still find Carol and Mike dispensing valuable life lessons. "There's this kid I work with who's 14," said Bradyphile Erin Smith. "I was talking to him about *Mork & Mindy* and he goes, 'That show from Nick at Night?'"

As a result of technology, teens of the 1990s not only have Gen X culture at their disposal, but a culture all their own that's in its infancy. In a survey published in *USA Today* in October 1995, teens 15 to 18 said that of the activities they enjoy most, half involved the entertainment industry. Will a show become a part of the next generation's TV lore as the Bradys did with Xers? Possibly, but it's less likely. So many more things out there are competing for kids' attention, not only more channels on TV but also the infinite realm of the Net. All Xers had were a few TV channels; there's no longer the possibility for any one thing to catch on because the culture has expanded to such a degree. As much as some parents of Xers used the TV as an electronic babysitter in the 1970s, today's kids get an even greater dosage from cable and the VCR. When older Xers were growing up, no one owned a copy of a Disney movie. Today, it's a given in some families that the moment the latest animated flick is on sale for $12.99 at the drugstore, it will be purchased and added to the home video library.

Future Nostalgia

Even the amount of time it takes a film or TV show to move through the windows of distribution has been accelerated to a hyperpace. In the early 1980s, it took much longer before a theatrical release was broadcast on network TV. *Jurassic Park* went from multiplexes to NBC in less than two years. Even *My So-Called Life,* a failed TV series by Nielsen standards, jumped from ABC to MTV before it was canceled by ABC. "That was instant nostalgia," Matt Roush said. "People already thought the show was history, but the show never got a chance to rerun on ABC. They ran the 19 episodes straight through without reruns; it was always new, and that's why they were done in January. Everything is very immediate with this culture, and it's all done on a multimedia level with everything so magnified and exaggerated. It either dies quick or hits big quick. The fact that *My So-Called Life,* within the cycle of its first season and not knowing whether it would come back for its second season, got stripped on a cable network, which usually takes a show a couple of years to do, shows the very disposable nature of television [because] there's so much of it now."

A cable channel devoted to flop TV shows, although certainly not on the immediate horizon, is conceivable. Xers will demand it. They want to be able to see shows they grew up watching that the networks took away after a short time. Unsuccessful programs have an inherent cult appeal. It can't be long before the Cult TV network is created to showcase the likes of *Once a Hero* and *The Nutt House*. Future flops would have a permanent oasis, and they could move from the networks to this specialized service within months. Such a network has yet to be developed, but a precursor emerged in April 1996 with the launch of Nick at Nite's TV Land network. TV Land even billed itself in ads as "the 24-hour network obsessed with TV."

Future Prime Time

It's not just Xers who are changing television. Baby Boomers, who made their greatest mark on the TV landscape in the 1980s, continue to change the rules. Just as *The Simpsons* makes fun of shows such as *Matlock,* Boomers are less likely to sit down for an hour with Jessica Fletcher. Like Xers, Boomers would rather tune in to see *Friends.* "In the past, when people got older they became old," said Charles Kennedy of Fox. "But as Baby Boomers become older, they haven't changed the rest of their lives."

Larry Gianinno of ABC agreed, saying there is both psychological age and chronological age, and for Boomers, psychological age is an important factor. Even as Boomers age chronologically, the age they consider themselves to be remains a strong governing force in their lives, Gianinno said. Following this logic, it should be easier for the networks to capture more Gen Xers and Boomers. Although the shows that targeted solely Gen X in fall 1995 flopped, the hits that have emerged since (*3rd Rock from the Sun*) have had great appeal to the mass audience that includes both Boomers and Xers.

For fall 1996, the networks went with this strategy, relying more on brand-name performers (Bill Cosby, Ted Danson, Michael J. Fox, and Brooke

Shields) rather than ripoffs of what's popular. These actors are all 1980s stars with mass appeal to both Boomers and Generation X. By creating vehicles the networks think will attract a broader spectrum of the viewing public, they hope to be in a better position to stem audience erosion. Ad buyers don't think they'll succeed. "Really, there's nothing here on the fall schedule to make people change their viewing schedules and come back from cable to broadcast," Gene DeWitt of DeWitt Media told Kinney Littlefield of the *Orange County Register* in May 1996. "I don't know what the networks can do, especially [when] cable keeps offering new options." Tim Brooks, coauthor of *The Complete Directory to Prime Time Network and Cable TV Shows* and senior vice-president of research for cable's USA Networks, predicted in April 1996 that by late 1997 or early 1998 the cable networks will have a greater audience share than the broadcast networks. Cable will be watched by 44 percent of TV viewers, Brooks predicted, surpassing the big three broadcast networks, whose combined share of the audience will be 39 percent. Brooks's study didn't account for Fox, WB, or UPN. While it's a near certainty that his prediction will come true eventually, 1998 may be a bit too soon. What about the threat from the Net? *Wired* magazine predicted in April 1996 that on-line ad spending would eclipse network TV ad spending by 2014. In the end, the Internet could prove to be more damaging to cable viewership than broadcast network viewership because it's still the broadcast networks that account for the bulk of TV culture.

TV talking about TV will likely end its epidemic soon too. Xers like their old TV shows, but they don't need to be reminded of them every time they watch a present-day sitcom. When shows like *Family Matters* start referring to other TV programs, it will be clear that this novelty has reached the peak of its popularity.

Future Computer-TV Integration

As changes in the media landscape continue, the one near certainty is the evolution of the computer and its integration with the TV. For today's children, this innovation will be akin to the impact cable TV and the VCR had on

Generation X. Soon the TV and computer video monitor will be one. On-line services may have to switch from using phone lines to more powerful cable lines, but the integration of the two tubes will happen. Not long ago it was predicted that consumers soon would have video-on-demand, and clearly, that is on the way. Viewers wil just dial up the cable company and the episode of *Seinfeld* they missed last week will be downloaded to their entertainment centers for the price of a video rental at Blockbuster. The big question is how long it will take before this technology is available to the general public.

In the meantime, TV and the Internet will continue to meld. Soon the Net will be more than promotional Web sites encouraging viewers to watch TV. Already, cybersoaps offer interactivity, and more programming for the Web is on the way. This is beginning to impact traditional television. In a 1995 survey by the Emerging Technologies Research Group, one-third of Internet users surveyed spent less time watching TV once they began hopping on the Net.

With the early 1996 introduction of Gateway 2000's Destination computer, viewers can surf the Net and watch TV at the same time on the same machine. This $4,000 entertainment center features a 31-inch TV screen with remote plus a keyboard and mouse. Even as the Net and TV continue to merge, the people pushing this new technology think traditional TV will survive. "There will continue to be a demand for passive entertainment," said Eric Hirshberg of *The Spot* World Wide Web site. "People like *Seinfeld;* people like *The X-Files;* they like to sit and not interact. It won't go away; it will be added to. TV didn't replace radio; it changed radio just like radio didn't replace print. What the Internet will create is a new demand that won't replace the existing demand." *Advertising Age* critic Bob Garfield is also certain the Internet will bring about profound changes. "It is going to change our entire relationship to our television, telephones, computers, entertainment, almost every aspect of our home and business lives," Garfield said. "What way that will happen, I don't have the vaguest idea. It's all being sorted out and it will be sorted out rapidly."

In the year 2010, the structure of television will likely be a far cry from what viewers see today. Maybe by then individual viewers will play programmer, scheduling what they want to watch when they want to watch it. Until that happens, the Net will continue to be used to rally around low-rated TV shows although as these campaigns become more numerous, they're likely to have less effect. How long will TV show producers continue to go to the Net? Will it remain a valuable source for feedback or become a realm dominated by only the most rabid fans? The evolution of copyright law will also impact how close fans can get to their shows. Will Web shrines devoted to *The X-Files* that include publicity stills be appreciated by the copyright owners for the free publicity, or will they be targeted by lawyers?

Future Gen X Culture

The spring 1996 sitcoms that tried to reintegrate black and white culture (*Buddies* and *The Show*) failed in the Nielsen ratings, which may or may not have had anything to do with their attempts to mend race relations. Depending on whether society returns to the "melting pot" theory or remains in the current "salad bowl" state, TV will reflect that decision. Either white sitcoms will stay white and black sitcoms will stay black or the two cultures will come together and there will only be sitcoms without a skin color modifier. If the chasm grows, viewers could even see a growth in the niche marketing of television networks aimed at specific groups of people. With the projected future growth of minority populations in America, TV will be a key indicator of the racial reality of American culture for better or for worse.

The improved economy is helping to change the fortunes of Generation X. Xers still can't get the jobs they want in corporate America, but instead of complaining about it, they're striking out on their own. These young entrepreneurs are finding luck in the growing technology fields, especially on the Net. Just look at the success of the twentysomethings behind the Netscape World Wide Web browser. They became millionaires overnight when they took their company public. Xers taking advantage of this technology work as Web page designers, a job that is becoming to the 1990s what advertising was in the 1980s.

It's likely that Xers will learn a lesson from the divorce-prone Baby Boomers and attempt to stick things out. The divorce rate may even start to fall as Xers, who are waiting much longer before marrying, create more stable family environments. They will likely monitor their children's' intake of television more carefully than Boomer parents did. Xers love their TV, but they also recognize that it can be abused. TV may have been their baby-sitter, but Xers know in retrospect that they would have been better off spending that time with a parent. With the creation of the V-chip, Xer parents will have more control over what their children watch and the ability to protect them from programming they deem unsuitable. But will they allow the Net to baby-sit their children as TV baby-sat Xers?

So it comes back to Generation X and television, two creations—one biological and sociological, one electronic—forever linked in a mutually shared culture. It's a journey that started 30 years ago and will continue for another 60 years. TV shows will come and go, technology will continue to change, and chronicling the results of the multimedia revolution will be left to the next generation.

Biblio-graphy

Articles

Alexander, Rob. "Metropolitan Diary." *New York Times*, Apr. 12, 1995, C2.

"American Internet User Survey." Emerging Technologies Research Group, 1955.

Associated Press. "Television's Loss Is Internet's Gain." *Richmond Times-Dispatch*, Jan. 13, 1996, B6.

Bash, Alan. "Cable May Top Ratings by 1997." *USA Today*, Apr. 2, 1996, 3D.

——. "Competitive *Living* among *Friends*." *USA Today*, Dec. 15, 1994, 3D.

——. "Once-Strong ABC Hungry for a Hit.," *USA Today*, Feb. 20, 1996, 3D.

Bellafante, Ginia. "Cyberspace, 90210." *Time*, Mar. 4, 1996.

——. "Stop the Inanity!" *Time*, May 13, 1996, 85.

Beller, Miles. "*Wild Oats*." *Hollywood Reporter*, Sept. 1, 1994.

Boeck, Scott, and Gary Visgaitis. "Teenagers Plug into Fun." *USA Today*, Oct. 19, 1995, D1.

Boehlert, Eric. "Buzz Been." *Rolling Stone*, May 2, 1996, 19.

Brown, Joe. "Silverstone's Sassy *Clueless*." *Washington Post*, July 21, 1995, Weekend, 38.

Carmody, John. "The TV Column." *Washington Post*, May 29, 1996, Style, F10.

"Cheers and Jeers." *TV Guide*, May 13, 1995, 8.

"Computer Users Turned On, Not Tuned In." *Richmond Times-Dispatch*, Oct. 16, 1995, A1.

Coupland, Douglas. "Generation X'd." *Details*, June 1995, 72.

"David Jacobs." *Daily Variety*, Jan. 25, 1993.

"Decision to Drop Actor Leaves Vacancy at *Melrose Place*." *Vancouver Sun*, May 21, 1992, C9.

"Defining the Internet Opportunity." O'Reilly & Associates, Oct. 1, 1955.

Duffy, Mike. *My So-Called Life* article. Knight Ridder News Service, Jan 26, 1995.

Dunn, Jancee. "The Fresh Ones: Video of the Moment." *Rolling Stone* Mar. 21, 1996 32.

Durden, Douglas. "CBS Chief Admits Mistake in Making So Many Changes." *Richmond Times-Dispatch*, Jan. 15, 1996, E5.

——. "Fox Scores with *Beverly Hills*." *Richmond Times-Dispatch*, Oct. 4, 1990, D6.

Enrico, Dottie and Bruce Horovitz. "Madison Ave. Rates the Ads of '94." *USA Today*, Dec. 29, 1994, B1.

Farhi, Paul. "On TV, Madison Ave. Sets the Dial for Youth." *Washington Post* Sep. 16, 1994, A1.

"50 Great Things about Television Now." *TV Guide*, Mar. 9, 1996, 23.

Fisher, Christy. "Mentos: Cool Advertising Freshens Older Brand." *Advertising Age*, Oct. 3, 1994, S3.

"For What It's Worth." *The Viewer*, June 1995, 5.

Frank, Betsy. "Primetime Program Development 1995–1996." Zenith Media, July 31, 1995.

"Fresh Faces '95." *People*, Dec. 25, 1995–Jan. 1, 1996, 127.

Fretts, Bruce. "British Invasion." *Entertainment Weekly*, July 21, 1995, 32–36.

Garfield, Bob. "Subaru Turns On to Grunge, But the Spot Is a Turnoff." *Advertising Age*, Mar. 22, 1993, 54.

Gay, Verne. "WB's Foxy Movies." *Newsday*, Jan. 11, 1995, B4.

Givotovsky, Nicholas, Mark Kvamme, and Ted Leonsis. "Boom or Bust? A Panel of Predictions for the Year Ahead." *Mediaweek*, Feb. 6, 1995, IQ24.

Gunther, Marc. "Television Meets Computing in a New Two-in-One Product." Knight-Ridder wire, March 21, 1996.

Harding, Janet. "Class of '96," *The Viewer*, Apr. 1993, 14.

Harrington, Richard. "Rock Around the Clock: From 'I Want My MTV' to 'Anything MTV Wants'—10 Years of Music Television." *Washington Post*, July 28, 1991, G1

Holbert, Ginny. "X Marks Spot for *Friends* on Thursday." *Chicago Sun-Times*, Sep. 22, 1994, sect. 2, 43.

Honeycutt, Kirk. "Kroffts' *Lost* Lands at Disney for Big Screen." *Hollywood Reporter*, Apr. 13, 1995.

"How America Really Watches TV." *TV Guide*, July 29, 1995, 26–30.

Huff, Richard. "Television News and Notes." AP Wire, Sep. 11, 1995.

"Internet Gender Gap—Myth or Fact?" Matrix Information & Directory Services, May 10, 1995.

Jicha, Paul. *"Party of Five* Aims to Tug Young Hearts." *Sun Sentinal,* Sep. 12, 1994, 1D.

Johnson, Peter. "Inside TV: Summer Slot." *USA Today,* Mar. 5, 1996, 3D.

Koehl, Carla, and Sarah Van Boren. "Periscope: Fads: Commercial Success." *Newsweek,* Sep. 11, 1995, 8.

Krofft, Sid, and Marty Krofft. Interview. Nick at Nite forum, Sept. 13, 1995, America Online.

Laurence, Robert. "On Paper, Premise of New *Party* Doesn't Do This Fine Show Justice." *San Diego Union-Tribune,* Sep. 11, 1994, TV Week, 17.

Leiby, Richard. "A Touch of Irony." *Washington Post*, Apr. 4, 1996, C1.

Littlefield, Kinney. "Television Ad Buyers React to Networks' Fall Schedules." *Orange County Register* via Knight-Ridder wire, May 28, 1996.

Lomartire, Paul. *"The X Files." Palm Beach Post,* Aug. 24, 1994, D1.

"Mail." *Entertainment Weekly,* Feb. 17, 1995, 6.

Marchese, John. "The Short Shelf Life of Generation X." *New York Times,* June 18, 1995, sec. 1, 35.

Millman, Joyce. "The Prime Times of Aaron Spelling." *San Francisco Examiner,* June 29, 1994, C1.

——. "TV Trivia Has New Set of *Friends." San Francisco Examiner,* Sep. 22, 1994, C1.

Murphy, Mary. "Why Anthony Edwards Is the Heartbeat of *ER." TV Guide,* Apr. 13, 1996, 16.

Owen, Rob. "'Placemats' Join to Watch *Melrose* En Masse." *Richmond Times-Dispatch,* Mar. 26, 1995, J1.

——. "Trash to Treasure: Morally Bankrupt MP Hits Gen X Pay Dirt." *Richmond Times-Dispatch,* May 18, 1994, D1.

——. "TV Fans Find Instant Gratification on the Net." *Richmond Times-Dispatch,* July 2, 1994, F4.

——. "TV's No. 1 Fans Turn On, Tune In to Cybernetworks." *Richmond Times-Dispatch,* Apr. 15, 1995, E4.

Perry, Charles. "You Are What You Order." *Los Angeles Times,* Dec. 29, 1994, H2.

Pescovitz, David. "The Future of Advertising." *Wired,* Apr. 1996, 68.

Quill, Greg. "The Young and the Shirtless." *Toronto Star,* July 31, 1992, G1.

Reader's Survey." *TV Guide*, May 4, 1996, 56.

Riches, Hester. "Vancouver Actor Wins TV Role Without Having to Starve in L.A." *Vancouver Sun*, Mar. 11, 1992, A3.

Rosenberg, Howard. "Fox's *Beverly Hills, 90210*: Zip Code for Cliches." *Los Angeles Times*, Oct. 4, 1990, F11.

Roush, Matt. "*Beverly*: Not Totally Cool in High School." *USA Today*, Oct. 4, 1990, 3D.

——. "Fox's Empty-Headed *Models Inc.*" *USA Today*, June 30, 1994, D1.

——. "*Melrose* Place Treads Middle of the Road." *USA Today*, July 8, 1992, D1.

——. "Muppets' New Caper: Prime-Time ABC Show." *USA Today*, July 19, 1995, D1.

Saunders, Dusty. "A Thoughtful Look at the Teen Years, *My So-Called Life* Is Anything But Fluff." *Rocky Mountain News*, Aug. 21, 1994, F4.

Schwed, Mark. "Melrose Moxie." *TV Guide*, July 29, 1995, 8–12.

Scott, Tony. "*Friends*." *Daily Variety*, Sep. 22, 1994.

Shales, Tom. "Fox Forgets the Zip in *Beverly Hills, 90210*." *Washington Post*, Oct. 4, 1990, 12.

——. "*Freshman Dorm*: Class Dismissed." *Washington Post*, Aug. 11, 1992, B1.

——. "The Pox on Fox." *Washington Post*, Sep. 3, 1994, D1.

——. "Well-Placed *Friends*." *Washington Post*, Feb. 23, 1995, C1.

Shister, Gail. "*Slacker* Author Langs Gig Writing for *Murphy*." *Tampa Tribune*, Aug. 19, 1995, 6, Baylife.

Smith, Erin, and Don Smith. *Teenage Gang Debs.* nos. 2–5.

Smith, Sid. "Live Onstage and Glued to the Tube; Reworking '70s TV Kid-Shows Is the Latest Trend in Theater." *Chicago Tribune*, May 8, 1994, c18.

Snierson, Dan. "It Came From Outer Space." *Entertainment Weekly*, Mar. 22, 1996, 42.

"Special Report: Black Television Viewing 1994/1995." *BBDO Special Markets*, Mar. 29, 1995, vol. 4, no. 3.

"Special Report: Black Television Viewing 1995/1996." *BBDO Special Markets*, Apr. 8, 1996, vol. 5, no. 2.

"Those Who Laugh Last." *Total TV,* Dec. 23–29, 1995, 9.

Tucker, Ken. "As the Free-Spirited Phoebe on *Friends*, She's Ready for Big-Time Heat: Lisa Kudrow." *Entertainment Weekly*, June 30, 1995, 46.

Unger, Arthur. "Fox Seeking Fourth Network Recognition." *Christian Science Monitor*, July 9, 1987, 23.

"Viewers Vote to *Party* On and Continue Exploring *Earth 2.*" *TV Guide,* Apr. 22, 1995, 51.

The Week in Rock. MTV, Aug. 4, 1995.

Williams, Marjorie. "MTV's Short Takes Define a New Style." *Washington Post,* Dec. 13, 1989, A1.

"Working Our Nerves: Those Stupid Frigging Mentos Commercials." *Sassy,* Nov. 1994, 80.

Zoglin, Richard. "Friends and Layabouts." *Time,* March. 20, 1995, 74.

Books

Bianculli, David. *Teleliteracy.* New York: Touchstone, 1992.

Block, Alex Ben. *Outfoxed.* New York: St. Martin's Press, 1990.

Brooks, Tim, and Earl Marsh. *The Complete Directory to Prime Time Network and Cable Shows.* 6th edition. New York: Ballantine, 1995.

Carr, Michael, and Darby. *The "I Hate Brenda" Book: Shannen Doherty Exposed!* New York: Pinnacle, 1993.

Cohen, Jason, and Michael Krugman. *Generation Ecch! The Backlash Starts Here.* New York: Fireside, 1995.

Coupland, Douglas. *Generation X.* New York: St. Martin's Press, 1991.

———. *Microserfs.* New York: ReganBooks, 1995.

Dunn, Sarah. *The Official Slacker Handbook.* New York: Warner, 1994.

Edelstein, Andrew J., and Frank Lovece. *The Brady Bunch Book.* New York: Warner, 1990.

Goodwin, Andrew. *Dancing in the Distraction Factory: Music Television and Popular Culture.* Minneapolis: University of Minnesota Press, 1992.

Holtz, Geoffrey T. *Welcome to the Jungle: The Why Behind Generation X.* New York: St. Martin's Griffin, 1995.

Inman, David. *The TV Encyclopedia.* New York: Perigee, 1991.

Jenkins, Henry. *Textual Poachers: Television Fans & Participatory Culture.* New York: Routledge, 1992.

Johnson, Hillary, and Nancy Rommelmann. *The Real "Real World".* New York: Pocket Books, 1995.

Kaplan, E. Ann. *Rocking Around the Clock: Music Television, Postmodernism and Consumer Culture.* New York: Methuen, 1987.

Kennedy, *Pagan. Platforms.* New York: St. Martin's Press, 1994.

Kim, Jae-Ha. *Best of "Friends."* New York: HarperPerennial, 1995.

Lewis, Lisa A. *Gender Politics and MTV: Voicing the Difference.* Philadelphia: Temple Univ. Press, 1990.

McNeil, Alex. *Total Television.* New York: Penguin Books, 1991.

Moran, Elizabeth. *Bradymania.* Holbrook, Mass.: Bob Adams Publishers, 1992.

Nelson, Craig. *Bad TV: The Very Best of the Very Worst.* New York: Delta Trade, 1995.

Pipher, Mary. *The Shelter of Each Other.* New York: G. P. Putnam's Sons, 1996.

Pourroy, Janine. *Behind the Scenes at "ER".* New York: Ballantine, 1995.

Ritchie, Karen. *Marketing to Generation X.* New York: Lexington, 1995.

Rubino, Anthony, Jr. *Life Lessons From Melrose Pl.* Holbrook, Mass: Adams Media, 1996.

Rushkoff, Douglas. *The Gen X Reader.* New York: Ballantine, 1994.

———. *Media Virus! Hidden Agendas in Popular Culture.* New York: Ballantine, 1994.

Strauss, Bill, and Neil Howe. *Generations.* New York: William Morrow, 1991.

———. *13th Gen: Abort, Retry, Ignore, Fail?* New York: Vintage, 1993.

Thompson, Robert J. *Television's Second Golden Age: From "Hill Street Blues" to "ER".* New York: Continuum, 1996.

Wild, David. *Friends.* Doubleday, 1995.

———. *The Official "Melrose Place" Companion.* New York: Harper Perennial, 1995.

Williams, John. *Entertainment on the Net.* Indianapolis: Que Corporation, 1995.

Wolff, Michael. *NetChat.* New York: Random House Electronic, 1994.

———. *NetGuide.* New York: Randon House Electronic, 1994.

Interviews

Ardell, David. Feb. 21, 1995, survey.

Astrof, Jeff. Mar. 7, 1995, Burbank, Calif.

Ayotte, Julie. Sep. 6, 1995, telephone.

Ball, Ian J. June 24, 1995, and July 11, 1995, telephone and e-mail.

Bergstrom, Holly. Feb. 21, 1995, survey.

Bianculli, David. Aug. 16, 1995, telephone.

Biggs, Kelli. Feb. 17, 1995, e-mail.

Bojdak, Sue. Apr. 20, 1995, survey.

Bosworth, Greer. Oct. 9, 1995, telephone.

Bowser, Yvette Lee. Aug. 2, 1995, telephone.

Bright, Andrea. Feb. 13, 1995, e-mail.

Bryant, Benjamin E. Feb. 12, 1995, e-mail.

Buchanan, Kristin. Feb. 10, 1995, e-mail.

Burnside, Mary. Feb. 16, 1995, e-mail.

Candilogos, Sandy. Mar. 30, 1995, e-mail.

Carreiro, Joe. Feb. 15, 1995, e-mail.

Casdin, Chris. Mar. 10, 1995, survey.

Cather, Jennifer. Feb. 22, 1995, survey.

Chase, Adam. Mar. 7, 1995, Burbank, Calif.

Collins, Russell. July 25, 1995, telephone.

Conlin, Rachel. May 4, 1995, survey.

Coplan, Helene. Feb. 10 1995, survey.

Cosker, Glynn. Jan. 22, 1995, survey.

Cosker, Joanne. Jan. 22, 1995, survey.

Costello, Kimberly, Mar. 9, 1995, telephone.

Cox, Jennifer Elise. Mar. 7, 1995, Los Angeles, Calif.

Crouch, Michelle. June 23, 1995, survey.

Davis, Scott. Jan. 13, 1995, survey.

DeFilippo, Sal. Mar. 31, 1995, survey.

Dillon, Joshua M. Apr. 20, 1995, survey.

Doerr, Heath. Aug. 22, 1995, telephone and e-mail.

Drellishak, Renee. Feb. 16, 1995, e-mail.

Durden, Douglas. June 23, 1995, Richmond, Va.

Ferrell, Ian. June 28, 1995, telephone and e-mail.

Fortier, Sheri. Feb. 10, 1995, survey.

Frank, Betsy. Aug. 7, 1995, telephone.

Frazier, John D. Feb. 13, 1995, e-mail.

Garfield, Bob. Sep. 16, 1995, telephone.

Geiger, Joey. Feb. 11, 1995, e-mail.

Gianinno, Larry. Aug. 14, 1995, telephone.

Goggans, Grant. Aug. 17, 1995, e-mail.

Gold, Tricia. Aug. 3, 1995, telephone.

Goldberg, Gary. Sep. 27, 1995, e-mail.

Goodnight, Terra. Aug. 25, 1995, e-mail.

Grams, Erika. Feb. 16, 1995, e-mail.

Greenblatt, Robert. Mar. 9, 1995, Los Angeles, Calif.

Greenstein, Jeff. Mar. 7, 1995, Burbank, Calif., and June 28, 1995, telephone.

Hadfield, Brian D. Feb. 17, 1995, e-mail.

Hale, Jennifer. Mar. 30, 1995, e-mail.

Hands, Robin. Feb. 15, 1995, survey.

Hirshberg, Eric. July 25, 1995, telephone.

Holzman, Winnie. July 1995, telephone.

Hom, Kenny. Feb. 12, 1995, e-mail.

Joyner, Steve. Sep. 14, 1995, telephone and e-mail.

Junge, Alexa. Mar. 8, 1995, Burbank, Calif.

Kaufmann, Marta. Mar. 7, 1995, Burbank, Calif.

Kennedy, Charles. Mar. 9, 1995, Los Angeles, Calif.

Knight, Chris. May 12, 1995, e-mail.

Komanasky, Elyssa. Feb. 15, 1995, e-mail.

Kopp, Beth. Jan. 20, 1995, survey.

Krofft, Marty. June 26, 1996, telephone.

Lesher, Chris. Feb. 16, 1995, e-mail.

Lippman, Amy. Mar. 14, 1995, telephone.

Lounsbery, Adam. Mar. 7, 1995, survey.

Mali, Sharmila. Feb. 13, 1995, e-mail.

Marcella, Jeff. Apr. 20, 1995, survey.

Mason, Mike. Aug. 6, 1995, e-mail.

McCarthy, Chris. Feb. 14, 1995, e-mail.

Milenky, Elissa. July 13, 1994, e-mail.

Millar, Alex J. Feb. 16, 1995, e-mail.

Murray, Brandi. Feb. 13, 1995, e-mail.

Murray, Jonathan. Sep. 25, 1995, telephone.

Muslin, Elizabeth. Feb. 14, 1995, e-mail.

Nebus, Joseph. Feb. 11, 1995, e-mail.

Padgett, Jol. July 27, 1995, telephone and e-mail.

Palm, Jacob. Mar. 18, 1995, survey.

Pelligrinelli, Jack. Feb. 18, 1995, e-mail.

Perry, Andy. Feb. 13, 1995, e-mail.

Pinkney, Rose Catherine. July 12, 1995, telephone.

Poltrack, David. Aug. 3, 1995, telephone.

Rechenmacher, Craig. Mar. 28, 1995, survey.

Ritchie, Karen. Aug. 1, 1995, telephone.

Robeson, Paul. July 20, 1995, e-mail.

Rosin, Charles. May 16, 1995, telephone.

Roush, Matt. July 1995, Washington, D.C.

Sauerwein, Kristina. May 4, 1995, survey.

Schwartz, Sherwood. July 26, 1995, telephone.

Scott, Kathleen. Apr. 20, 1995, survey.

Sebelius, Steve. May 4, 1995, survey.

Sender, Craig. Feb. 10, 1995, e-mail.

Singer, Jon. July 10, 1995, telephone and e-mail.

Smith, Erin. July 10, 1995, telephone.

Spangler, Jonathan. May 3, 1995, e-mail.

Sridharan, Prashant. Feb. 15, 1995, e-mail.

Stipp, Horst. July 12, 1995, telephone.

Stock, Parley. Feb. 17, 1995, e-mail.

Stratakis, Jennifer. Feb. 22, 1995, e-mail.

Strauss, Jeff. Mar. 7, 1995, Burbank, Calif., and June 28, 1995, telephone.

Suerdieck, Mike. Feb. 3, 1996, e-mail.

Swanson, Dorothy. July 20, 1995, telephone.

Sydlansky, Laurel A. Feb. 22, 1995, survey.

Taube-Schock, Craig. Feb. 13, 1995, e-mail.

Topolosky, Ken. Aug. 18, 1995, via e-mail.

Ungerleider, Ira. Mar. 7, 1995, Burbank, Calif.

Vitale, Karla. Feb. 22, 1995, survey.

Waldman, Paul. Feb. 15, 1995, survey.

Walters, Tena. June 4, 1995, survey.

Warner, Michael. Feb. 21, 1995, survey.

Weight, Gregory M. Feb. 13, 1995, e-mail.

Wells, John. Aug. 23, 1995, telephone.

Whitford, Sara Emily. Feb. 18, 1995, e-mail.

Wicklund, Petra Renée. Apr. 20, 1995, survey.

Wilkinson, Kevin. Feb. 12, 1995, e-mail.

Williams, Andy. June 28, 1995, telephone and e-mail.

Woodjetts, Joyce. Feb. 22, 1995, e-mail.

Yohe, Tom. July 10, 1995, telephone.

Zakarin, Scott. Sep. 18, 1995, telephone.

Zoerner, Tom. Oct. 11, 1995, e-mail.

Index